Book One
Early Years

THE PILGRIM CONTEMPLATIVE

THE
PILGRIM
CONTEMPLATIVE

Book One - Early Years

Herbert F. Smith, S.J.

COLLEGEVILLE, MINNESOTA

THE LITURGICAL PRESS

By
Herbert F. Smith, S. J.
LIVING FOR RESURRECTION
THE LORD EXPERIENCE
GOD DAY BY DAY

FIRST PRINTING, 1977

SECOND PRINTING, 1980

To Jesus
and His Vicar
Paul VI

Introductory Briefing

Once at twilight I walked alone down a road marked *Dead End*. The sign did not deter me because I dimly remembered going that way before. Soon, out of the shadows loomed a fence that seemed unbroken. Up close, I discovered it was composed of two sections, one beginning where the other ended but *set back slightly*, so that the space between provided an opening not from the front but from the side. I passed through and continued on my way.

Such wayfaring episodes bear an uncanny likeness to the ones experienced by those wayfarers of the spirit, men and women of prayer. Their way seems ever beset by hindrances and dead ends. Only the most dogged pilgrims proceed undeterred, probe, penetrate, and eventually pass beyond.

Through the ages hardy spiritual explorers have marked out the detours, warned us of the danger points, and described how the rapids can be forded and the mountains scaled. They have left us their compasses and their maps. They have pointed out paths which we would otherwise find with difficulty or never find at all. They are the Mystical Body's explorers, pathfinders destined by the Lord of history.

There remains one path of prayer, however, for which the maps seem to be discouragingly inadequate. I refer to the way of the *contemplatives in action*, the way of praying apostles who struggle all their days to find a path that closes the gap between prayer and action so that they may act contemplatively and contemplate in harmony with their action. Much is written on the subject, and some of it is helpful, but nothing seems adequate. Certainly, nothing has been adequate to my own needs.

Why are the writings on contemplation in action inadequate? Only after lengthy reflection on this question am I able to propose the following answer: Contemplation in action is existential and intuitional in nature, while the writings tend to be theoretical. They too infrequently describe the actual practices and experiences which teach us *how to* become contemplatives in action. When they do descend to particulars, they usually lump together, without order or priority, a series of practices which give no hint that certain of them are possible only when certain others have already been mastered. Thus such helps can mislead the unwary spiritual pilgrim.

Then, too, there are manifold subtle and complex difficulties along the way of contemplation in action which cannot even be properly understood, much less solved, until they are seen embedded in the concrete conditions out of which they arise. The result is that an abstract treatment cannot adequately deal with these difficulties.

What can be done to improve this state of affairs? If we are led by these preliminary considerations to focus on the fact that, like other living things, contemplation in action is a *growth process*, and must be treated as one, we are on our way out of the impasse; and if we pause for a moment to consider how other growth processes are plotted, we should be lighted on our way to formulating a more life-like account of contemplation in action.

The growth of a tree is studied according to the concentric circles which annually accrue to the bole as it grows. The maturing of a human being is studied according to the well-known stages of growth which begin at conception. Purely *interior prayer* has long since been studied according to its stages of development: meditation, prayer of affection, prayer of simplicity, prayer of faith, prayer of quiet, and so on. What we can do, then, to improve our understanding and mastery of contemplation in action is to recognize it as a *life process*. We can try to trace out its development and discern its stages, and describe what happens in each stage, and what practices are helpful in each. We can study it along its time-line of growth, we can investigate its mysterious inception and examine it in its sturdy maturity.

In the pages that follow I have made a preliminary attempt to execute the program I have just outlined. The divisions and stages are presented as tentative and experimental. It will take the pooling of much more experience to raise the art and science of contemplation in action to the level of refinement long ago achieved in the study of purely interior prayer. Let us make our beginnings and collect the data which will be necessary before the Lord can send a Teresa of Avila and a John of the Cross *of contemplation in action* to carry the work forward to a more definitive stage of development.

In writing this account I have tried to bear always in mind and continually refine the distinctions between the vocation to cloistered contemplation and that to contemplation in action. A contemplative in action is one whose *core* calling is to find God in all things, especially in the course of action. The cloistered contemplative also aspires to find God in everything, but his *core* calling is to find God in Himself, beyond all things. The difference is one of emphasis, but it pervasively influences the way each spends his life. The life of a cloistered contemplative is organized to focus his primary energies upon God Himself and to promote unmediated union with God. The life of the contemplative in action is organized to focus his energies on secular activities so as to promote union with God through the mediation of these activities. Of course, both long for unmediated union with God, but each renders his own unique and distinctive service along the way to God. The cloistered or passive contemplative most purely offers and symbolizes the free human response that opens the way for God's continuing entrance into humanity. The contemplative in action most purely offers and symbolizes man's readiness to be the helpmate of God in the work of completing creation. The former is the prime avenue of God's transforming union with humanity, and the latter is the prime avenue of God's transforming union with the cosmos. The cloistered contemplative follows Christ into the desert to pray for the world; the contemplative in action follows Him into the world to carry out the transformation that is being prayed for. The cloistered contemplative's self-giving to God is also his service to man, and the contemplative in action's service to man is his self-giving to God.

We would be unrealistic if we did not admit that the cloistered contemplative, *also*, lives in the world—however circumscribed his ambit—and has his own range of secular activities and works of charity for his fellowmen. In this regard, one Carmelite nun wrote me as follows: *Carmel itself is a little 'cosmos' that needs constant transformation. Consequently I easily apply to myself most of your phrases describing contemplatives in action. . . .* But we would be equally unrealistic if we did not see that the uncloistered contemplative (that is, the true contemplative in action) has an immense and unrestricted range of apostolic opportunities and apostolic demands made upon him that call for a life-style and spirituality radically different from that lived by the cloistered contemplative. The cloistered contemplative sacrifices apostolic mobility and availability in order to better pursue his vocation to unmediated union with God and the new life that union infuses into the kingdom of God on earth; the contemplative in action sacrifices this intense life of unmediated union with God in order to serve more fully as God's fellow worker in laboring with head and hands for the Kingdom. Each has made his sacrifices, and each must avail himself of the opportunities his sacrifices promote, or those sacrifices will be in vain. Cloistered contemplation is one branch of contemplation, and contemplation in action is another.

Now that we have located ourselves within the framework of contemplation as a whole, it is time to focus on contemplation in action. One who turns his attention to contemplation in action for the first time is very much in the position of a city dweller going for an unaccustomed walk in the woods. He sees nothing but trees, and has no way of securely finding his way. Only after many walks is he likely to begin seeing not merely trees, but oaks and elms and pines and birch and maples. Later still he will perceive that there is more than one kind of maple, more than one kind of oak, and so on. If, however, he is from the first accompanied by a skilled woodsman who points out the distinguishing marks of the various flora and fauna, he will become a real woodsman himself much sooner. So too will it be to the advantage of most readers who accompany me into the realm of contemplation in action to have it pointed out to them here and now what it took me long to discover—that contemplation in action must be compared not to a tree but to a woods with many trees. This is a critically important fact, because just as each kind of tree has its own laws of growth, so does each kind of contemplation in action. As a result, when we discuss contemplation in action, we have to say whether we are referring to the forest or to a particular kind of tree. That is, we will never be able to understand or plot out the growth process of contemplation in action until we first distinguish the various types, and identify the one we are describing. My next task here, then, is to point out the more common varieties of contemplation in action, and then single out the one which will be the central concern of this treatise.

Let me proceed as though I were calling to mind actual types of contemplatives in action from among my acquaintances. Over there is a Christ-centered person I know who is active in the world, but who does not really seek God in and through all things as do some contemplatives in action. Rather, he is always trying to communicate with God through direct prayer, even while he is engaged in other activities. No matter what career he pursues his only real interest is God. The moment his work permits, his mind gravitates to God. Since God is his focus in work and play and prayer, let us identify him and his kind as *the active contemplatives of God's presence.*

Over here is a Christ-centered person who is always pondering and discussing the religious implications of everything around him. Everything he experiences is ground in the mill of his reflections on what God is about in the world. Let us name him and his kind *the active contemplatives of God's providence.*

Over there is an acquaintance of mine who is given to systematic pondering of what is most meaningless and absurd on the face of it. His purpose is to use the weapon of reason against everything that threatens to undermine our rational vision of the cosmos, and to use the weapon of spiritual insight against everything that darkens the vision of faith. Whatever he does he makes part of his exploration in search of a more integrated perception of God and His cosmos. Let us call him and his kind *the active contemplatives of enigma.*

Let me next point out a thoughtful, artistic, contemplative friend who is forever probing the inner reality of things. She shows a facility for coaxing ordinary things to yield up the mysterious message of the Beyond which no one else even suspected they held in trust. She is a veritable spiritual tracker on the trail of the Divine Personage who has left His spoor on the paths of creation. Let us call her and her kind *the active contemplatives of creation.*

I now point out a man who very faithfully nurtures a daily time of withdrawal into meditation despite the pressures of his busy life. I have learned by conversation with him that it is no accident he chose a teaching career. He entered by choice a profession by which he could sow in the minds and hearts of others the seeds of thought and of love which mature within him during his daily meditation and contemplation. He has organized his whole life to facilitate his daily rhythmic passage between contemplation and action. Let us identify him and his kind as *the contemplatives of the mixed life.*

Now please pay careful attention to this man I am presently pointing out. He is dedicated to God, but his goal is not merely to find God in all things but to work to advance His presence and visibility in all things. Long since he has felt the call to do this. The result is that he has trained himself to be a man of deep prayer and of competent action. Mysteriously, his contemplation concentrates not only on God but on his own ambit and sphere of influence, and on himself as God's worker within that ambit.

Perhaps not dramatically, but still definitively, he knows he has been called to deep prayer to help him penetrate to God Himself in some undefinable way. Out of that prayer he finds that he returns to his world as one *sent*. Furthermore, as a result of his deep contemplative prayer, he knows at least in a general way what he is sent to do. He is an apostle by Divine appointment. Let us identify him and his kind as *the sent contemplatives*.

The sent contemplative recognizes the urgency of his contemplation as the means of hearing his call and learning his mission. Without contemplation he is like an ambassador whose communications with his leader have been cut off. When he neglects his contemplation he not only ceases to be contemplative; he ceases to be *sent*.

As long as he continues to be sent, he remains God's missioner, His apostle, His agent in human affairs. Ideally, the sent contemplative knows God's will by perpetual contemplative attunement to God in all circumstances. Thus his contemplation is in some sense a charism of discernment given for the sake of directing his mission. This means that the sent contemplative is a charismatic apostolic contemplative. He is servant, son, and fellow worker of God. No name can fully identify his role. When we focus on the *source* of his mission it seems congenial to call him the *sent contemplative*; when we focus on the *execution* of his mission it seems preferable to call him the *pilgrim contemplative*. I shall call him by both names—and others—for it is he who is the direct focus of this treatise. Others can be helped by it, but it is his story, and it is his growth process which will unfold before us.

So far I have described the whole realm of contemplation, and I have identified and located the sent contemplative within that realm, in order to orientate the reader. To do what I have so far done in as brief a space as possible, I have had to use many abstractions. The treatise which follows this introduction curtails abstractions. It rather describes actual experiences of growth and service, and of contemplation in service to both—though it is greater than both. The treatise presents the pilgrim's spiritual awakening and the gradual development of his inner resources, the resources necessary to grow in contemplation and in the use of the charism of the discernment of spirits. For the pilgrim contemplative must focus on improving his apostolic yoke to God in the course of his activities by habitually discerning the impulses that motivate him (and to some extent, those around him). Only by growth in this process can he become God's agent in a mature, living, day-to-day way. For the pilgrim contemplative is not one who was sent by God once upon a time. He is being sent and guided anew in this instant. He is servant and son ever eager to do the Father's will.

The six types of contemplatives in action already described— and probably any others that could be described—overlap in the life of any one contemplative in action. The type which predominates in one's life may shift as one grows or changes to a different work—or enters a crisis; it may shift somewhat with the hours of the day and the various daily activities. Still, the distinctions are more fundamental. Even as many garden plants look quite similar to the unpracticed eye, but in the end produce different vegetables, the different varieties of contemplation in action are rooted in differing personal gifts and graces and charisms, and produce a variety of services in the Church. Each type is essentially a vocation in the Mystical Body. Reflection on the types can help each spiritual pilgrim discern where he is being drawn, so that he can respond more sensitively.

Now back to the other problems we face in this treatise. The lack of adequate guidance for the pilgrim of contemplation in action was referred to earlier. Let us unravel this lack into the various problems it causes. The first problem is that many potential contemplatives in action have not *identified* their problem. Activist in an activity devoid of sufficient meaning, they are driven on to an even higher pitch of activism. Alternatively, they take the route of the cultural dropout—all because no one has even told them of the *possibility* of contemplation in action. Divine providence appoints them to work in the world, yet not apart from God, but their religious training has failed to help them understand this.

Other potential contemplatives in action have a dim sense of a divine vocation to work in the world, but at the same time they feel hounded by the world's meaninglessness—to them at least. Akin to these are youths who feel called to active religious orders, but desire a cloistered order because they find God in prayer and not in action. They do not yet know they are being called to find Him in all things.

The tragedy of many of these people is that they have never even heard of the *possibility* of finding God in all things. Things are things and God is God. Those who have been spiritually awakened the least bit want to be with God more, but they dismiss this longing as something to be fulfilled in heaven. They settle for Mass and Communion, and prayer when they have a chance. For the rest, they carry on their boring duties, hoping not to offend God in the meantime. The present account would be a revelation to them.

Others have been more deeply touch by God and now find the world an exile. They have not even heard the theory of contemplation in action, but already they weep with desire for the fact of it.

Others still have been psychologically and spiritually divided and devastated by the multiple activist demands which harrass them and compartmentalize their lives. They cry out for a way to unify their lives—they cry out for knowledge of the path of contemplation in action.

Others have been introduced to the theory of contemplation in action, but have been shown no way of reducing it to feasibility. They either conclude that it is impractical, or they reserve judgment and mark time. Some continue to try and to search.

Pilgrims more advanced find themselves with the problem of maintaining a faithful commitment to both prayer and action, and they are in search of an answer. The endless ramifications of this problem, and the efforts to solve it, are woven through the treatise that follows.

Many other problems arise. If we are to be God's agents in any meaningful way, we need to know His will in all circumstances. How are we to learn it? That is, how grow sensitive to the leading of the Holy Spirit? And again, to what types of works are agent contemplatives called? Are purely secular works capable of promoting the kingdom of God? If so, how escape secularism? Are there any guiding principles for the choice of an apostolate? What is the cause and cure of that contemporary disease in which zeal degenerates into unrest and instability of apostolates and states of life?

How remain faithful to the sometimes unworldly demands of God without feeling a traitor to the very worldly demands of men?

How reconcile the desire to serve effectively the oppressively urgent needs of starving and warring peoples with the yearning to be joined to Christ whose labors were rejected—who was spat on, scourged, and led to die in disgrace? How conduct the dialectic between efficiency and asceticism, between work and play? How maintain hope in one's work for God when the futility of one's efforts becomes evident?

In the confusion of our day, can we draw up reliable norms for sure union with the true Revelation? How determine which theologians to utilize and which to shun? How can the agent contemplative harmonise, in his own life and apostolate and relationship with the Church, the charismatic and institutional elements of Christianity?

These problems and many others will be faced one by one as they arise in their natural setting in the course of this effort to treat comprehensively the growth process of an agent contemplative.

To minimize abstractions and present the growth and development of an agent contemplative in life-like detail, I have adopted biography as a literary form. The experiences described are actual experiences, but they come from the lives of many different men and women. The text will clearly indicate this. All of these people are our contemporaries. The people who are the source of the more extraordinary experiences are almost all long-term acquaintances of the author, who judges that their lives over the years vouch for the genuinity of their experiences. This practice of drawing on experiences from many different lives helps to broaden the base of our account. It makes our imaginary agent contemplative a composite figure who approaches the ideal of being a "concrete universal." Still, he only approaches that ideal, and so the limitations of this account are best pointed out here and now to forestall disappointments which could obscure the value the work does have.

The first limitation on the value of this work is imposed by the fact that each individual is unique. No two experiences of growth in prayer or anything else can be expected to correspond exactly. Secondly, in the growth process accidental obstacles to growth differ from one person to another. These happenstances can suppress certain stages of growth or transfer them to an abnormal time. A third limitation on the value of this work derives from the differing charisms and apostolates of various individuals. These modify personal experience immensely. One whose apostolate is a humanitarian service will find far readier acceptance and approval than one who is called to preach the Gospel with all its other-worldly demands. These demands are bound to trigger a confrontation between the agent and the naturalists and the little-faiths. Even so, the differences in experience will be less than the common bond, for no apostle escapes the cross of Christ in one form or another. Put broadly, we can say that the value of this account will be limited by the diverse circumstances and natural and supernatural gifts of different agent contemplatives.

What value can we realistically expect this account to have? I think there are many values which each reader should be left to discover for himself. I will only point out what I consider its prime value. If a tuning fork is struck, one nearby of like frequency will be set vibrating. So should this work render to the reader the service of setting his own experiences resonating, experiences he has neglected, or forgotten, or perhaps not understood before. He can relive them and, helped by the reflections and connections he reads about, he can better interpret and understand his own experiences, and better cooperate with his own call. To that end, the reader should ponder his own experiences as he reads. Then this vicarious autobiography will help him to construe his own, and perhaps foresee something of what lies ahead of him. Then he will advance with greater sureness along a wild trail which yet is occasionally marked with the tracks of other pilgrims who have been in the same regions of the spirit.

I conclude this introductory briefing with a prayer to You, Lord Jesus, for all my fellow pilgrims who walk along with You, the True Way. I pray for all pilgrims who will ever read these words; I ask You to light their path.

Of you, my fellow pilgrims who receive this communication, I ask prayers in turn, that we may one day meet at the confluence of all true ways, and exchange our delighted greetings in, through, and with the Father, Son, and Holy Spirit. Amen.

Outline of Contents

Part One
AWAKENING TO GOD

1 ORIGINS

Explains how contemplation germinates in an atmosphere of faith and how religious practice begins to assume its rightful place. Describes the initial impulses to prayer and service and the gradual change these effect in the pilgrim contemplative. New insight into the terribleness of sin. Cites other experiences which awaken a longing for eternal things and lead to a choice of enduring values. Treats of new religious practices which are taken up despite opposition. Deals with the joys and sufferings of friendship at this juncture. —page 3

2 THE AWAKENING

Tells of an unpredictable experience of God which is given, not produced. Describes the response which is called for and the new relationship made possible by this visitation. Makes clear the consequent loss of interest in the world of action and the necessity of this temporary interior withdrawal. Considers how this divine visitation frees the budding agent contemplative from insoluble problems while leading him to new ones. *Spiritual Project One*: Plumbing My First Name of Grace.

3 GOD'S ABSENCE IS DISCOVERED

Describes how the pilgrim's taste of God changes absence of the knowledge of God into knowledge of the absence of God, making the pilgrim suffer the pangs of the birth of contemplation. Explains why God is absent now in both the pilgrim and the world, and why this is necessary. Treats of forces which tempt him to withdraw into prayer and rashly abandon his true vocation in the world. Notes the authentic role of the spiritual director in helping him discern rightly. Describes how secular affairs are experienced only negatively, and how God is the only good and sin the only evil, so that the horror of sin mounts and scruples threaten. Pilgrim and director must trust God's ways, not fight them. The experience of God will in the long run lead back to creation at a new depth of love. *Spiritual Project Two*: Searching for Interior Freedom.

4 THE KINGDOM OF THE WORLD GROWS MANIFEST

Differentiates between two uses of the term "world" and tells of the pilgrim's struggle over divided loyalties. Speaks of the hatred and hostility he faces, and warns against returning it. Cautions against alienation. Shows how the Scriptures will help. Explains the importance of having faith in the goodness of God's creation. Describes how the pilgrim is gaining a realistic knowledge of the world and an understanding compassion for it which are essential. *Spiritual Project Three*: Attitudes Toward the World.

Part Two
AWAKENING TO THE KINGDOM OF GOD

Part Three

THE KINGDOM OF GOD COMES IN POWER

1 EXPERIENCES OF THE INCARNATION

Describes the advent of Jesus which intensifies the pilgrim's love, absorbs him in the mystery of the ongoing Incarnation, and makes him see Jesus as the key to the union of heaven and earth which makes contemplation in action possible. Tells how the Eucharist dominates his life under Mary's tutelage.   —*page* 85

2 EFFECTS OF THE ADVENT OF JESUS

Tells how the Scriptures become a privileged place of meeting Jesus, and the guide to a lowly and therefore secure relationship with Him. Confirms the importance of this lowliness in an agent of God. Describes other virtues which flourish now. Considers other trials, and posits meditation on the Passions as a kind of universal remedy for desolation.   —*page* 88

3 FURTHER EFFECTS OF THE ADVENT OF JESUS

Considers and plays down certain sensible effects of prayer at this time. Describes right conduct when subject to erotic feelings in prayer. Tells of the gift of tears and its power to purify the affectivity and to enhance the ability to discern spirits. Raises the problem of the two and the many in love, a problem at the heart of contemplation in action.   —*page* 94

4 EXPERIENCES OF THE LORD OF NATURE

Describes how nature becomes a meeting with God. Shows how familiarity with Jesus and His teaching helps this to happen, as does the pilgrim's own conscious effort to promote the meeting. Points out how this is an advance in contemplation in action.   —*page* 100

which invades the pilgrim's world, work and prayer. Tells how meditation and spiritual direction unearth the cause, relieve the pilgrim's anxiety, and help him cooperate with this austere new growth. Locates this growth in the gift of knowledge, which turns him to Sacred Scripture.　　—*page* 125

10　THE WORD OF GOD IN THE LIFE OF THE PILGRIM CONTEMPLATIVE

Gives examples of the types of external experiences which lead a pilgrim to the Scriptures, but locates the real cause in the gift of knowledge had within. Explains how the Scriptures enhance the pilgrim's growth both as a contemplative and as God's agent in practical affairs. Cautions against abuses of Scripture, and cites ways of avoiding them.　　—*page* 128

11　A LAMP TO THE PILGRIM'S FEET

Portrays the pilgrim's perception of Jesus as the one who shows us how to use Scripture to build the Kingdom. Describes how the pilgrim is taught by the Scriptures to avoid wayward theologians and to seek Church guidance in interpreting Bible passages. *Spiritual Project Five:* Lecto Divina.
　　—*page* 135

12　THE APOSTOLATE OF TRUTH

Reports how truth sought in both creation and divine revelation becomes central now, and the search for and the spreading of truth become the means of growing personally and of spreading the Kingdom. Describes the pitfalls of the apostolate of truth. Speaks of the all-pervasive relationship between truth, God, and faith.　　—*page* 140

13　THE PILGRIM AND DIVINE REVELATION

Explains how the pilgrim contemplative's charism is to be Spirit-led in his role as God's agent. Raises the problem of harmonizing inner, Spirit guidance with outer, magisterial guidance. Begins the search for answers in revelation, and shows why the pilgrim must become more and more ecclesial adequately to respond to the Spirit. Lays plans for surveying, in the next three chapters, the magisterium's teaching on its own

his apostolate of truth and bold quest for Christliness. Regrets that some pilgrims are deterred by hostility, but declares that the wise pilgrim profits by it, however much suffering it causes. —*page* 173

18 DIFFICULTIES IN THE APOSTOLATE

Considers the ways the pilgrim's strained personal relationships affect his apostolate, but warns against false ways of judging apostolic success or failure. Calls to mind the true norm of judgment. Considers the dialectic between various conflicting values: desire for acceptance and success versus the desire to share Christ's rejection; learning versus uncultivated simplicity; asceticism versus efficiency; work versus play, etc. Describes finding new need for and new uses of the daily examination of conscience. —*page* 178

19 PRAYER IN PROCESS

Describes persistence in hard prayer, and the enduring importance of Mass and Communion. Testifies to the importance of the Eucharist for the apostolate, for community, and for the Kingdom. Tells of the joy of having companion pilgrim contemplatives who share these experiences in the Lord. Reports that former ways of finding God cyclically recur, teaching him to find God in all things and thus grow toward maturity. Rejoices in the many freedoms gained and the liberation experienced by the pilgrim who has come this far. Rejoices in his privileged vocation as divinely commissioned to be an apostolic contemplative in the world. —*page* 184

Credits

Many men and women have put me in debt for their contributions to this book: the donors of testimonials to religious experiences too personal to be quoted except anonymously; the theologians and personal friends whose criticisms and valuable suggestions led me to undertake a much more comprehensive treatment of contemplation than I had intended; Fathers George Schemel, Thomas King and William Dych of the Society of Jesus; the members of the Xavier-Damians Christian Life Community, especially Dr. Michael Vaccaro and Dr. Joseph Di Ienno, whose critique of the manuscript from their vantage point as practicing psychiatrists led to some clarifying additions and revisions.

My work load was lightened by the help I received in proofreading the work and/or marketing it. In particular I mention Father Philip V. Sullivan, S.J., Brother Bart Sheehan, N.S.J., Ms Catherine McInerney, Sister Mary Jude, C.S.F.N., and Sister Catherine Mary Dambach, M.S.C.

Grateful acknowledgment is made to The Jesuit Center for Spiritual Growth, Wernersville, Penn., and its Director, Fr. George Schemel for the use of the "Spiritual Projects," and to the following for permission to quote copyrighted material:

Revised Standard Version of the Bible, copyrighted 1946, 1952, © 1971, 1973, published by the National Council of the Churches of Christ, New York, New York.

The Pope Speaks (autumn 1966, pages 351-352), published by Our Sunday Visitor, Huntington, Indiana.

The Teachings of Pope Paul VI—1970, published by the United States Catholic Conference, Washington, D. C.

The Teachings of the Catholic Church by Josef Neuner, S.J., and Heinrich Roos, S. J., published by Alba House, Staten Island, New York.

The Confessions of St. Augustine in the translation of F. J. Sheed, copyright 1943, Sheed & Ward, Inc., New York, New York.

Excerpts from the text of *The New American Bible,* copyright 1970 by the Confraternity of Christian Doctrine, Washington, D.C., are reproduced herein by permission of said Confraternity of Christian Doctrine. All rights reserved.

Abbreviations

Gen.	Genesis	Ezech.	Ezekiel
Exod.	Exodus	Dan.	Daniel
Hos.	Hosea	Rom.	Romans
Lev.	Leviticus	Cor.	Corinthians
Deut.	Deuteronomy	Gal.	Galatians
Sam.	Samuel	Eph.	Ephesians
Ps.	Psalms	Phil.	Philippians
Prov.	Proverbs	Col.	Colossians
Qoh.	Ecclesiastes	Thess.	Thessalonians
Wis.	Wisdom	Tim.	Timothy
Sir.	Sirach (Ecclesiasticus)	Hebr.	Hebrews
Is.	Isaiah	Apoc.	Revelations
Jer.	Jeremiah		

CV	Confraternity Version
JB	Jerusalem Bible
NAB	New American Bible
RSV	Revised Standard Version/Catholic Edition
NR	Neuner and Roos (Ed., Karl Rahner, transl., Geoffrey Stevens), *The Teaching of the Catholic Church*.

Part One

AWAKENING TO GOD

1.

The Origins

One man at least knew from His boyhood that He was sent into the world on mission from His Father, and that one was Jesus. When His parents were perplexed because their twelve-year old Son had stayed behind in Jerusalem, He seemed surprised that they did not already understand: "Did you not know that I must be busy with my Father's affairs?" (Luke 2:50 JB)

Jesus repeatedly identified Himself as the *sent one*. He declared expressly that He was the fulfillment of the Isaian prophecy concerning the one to be sent on a mission which involved so much suffering he would become known as the *suffering servant of Yahweh*. But Jesus revealed that His was the service of a loving Son. And so His dedication was complete: "My food is to do the will of him who sent me, and to accomplish his work" (John 4:34).

Jesus lived at such a depth of prayer that even in His work He was in on-going communication with the Father, consulting Him, always learning what came next. In traditional terms we call this depth of communion and communication with God *contemplation*. Jesus was a contemplative.

Jesus was a contemplative sent on a mission by the Father. As is already clear, His contemplation was not solely a prayer of union. It was a prayer of ongoing communication in the interest of His mission from the Father. Jesus illustrates this by expressing His *awareness* that He is constantly carrying out the Father's will: "He who sent me is with me; he has not left me alone, for I always do what is pleasing to him" (John 8:29). Jesus was a *sent contemplative*.

Are there other contemplatives sent by the Father to continue

3

Jesus" mission? Who could doubt it! When Jesus completed His mission He said to His apostles: "As the Father has sent me, even so I send you . . . Receive the Holy Spirit" (John 20:21-22).

The purpose of this book is to show the evidence for this vocation today, and to trace out its nature, and above all to make manifest its growth patterns to help in the formation of those called to it. Let us begin tracking our quarry.

Each growing thing needs its own nurture for it must grow in accord with its own life force. So it is with the sent contemplative. He does not spring unheralded from a climate of unbelief. He grows organically out of the soil of religious faith. To set limits to the vast expanse of religious experience lying before us as we open our search for the growth patterns of this vocation, we will focus our attention on the patterns as they manifest themselves within the Catholic faith. Further, we will single out from the vast company who share this vocation one sole spiritual pilgrim being readied by God to be sent on mission. We do this not to narrow our sympathies but to eliminate vague generalizations.

The youth on whom we train our gaze has not yet awakened to his call. He is still in the early stages of religious experience and growth in Christian holiness and service. It is not to our purpose to observe whether he is faithful beyond the norm, or more than normally unfaithful. What we observe in him at this stage is a living faith that is shepherding him through experiences of grace, of sin, of hope in God. He is conscious that he has pledged an allegiance and because of that, though sin may abound, he knows it to be sin and finds it hard to bear, even finds it torture. Faithfulness is joy. Thus for him there can be no neutrality. Though he does not yet understand what he is experiencing, he is in fact experiencing the impact of the Spirit.

Contemplative awakening lies in his future, but its seeds are germinating. Sundays find him at Mass, listening to the Gospel, receiving Holy Communion. Undramatically, almost imperceptibly, these experiences deepen in meaning and he begins to carry a diffuse sense of prayerfulness home with him. Rarely, however, does it reach the level of formal prayer apart from communal worship. The Gospel message is slowly beginning to trouble him with its call to apostolic responsibility. He tries to quiet it by increasing his offering at the collection, or by some other gesture whose inadequacy he senses. The new awareness refuses to go away.

Just as seeds continue to germinate even in poor soil, his new sense of a call to prayerfulness and to service grows with its own life, whether or not he gives it its due. The impulse to both prayer and to action are growing out of the one seed of his call, and the day will come when they will be one in their manifestation as they are in their seed. If he cooperates with these impulses he will grow rapidly in prayer, in action, and in union with God. As long as he does not viciously suppress them, he will continue growing into a man of faith. "My righteous one shall live by faith, and if he shrinks back, my soul has no pleasure in him" (Hebr. 10:38).

What comes out of these impulses is an inclination to reexamine his whole relationship to God. Where before he had been acting as though religion were merely a part of man's activities, it is being driven home to him that all other activities are—or should be—a part of religion. He comes to accept this new realization as a fact, but it is only an intellectual fact. He may not yet be willing, and he is certainly not able, to make it a fact of his whole existence.

The fact is, nevertheless, beginning to affect his whole existence. Values are shifting, old meanings are decaying like last year's vegetation. Activities formerly important to him are losing their significance. His interests are changing. He can spend an evening sitting reflectively on the porch gazing at the stars. He picks up some spiritual reading—a pamphlet from the Church vestibule, or a life of a Saint long lying around unread. His former interest in secular activities and adventures is losing its hold.

This decline in the importance of the secular will continue and reach a dangerous low unless he finds new meaning through new understanding of the place of the world in the Kingdom of God. And even that new understanding will not suffice unless he continues to progress in the fusion of prayer and action.

His personal sins take on the ugliness of gargoyles and his horror of them mounts. Morally they are evil enough, but worse, they are a betrayal of his Lord. The fight against sin—and he may still fall into serious sins—usurps vast energies. It becomes an all-pervasive battle.

Events in his life and around it set in motion confrontation with the whole meaning of his existence. Attainment of a cherished goal such as a college degree or an advance in his career shocks him by leaving him as empty as ever—or gives him a sense of accomplishment that rings with finality, intimating that he can be done with such things now, and turn to others more meaningful—those which have to do with the Lord.

A failure brought about by events beyond his control teaches him the precariousness of human existence, and the folly of devoting a lifetime to some goal which can be swept away in a moment.

The death of a loved one stuns him by undermining the fabric of his life. Heights and depths foam and surge within. Of what worth are transient things, and who can measure the greatness of the loss of everlasting life? He experiences even a physical hunger for enduring meaning. The importance of most things declines, but he feels the awakening of a deeper need for enduring friendships, for deeper, warmer human relationships, for sharing and love. In these, at least, he feels contact with something that cannot die.

He has thought himself close to God, and full of faith and hope, but now in some moment of true closeness, in some taste of His love, he discerns great gaps in his faith and his hope. It may be that at Mass he gazes at a crucifix or other image of Jesus, and discovers how far his love exceeds his expectations and his deeds. Why? One pilgrim found the reason exposed in the words that burst forth from him to the Lord: *If only I really believed you give yourself to me. . . .*

Impelled by the growing force of his religious needs, the pilgrim begins to act on his old yearning for more prayer and worship in his life. Until now he has been deterred by what others might think. He had no desire to cast the image of a "Holy Joe." Now he puts aside this cowardice and foolishness. He will do what he must do. He adopts the practice of daily prayer. Or he may at last fulfill a long hunger for daily Mass and Communion, and taste the sweetness of the Lord.

Before long the cost of the pilgrim's new course begins to surface. Its name is *alienation*. He finds himself moving away from the common interests of even those dearest to him. In the daily drift of conversations about money and business, cars and possessions, he is no longer at home. He ponders deeply. The rift will grow. Is he ready to pay the cost? Can he endure it? Is there some other way? Should he forget what he longs to become and where he longs to go rather than be separated from those he loves by a distance that miles cannot measure? On this little-traveled path which promises so much he has already been beset by loneliness, division, separation. If he continues to make God his first thought in everything, this sense of alienation will grow—he knows it. *Does he want to go on?* The answer that comes to him is that to go back is to give up what is sweetest and most meaningful to him. To go back is to be united with others only by alienation from himself. He must go on.

Only long after he formulates his resolve does he catch a glimmer of the truth that he had made his decision long before he articulated the question. Had he not long felt, on occasions of no moment as when passing grown men on the street, that he was like a child before them, and yet it was their interests that identify them with a child's world? It was a momentary contact with hidden realities full of loneliness yet full of wonder. He had never inhabited their world at all. It was an experience with no fear and no regret, for it was simply the way things are, no more to be changed than the givenness of sand and soil and stars. Much later still, he would wonder whether all men do not at times share the experience, unless they go out of their way to crush it, the way a pedestrian sometimes goes out of his way to crush a living acorn under his heel.

The joys and sorrows of friendships increase. The pilgrim who is fortunate enough to find a like-minded friend, a fellow pilgrim of the spirit with whom he can talk of all these things, finds his loneliness eased. But what suffering to have a close friend who would like to draw him to useless things! What agony to have an intimate friend who would entice him to sinful ways! Unless an understanding is reached, the suffering is unbearable and the companionship must end, though not the love.

Christ the Light of the world is drawing the pilgrim, and the Holy Spirit is at work within. Spiritual seeds are quietly germinating in his soul, and tender shoots are sprouting, but their nature is not yet manifest. It is faith's springtime.

2.

The Awakening

Of the day, the hour, and the moment which must now be described, no man knows beforehand. No heralds trumpet its arrival. No tell-tale signs precede it. Like every other moment, the moment arrives, and then a man tastes the taste of God. For the most part, the experience is not even spectacular. In his simplicity, the recipient does not appreciate what has really happened. He does not know his life has been changed forever.

The moment before, his soul may be heavy and overcast, with no hope for a sunny day. Then the sun bursts through, giving warmth and comfort. Often the event will occur in the Christian assembly: at Mass, or in shared prayer, or during a retreat.

It can be the moment after Holy Communion. The pilgrim tries to make thanksgiving, but feels unconsoled, sad, unworthy, even troubled in conscience. Out of nowhere a quiet falls on him—the Lord is there—and without ever a lesson he learns to fall silent and communicate at a depth beyond words in a peace beyond telling. The visitation may come after a troubled and prolonged torture of conscience. There is confession, and at once like full day arriving without a slow sunrise there is the impossible experience of a forgiveness deeper than his sin. Many times before this he has experienced the restoration of union with God, but now he is coming to know the union of the sweet embrace of God. Its after-effects linger for months.

It can occur during sorrow-laden thoughts of the Passion of Christ. The pilgrim walks the way of the Cross, lays Christ in the tomb, kneels before the Blessed Sacrament—and is given a taste of the resurrection.

This visitation is what God invites us to through the prophet David: "O taste and see that the Lord is good!" (Ps 34:8). This invitation is a visitation, for it is given not in words but in a taste of His presence.

The visitation shows signs of occurring most frequently during times of suffering and heavy burdens endured for the love of God. The burden may be the burden of sin, for he alone willingly entertains sorrow for sin who loves God dearly. God "comforts us in all our afflictions," St. Paul writes (2 Cor. 1:4). These visitations of which I write here come not to saints but to sinners. One such visitation rescues the pilgrim from the loneliness of his solitary journey.

The visitation may come at the very time it is needed to rescue a pilgrim from the grip of despair. One young man attending college was studying the many faithless, hopeless, loveless analyses of reality popular today. His faith ebbed away. His belief in love collapsed. He doubted that selfless love existed at all. He became convinced no one loved him for himself, not even his parents. The desolation of meaninglessness flooded him, tied his stomach in knots, and introduced him to thoughts of suicide. Out of nowhere he was given an overpowering realization: *Jesus loves me!* Tensions dissolved, unbelief fled, hope was reborn, meaning returned, and the joyous consolation of love flooded his life with peace.

Is the authenticity of such an experience open to question? Undoubtedly. The psychiatrists frequently describe similar experiences which prove to be religiously non-authentic, and some of which have been demonstrated to be paranoiac. What a thing produces tells what it is, and here long-range effects of the experience are valuable norms for judging it. In the case of the pilgrim just described, the author has knowledge of his enduring subsequent fidelity to Christ in a religious vocation.

The profound effects that can be expected to issue from a deep religious experience are quite evident in the following testimonial by a woman whose tottering marriage turned her more fully to God:

> I cannot remember not praying in my life, but I think my first earth-shaking experience of God and prayer was when my husband became an alcoholic. I don't have to go into all the details of the patterns of an alcoholic or the pain caused by the effects of alcohol. I know that a husband, wife or family of an alcoholic go through many nights of anguish and prayer. I mean the down-to-the-bone repetition type prayers of OH GOD, HELP ME! and

prayers without words asking God to watch over the one that is lost. I could not even consider divorce, it would destroy my husband completely and the threat of divorce would be of no value if the plan was not carried out. The children needed a father and basically he was a kind and good person.

I was concerned about helping him and I was concerned for the direction that our souls could go, so once again I asked Jesus for help. I really learned the meaning of placing my trust and whole being in Jesus Christ.

By placing my entire will in Christ, He took my hand and showed me the way. He gave me the courage to say the things I had to say and make the preparations necessary to leave our home. My husband HAD to leave the environment and friends he could not say "No" to.

We moved thousands of miles away where I knew not one person! How did I know that my husband would not start his drinking all over again? I knew, because I had asked in the name of Jesus. I thank God that my husband has not drank in excess since.

Without the direction of God in my life I cannot love, I cannot live, I cannot be; without Him, I am the one who is lost.

God alone knows the right moment and the right circumstances to make His visitation and awaken the pilgrim's love. Three times in the Song of Songs does the lover repeat his solemn admonition: "I adjure you . . . that you stir not up or awaken love until it please."

This single experience of the Divine, if it is genuine, is a seed out of which germinates a new relationship with God. With a whole new meaning the pilgrim repeats one of the old words: JESUS! or SAVIOR! or FATHER! If God ever was simply an act of faith or a polite experience for this pilgrim, he is no longer. He is an ardent, intimate personal acquaintance and longed-for companion. He is the experience of a moment's taste of the love for which everyone longs as in a dream. He is the taste of a childlike innocence which seemed as impossible as reversing the flow of time. He is a moment of certain hope in an immortality that is momentarily touched.

Is this experience the birth of a sent contemplative? The answer seems to depend not only on whether he is called to that vocation, but also on the condition and the will of the pilgrim himself. The visitation involves not only the advent of God but the response of man. The man or woman may in fact be still only a boy or girl, still incapable of making a whole and unified response because his or her personality has not yet grown integral. Then a sweetness can grow between this youth and the Lord, but the birth of contemplation and of vocation are not meant to be as yet. There will be another, and perhaps many other, such privileged moments, until the youth can respond wholly and freely. Again, the pilgrim may indeed be self-possessed, but draw back, sensing in the gentle breeze of love a whirlwind that means to sweep him away with itself. If he is fortunate, if he is destined, another hour will come when he is willing and ready.

One pilgrim tells of her experience and her inability or unwillingness to respond to it for a long time:

> Because I was one of the officers of a group which decided to make a weekend retreat, I went along. During the retreat I had a staggering realization of the awesomeness of the incarnation. In some way, I felt disturbed and upset by the realization that God had become man. I didn't understand why I should feel whatever I felt because I had been taught about the incarnation since childhood and I was now past thirty.
>
> After the retreat I left for Washington to attend a White House conference in an official capacity. Though accustomed to playing an active and vital role in such affairs I couldn't sit through the meeting. I made excuses and left. For lunch I had only drinks, and when I left the session I again went to the bar. I was very tense and the drinks had no effect. I went for a manicure and the girl asked me to please try to relax. I was scheduled for supper at the White House, and cared so little to attend that I missed the bus. A good friend asked about the dramatic change in my demeanor. When I tried to explain what was bugging me she said: "So you've had a deep spiritual experience. That doesn't excuse you from making a contribution here."
>
> I was tired but I couldn't sleep or eat. I was completely ill at ease with these feelings never before experienced. My efforts to return to the more comfortable familiar routine were fruitless; I couldn't escape. I bought a bottle of scotch and took it to my room —something I'd never done in my life. Drinks seemed powerless. I even sought out a priest to "de-brief" me.
>
> Whatever it was that happened, the intense discomfort lasted for about a week. For the year that followed, however I tried to "secularize" myself, something of the experience recurred. The next retreat brought me face to face with a man so deeply involved with and committed to the God-man that I could no longer deliberately run from Him.

Whether it is one or a series of encounters which issues at last in the birth of a sent contemplative, when he is born he begins a new life coalescing around love. He has always known that God's command is to love, but now the Lord has communicated the reality behind the words, and the command is no longer needed.

Unless I interject a brief explanation here, confusion may result from my saying that out of such an event a sent contemplative is born. Are not other varieties of contemplatives also born of such experiences? They are, but here and all through this treatise as I earlier observed, I am attending to the meaning of such events in the course of the growth of one who is destined to be a sent contemplative. Just as the stems of many different plants are similar, many of the experiences—especially the early experiences—of a sent contemplative will be similar to those of other contemplatives, but their meaning is different for each. The meaning is given by the Divine vocation of which they are a part, and it is only as the Divine call unfolds that the differences will appear. In almost all of the instances I cite, I know from the later course of the person's life that the experiences are genuinely related to a call to be a contemplative in action; as in life, the fuller meaning of these events can appear only as the treatise unfolds.

These divine visitations cause the germination of a whole new life of prayer. It is not yet, however, the contemplation of one who has been sent on mission, but rather the contrary. It is simply the contemplation of communion with God. It is the purely passive contemplation which is at the root of all contemplation. In passive contemplation, God takes the total initiative, comes personally, and makes Himself known. It is the heart of the contemplative experience. It cannot be self-produced any more than man can see in total darkness.

Such moments of divinely initiated passive contemplation will seem to call the pilgrim away from his real vocation to activity in the world. The pilgrim cannot put it in those terms since he usually knows nothing about contemplation, but he may wonder about this turn of events which entices him away from secular interests in a powerful way even while he feels that he ought to be interested in secular events. Once again the ways of God seem strange to man: "Consider the work of God. Who can make straight what he has made crooked?" (Qoh. 7:13).

Since it is our part to cooperate with God's wisdom—not to fight it—we ought to search into His ways as best we can. Why has God given to this man destined for work in the world such an otherworldly interest in Himself that for a time he is destined to lose all interest in the world?

We ought first to be clear and insistent on the point that this loss of interest takes place in one destined to be a sent contemplative, and is inevitable, and therefore is in itself no sign that a person is called to cloistered life. Anyone who has experienced it knows that it is so.

It is not only the prayer life of the pilgrim that changes, but everything about him. The change is permanent and inescapable. He has met God, and the meeting is tantamount to a command: "Go from your country and your kindred and your father's house to the land that I will show you" (Gen. 12:1). Like Abram, many sent contemplatives are called to far-away places to carry out God's purposes; but what is more important, every sent contemplative, the moment he begins to respond, has already entered a new land and a new world within himself.

Why has God done this thing? If we turn to the pilgrim's plight before the event, we can gain help in understanding why it *had* to happen—why, despite effects seemingly contrary to his call to be a contemplative in action, it was necessary to make possible that vocation.

The pilgrim had long wanted to find God in work and play— and at times had even struggled to do so—but for the most part he had no idea it was really possible since in these matters he usually found only the attraction of his worldly interests and pleasures. He had wrestled with the world to subdue it to his spiritual purposes, but it was too often he who was overpowered. Even if at times he rose to the high resolve of wanting to be inebriated with God, he too readily became inebriated with what God had made, forgetful of God for a time. He would begin well enough to use things as their master, only to end not as master but as slave.

Paul described to the Romans the laws of this struggle: "Do you not know that if you yield yourselves to anyone as obedient slaves, you are the slaves of the one whom you obey, either of sin, which leads to death, or of obedience, which leads to righteousness?" (6: 16). Paul exposes the mistake of fledgling spiritual pilgrims. They think to become absolute masters, and because this is an impossible goal, they lose their freedom to what they took to be their slaves. Only those who give themselves over totally to obedience to God in love are delivered into the freedom of the sons of God: "But now . . . you have been set free from sin and have become slaves of God" (Rom 6:22).

Man faces the problem of *how to become a slave of God*. It is not within his own power. We are easily enslaved to sensible things because it is easy to come to know them and grow attached and addicted to them. It is not equally easy to come to know God well enough to become a slave of love for "No one has ever seen God;

the only Son, who is in the bosom of the Father, he has made him known" (John 1:18).

Man is a traveler sinking into the quicksand of material pleasures and satisfactions. His struggles make him sink the quicker. If only a helicopter would come, drop him a rope, lift him out! The visitation of God is that helicopter. It lifts a man out of the mire of his entanglements and sets him back on the road of his pilgrimage.

Or a man can be compared to an iron filing held by a small magnet which represents the attractiveness of creatures. Break loose as he may, he will soon become enslaved to another magnet, for the magnetic beauty and goodness of creatures is everywhere. It is only at the approach of some great and mighty magnet that the filing can break loose once and for all and fly toward the great one. God alone is that great magnet.

One pilgrim had a profound experience of this need for God's help to go to God. He recounts it for us.

> I decided to become a religious. A close personal friend accused me of doing it out of pride. In the course of our conversation he made such a powerful case for it that when I tried to answer I was like a man struck dumb. My mouth opened but no words came. When I was alone I reexamined my whole motivation, but my mind could find no solution and no rest. The problem got worse, the pain was terrible. I tried to solve the dilemma by putting before myself everything involved: God, the whole world, and myself and my sinfulness. As if by itself, the world dropped out of the picture. Then my sin dropped out. There was only God and I, and I felt a vast sense of exhilarating freedom. The choice of God and all reasonableness stood on one hand, and chaos on the other. Even so, I COULDN'T MAKE THE CHOICE AND THE RIGHT ONE! I said: GOD, I NEED YOUR HELP. God's hand came down and reached out to me and I raised my arm and took it (I saw nothing, but felt his hand). From then on there was great peace and my resolve to be a priest was stronger than before. I have now been a most happy religious for a quarter of a century, and have never had a serious temptation against my vocation since.

This new freedom from sensible things brought about by a divine visitation is necessary to every spiritual pilgrim's advance, but it is doubly necessary for the sent contemplative. No one sent by God to do His work in the world will be of much use if the world is stronger than he at every turn, or if it is more attractive to him than his unseen Lord. He cannot be constant in his vocation or effective in his work until he is so devoted to God and so free that he can master every other impulse sufficiently to be constantly attentive to the gentle impulses of God within. He can find God in all things only when he is no longer hypnotized by the desirability of things. Only when he has known Beauty and Goodness Himself can he look beyond the goodness and beauty of things to the glorious hints they give of their origin and their destiny.

The new-found strength of one who meets God is often quickly tested, because the forces of the world and the devil do not easily surrender an old acquaintance of theirs. One popular young man who was successful academically and socially, dating regularly, had the following experience:

> I decided to enter the religious life—though some probably thought me a worldly man, and I myself had doubts and misgivings about my suitability. One evening I dressed for a date, and as I was leaving the house it was as though somebody had said: HEY! (though I heard no sound). I jerked my head around in surprise. There in the doorway at the top of the steps it was as though I saw something which was not really visible. The devil stood there, observing me and sneering. I thumbed my nose at him and walked out, but I was shaken and afraid. After that there was much resistance to my vocation from my own mother and from a dear friend who had first told me how at last I had discovered my true calling.

It seems desirable to insert here a note of interpretation concerning the reason for recording such extraordinary events. Their purpose is this: these dramatic events which actually took place serve to illustrate emphatically what most of us experience more prosaically: that we do need God's help; that the devil is at work against us; and so on. The most dramatic authentic form of each kind of experience that has come to my personal attention is used on the principle that the most intensive example of a given experience includes in itself all lesser forms of such an experience. Thus this treatise is rendered more universally applicable, if only the reader does not fail to see himself in these events simply because he has not experienced them as dramatically.

I also ask the reader to perceive that in constructing this "composite autobiography" I am depicting a kind of *super sent contemplative*. He portrays the best and the most terrible things that happen on the pilgrimage of the spirit. It would be *unrealistic* for anyone to expect all these things to happen to one person. It would be *wrong* to feel that *any* of the more extraordinary events need happen to anyone to make him a sent contemplative. But they do happen to some, and it is good to know that they do in case they should happen to us or to those whom we direct; and it is instructive to realize that in their essence but not in their drama they happen to all of us. We are all visited and strengthened by God. We are all subject to resistance and diabolical temptations.

The pilgrim's meeting with the Master will give him joy and free him from many of the old problems, but it will give rise to new ones which he will discover quickly enough as he continues his pilgrimage. That should surprise none of us, for the Father Himself has said that it would be so: "My son, if you aspire to serve the Lord, prepare yourself for an ordeal" (Sir. 2:1 JB).

SPIRITUAL PROJECT ONE:
Plumbing My First Name of Grace

"The Lord called me from the womb, from the body of my mother he named my name" (Is. 49:1).

By reflecting on your grace experiences you can draw a spiritual profile of yourself that will help you discover your "grace name," your spiritual identity before God. Your reflection can be helped by meditating on the following questions, and writing the answers. When you have finished, read them over and see if you can learn anything new about your identity before God.

1. What is the etymological meaning of your baptismal name?
2. What is the taste of the springs of your first spiritual experiences?
3. From what disordered spirits were you converted? From lovelessness? Meaninglessness? Suicide? Lust? Greed?
4. What unique constellation of divine favors constitutes your grace identity? What virtue especially draws you? What do you desire to be? To accomplish? What gifts do you have? What apostolate is most meaningful? What divine name most appeals to you?
5. What does your relationship with God tell you about Him? Is He near or far away? Tender or severe? Intimate or standoffish? Matter-of-fact or romantic?
6. In what crisis did God most evidently come to your rescue?
7. How can you best serve God and the world? Are you attracted to enter the world and work for it in Christ—or to withdraw to pray for it?
8. Do you feel God neglects you and refuses to give you what He gives others? Do you face Him openly in prayer, or bear secret grudges against Him?

9. Did this reflection expose any unfinished spiritual business to which you ought to attend?
10. Did this reflection help you to discover you have more in common with the experiences of a sent contemplative than you had realized?
   (Recall that a sent contemplative is one whom God sends on apostolic mission with the special ongoing guidance of the Holy Spirit).

3.

God's Absence Is Discovered

The pilgrim who comes this far now begins to suffer in earnest the birth pangs of contemplation. From the moment of God's visitation he begins to discover *the absence of God in all things*. It is a true discovery by a spiritual explorer. It will transport his soul into a new land. From now on he will no longer be a child of his times, no longer consciously and unconsciously identified with every current whim and aberration. His religious experience has dislocated him from the reality he knew and loved. He has been called from his fatherland to go in search of the absent God.

We must try to discover why this discovery of the absence of God is a true discovery, and a necessary one, and what its meaning is for his vocation. Why is it that the world made by God no longer reveals to him the traces of God he used to find in natural beauty and goodness?

The psalmist too asks this question: "O Lord, why dost thou . . . hide thy face from me?" (Ps. 88:14). It is not that the psalmist does not know God is present for he begins his prayer by saying: "O Lord, my God, I call for help by day; I cry out in the night before thee" (88:1). But note that he finds God's presence in the *night*—that is, in the darkness of the soul's interior, by faith. It is in the daylight of the world that he can no longer find God's presence. He is not pleading to see the uncreated Face of God for he knows it has been revealed to Moses that "You cannot see my face; for man shall not see me and live" (Exod. 33:20). Like the pilgrim, the psalmist wants at least to see God's "created face" in His works and in His providence, but he cannot as he makes clear: "Thou hast caused my companions to shun me . . . I am shut in so that I cannot escape" (Ps. 88: 8). That is, the persons and the things through which he used to experience God's kindness and His "presence" now either show alienation from him, or oppress him by tugging at him to draw him away from God.

Before we can throw light on this experience, we must look more carefully at what preceded it. The pilgrim used to find God in the world until he met Him for a moment within. Then he found Him neither within nor in the world. Why? Let us notice first that the pilgrim is experiencing a two-fold absence of God: the one within, which he had never noticed before, and the one outside, which he had never experienced before—this is the first time the light of the beauty and goodness of the world has ever gone out so completely.

Now we will try to understand what has happened. Before God's visitation within the pilgrim knew God only at some distance, as it were. He knew Him through created things and through spiritual experiences that had never revealed to him in such depth how intimately and delightfully God can be present. One moment changed all that. That one moment changed *absence of the knowledge of God to knowledge of the absence of God*. The pilgrim longs to recover that moment of God's interior Presence, and it is not in his power. It was a gift.

This is the first way he is experiencing God's absence. His plight can be compared to that of a young man who has always known the girl down the block, but only casually, in a distant sort of way so that he never missed her when she was away. One day they date, and he comes to truly know her and he falls in love and now a single hour of her absence is greater than all her former absences combined. So does the soul pine for God once He has made Himself known interiorly even for an instant.

What explains the second form of God's absence, His absence

from created things? Why can the pilgrim no longer find in the goodness and beauty of created things some joy and some knowledge of how Beautiful and Good He must be who created them? Why have all things grown plain and frowsy? Why have they lost their appeal? A simple and accurate (if only partial) explanation is that things are lovely and good because they reflect the qualities of Him who made them, but once the Artisan is present, the artifacts are seen to be nothing by comparison. That is why Jesus said to the man who saw only His humanity and called Him good: "Why do you call me good? No one is good but God alone" (Luke 18:19).

To clarify what has been said it is helpful to add that in reality God is no less present than He has ever been, with the exception of the one moment of His inner visitation; but that one moment has made all the difference. The experience of it has made every other experience "no experience" by comparison. The truth is that God is probably more "present" to the pilgrim than ever, but it was only the moment of God's new depth of entrance into his soul that gave rise to the experience of Him—just as we are more conscious of moving things than of things at rest. What we are talking about, then, is not a real absence of God but an experience which registers as absence.

This whole experience of God's absence from created things can be made plainer by a similitude. A man sees his surroundings clearly in broad daylight, but let him glance at the sun and for a time he will see the earth only dimly or not at all. So too the pilgrim turning his gaze from Creator to creatures sees more their darkness and deficiencies than their assets. He sees a world disfigured by sin.

The changed aspect of things is most notable in human affairs. Until now he has cherished human love and its fulfillments, but now he has tasted the fountainhead of love and he feels the need of a love no human can give. His eyes have been opened to the sickness afflicting human love. Where before he found love, now he more readily finds its absence. It is not others but he who has changed. Philosophers explain this kind of change with an axiom: "Everything is experienced according to the condition of the one who experiences." Sin has wounded mankind's likeness to God and the pilgrim now sees the ugly wound.

Engagement in secular affairs takes on a certain negative characteristic. Since at this time God chooses to make His divine visitations within, apart from the world, in the heights of the soul, the pilgrim cannot find Him in the jejuneness of earth. Human affairs become tedious, profitless, childish castle-building in the sands, washed away by the tides of time before ever anything is finished. God alone counts. *Our Father, who art in heaven!* Work is both necessary and useless, a burdensome distraction. God is to be found in the high mystery of the Mass, in the silence of Holy Communion, or in the depths of prayer. This is his experience.

It would be unjust to lay heavy blame on the world. Not merely the world's sinfulness but its nothingness underlies this development. Nor can the pilgrim himself be exonerated. He fails to find God in creatures because he does not know how to look with the clear eyes of selfless love. He fails to find love where it can be found because he does not know love well enough to recognize it in the rags of its imperfect state. He has tasted God's love, but love is known fully only when it is fully given as well as received. He desires to love and to give, but he must wait patiently for love to erase all his old habits of selfishness.

If the pilgrim knew these things it would help, but he does not know them. As yet he does not know that he is being called in order to be sent into the world whose grip is losing its hold on him to make God's presence in the world more manifest to others by helping to develop it into the Kingdom of God.

Other factors may compound his problem of finding God in his secular pursuits. He may be in the wrong state of life, the wrong academic course, the wrong career; he may be pursuing the wrong objective still. In short, he may have set his course without consulting God's purpose for him. For some, that purpose will include the religious life and the priesthood, and this is likely to grow manifest now. If so, it will be a joy to respond, though there may be suffering in surmounting the obstacles.

One caution concerning life style changes may be profitable. Since pilgrims in this stage long for solitude and prayer they must not take as from God every impulse to abandon their current positions and responsibilities. Such impulses need to be discerned wisely. A pilgrim whom God intends to dispatch as one of His sent contemplatives could easily prefer to join cloistered contemplatives, and mistake his preference for the will of God.

One pilgrim writes:

> I had thought God wanted me to join a certain active religious order. Before entering I received a gift of deep prayer and was attracted to the Trappists. For a time I was cast into doubt about which course to follow. One day, beset by the problem, I knelt before the Blessed Sacrament and an image of Our Lady. Without knowing how I came to a decision I spontaneously promised Jesus

and Mary I would enter the active order. Since it felt to me a little as though I was giving in I suspected the confusion was brought on by following my own desire instead of what, in my deepest heart, I knew God wanted. I entered that active order years ago and have been at peace ever since.

Another religious desired to leave her active order and join cloistered contemplatives. Her director advised her to try giving more time to prayer to see if that would suffice. It did.

A religious woman eager to grow in prayer became upset at what she felt was the low priority given to prayer by her community. She writes:

> I became increasingly dissatisfied with what I viewed as a strong emphasis placed on conformity and the apparent lack of concern for the individual as well as the seemingly patterned approach to prayer . . . I felt impelled to speak out . . . After doing so, I began to realize more and more that not only were my words falling on deaf ears but that they were primarily giving rise to feelings of hostility within myself. . . . Unrest, hopelessness and despair refused to leave . . . I felt and knew I was retrogressing rather than progressing and that I was helpless to change the tide. I believed I could respond to His "call" elsewhere.

At this point the religious consulted her spiritual director, who saw at once that she was wrongly making an important decision in a time of desolation and confusion. He suggested that she pray over the passage: "Now is my soul troubled. And what shall I say—Father, save me from this hour? No, for this purpose I have come to this hour. Father, glorify thy name." Startled, the religious told him that this was the passage the Lord had always brought to her mind in the past to weather her vocational storms. Prayer over the passage restored her peace.

In one diocese fifteen religious women in turn transferred to congregations of cloistered contemplatives. In the end all left religious life.

These testimonials and examples make it clear that when new religious experiences come, the obvious thing to do is not always the right thing to do. Life styles should be changed only after sound reflection and the consultation of a reliable spiritual director. It is necessary to avoid making major decisions in time of desolation, and to choose one's path wisely even in times of consolation. Often a great good is lost in the name of a greater good—which proves spurious.

It is in order to consider now the resistance to this inner experience of God and its unworldly effects. This resistance is certain to arise in the pilgrim or in those around him, whether through fear or temptation or by reason of some ideology, some preconception of the way religious experiences ought to conduct themselves. It looks like a dangerous thing, this dislocation from the world, and it is! *Then better to turn away from it! Better to stay on the beaten path and shun this impractical, this visionary state of affairs!* So are the spirits within a man and within his companions likely to reason against him. To overcome them a pilgrim must turn to prayer, to a good spiritual director who knows about these things, and to the assurance he can find in the writings of the Saints and good spiritual theologians on prayer.

An unwise spiritual director can himself mount this resistance against the pilgrim. The authentic role of a spiritual director is to help the pilgrim discern where God is leading him, and to support his response. Blind guides lacking knowledge of contemplative growth—and worse, infected with some inflexible activist ideology that takes a dim view of prayer and its mysteries—can cause intense suffering. Such guides resist both the Holy Spirit and the yearning spirit of the pilgrim. They will thrust the pilgrim into ways he cannot travel at this time, ways that will starve the new life within him. And what a persuasive argument they have when they point out that the fledgling apostle's prayer is "alienating" him from the world which he himself feels sent to serve. The sent contemplative is like the baby claimed by two mothers—contemplation and action—but the spiritual director, instead of giving the wise decision of Solomon, is for hewing the baby in two!

Once again it becomes evident that the sent contemplative is not called to a set of practices but to a living, growing way of life that does not always move in a straight line toward apostolic goals. The pilgrim's journey is like that of the Israelites through the wilderness. The stages of their journey were not plotted by men but by God, who made His will manifest by a cloud that hovered over His tabernacle in their midst: "Whether it was two days, or a month, or a longer time, that the cloud continued over the tabernacle, abiding there, the people of Israel remained in camp and did not set out; but when it was taken up they set out. At the command of the Lord they encamped, and at the command of the Lord they set out" (Num. 9: 22-23). Those who moved by other norms were lost.

Both the pilgrim and the director have their duties and their rights. The pilgrim should either follow the director's guidance or leave him. When tempted to leave, he should be aware that he may be looking for a guide he can lead rather than one who will lead him.

The director should not continue with a pilgrim who does not accept his advice. The director should also remember that he is only an auxiliary discerner helping the pilgrim to hear and do God's will in Christ. His knowledge of revelation and of the wisdom of the Church, and of the pilgrim and his condition and the spirits that move him, is what he should use to judge the trueness of the way along which the pilgrim feels called. The director should guide within the objective boundaries of God's revelation and he should make use of the Lord's own norm for judging whether the pilgrim is on the right path within those boundaries: "You will know them by their fruits. Are grapes gathered from thorns, or figs from thistles?" (Matthew 7:16). A discerning director will recognize in the pilgrim so far described one who is bearing the rich fruit of the greatest commandment: "You shall love the Lord your God with all your heart, and with all your soul, and with all your strength, and with all your mind" (Luke 10:27). Unless he is neglecting his duties, it is not time to remonstrate with him about greater service to neighbor. It is the hour of opportunity, the hour to nourish the mustard seed of divine love. If that seed sprouts in him it will make him a man of God and therefore a man for others. If it does not sprout, neither will he ever become a man for others—only for himself.

No man of sense loads a young colt with the burdens of a full-grown horse. No man of judgment asks a bridegroom to carry on his normal duties in the season of his marriage. That is why Hebrew law exempted a bridegroom from military service (Deut. 20:7). Such laws were written for our spiritual instruction. If a man and woman who fall in love are for a season dislocated from their normal lives, are we not wise enough to expect something similar of one who falls in love with God? Think of Paul of Tarsus meeting Jesus and then going off to the Arabian desert. Who could think it subtracted from the love and service he gave his fellow men in the long run? Jesus spent thirty years in private life, and when His public apostolic work seemed overdue, He went off for forty days of prayer.

It should be openly admitted that this grace of passive contemplation produces such a need for prayer and solitude that it *seems* suited only to those destined for cloistered lives. Why then is it given to all types of contemplatives? That is like asking why flesh is given to everyone who is to have a body. For as flesh makes up the substance of the body, passive contemplation is the root and substance of all contemplation, even that of the active contemplative sent on mission by God. The root of contemplation is passive because contemplation is in essence loving attention to the gift of God's presence.

How this gift of contemplation takes on a special form to make possible the vocation of one sent on a Spirit-guided mission will be seen as this treatise progresses; but here we will look at the value of passive contemplation for any spiritual pilgrim fortunate enough to be graced with it. Passive contemplation is a great gift of prayer, and growth in prayer is necessary for and is itself spiritual progress. Prayer joins a man to God in that union that makes a man both know God and share in His wisdom and power. Furthermore, just as it is the experience of creatures that first leads a man to God, it is the experience of God that leads a man back to creatures at a new depth of discovery of their goodness. *This return will appear later in the pilgrim's development.*

Deep prayer and meditation will also serve to make the pilgrim know Christ more interiorly. Prayer is the transformer that converts faith information about Christ to various forms of inner experience of Christ. Meditation converts the pilgrim's sensibilities: statuary, pictures, and stations of the cross fill his vision with likenesses of Christ while faith and intellect are aware of the Divinity inhabiting His body. As the pilgrim grows, imaginative meditation replaces the statuary and other external images. The more these images of Jesus and His mysteries penetrate the psychic life, the more feelings and emotions, intelligence and freedom are gently converted to the life of faith.

Senses, feelings and imagination continue to store up images, experiences, habits and memories conducive to a life like Christ's own. In due time, the pilgrim will begin to respond spontaneously with the mind and heart of Christ in the course of ordinary affairs. What we are describing here is not a mere self-induced assimilation to Christ but a cooperation with the Holy Spirit who is the Author of our transfiguration: "We all, with the unveiled face, beholding the glory of the Lord, are being changed into his likeness from one degree of glory to another; for this comes from the Lord who is the Spirit" (2 Cor. 3:18).

We ought not to omit one further purpose of the divine visitation which produced the events considered in this chapter. The purpose of the divine visitation is love. It is what love must do. The true lover must come and manifest himself to the beloved—and God is the truest lover of all. And even if (contrary to fact) the visitation did not help the pilgrim to be a better apostle, it must still take place. True lovers love and bear all the consequences.

Just as God is the only good of the pilgrim at this time, sin is the only evil. Sin is what kept the Beloved from coming for so long, and sin is the only threat of losing Him. Does this not terribly worsen the burden of life in the world? The world is no longer a place where God can be found and so it is useless, but it is a place where He can be lost and so it is worse than useless! "Terror, and the pit, and the snare are upon you, O inhabitant of the earth! He who flees at the sound of the terror shall fall into the pit; and he who climbs out of the pit shall be caught in the snare" (Is. 24:17-18). While the pilgrim remains in the grip of this experience, ordinary responsibilities become a heavy burden. He is in real spiritual danger, for he is still not free enough to use things well. Things he used to cling to but now wants to renounce cling to him like stubborn bloodsuckers.

Of course, he is aware of the biblical injunction to serve his neighbor but it cries to him from a distance weakly while God is a burning experience and sin is a raging tyrant. He is on a futile earth, and God is in heaven, which is sometimes within. What meaningful thing can he do but enter within when duty does not demand otherwise?

Growing horror of sin may rebound on him. Specters of past evils done rise up against him. Rumors of old sins poorly confessed haunt him. Sin is so shameful he can hardly broach such matters in confession. When the torture of telling them is less than the torture of concealing, he re-confesses doubtful matters. Even so, he can never remember rightly, never be sure. It is an endless process. Never again will he have peace in this life. So he thinks, but a marvelous grace can come by which he resigns himself to God's will, and trusts he will come home to Him in death, washed clean in the blood of Christ.

An understanding confessor is a great blessing not only for the pilgrim but for the sake of the Church. This turmoil exhausts a man's energies doing inner battle and it makes him unfit for service. Unless he overcomes this problem the pilgrim's contemplative call to service may be vitiated by a running battle with these inner enemies. Some religious in this plight are dismissed as unsuitable for religious life. One religious suffering from religious scruples tells how he avoided this fate: "The novice master cautioned me that my scruples could hinder my vocation. Since I had implicit trust in Mary I went to her and told her confidently of my need. The scruples left me at once and have never returned." His experience illustrates the truest remedy for all spiritual maladies: Confident prayer.

Some pilgrims abandon religion in their torture. If that gives them relief, it is a good sign they were subject to the machinations of the devil, not to authentic problems of sin. The devil can take an overly sensitive conscience and turn it against a pilgrim. That is why St. Ignatius counsels the scrupulous person with an over-sensitive conscience to act courageously to de-sensitize it by acting exactly contrary to its unreasonable mandates. Courage is necessary to win against scruples, but so is a certain sternness with oneself. Narcissistic self-pity can be dosed with the severe but potent dictum of one writer who called scrupulosity "the bleeding wound of self-love."

A good confessor will explain to a tortured pilgrim who is manifestly scrupulous that all sins are forgiven, even forgotten ones; and that no past sins need be nor should be confessed again unless there is *sure knowledge* that some sin was certainly mortal and certainly never confessed. If the person is in bad enough straits, he can even be told that his condition excuses him from *any* further effort to confess past sins; and as spiritual director, the priest can forbid it. This is an extreme remedy and should be reserved for extreme cases, such as psychologically disturbed persons. The reason is that instead of helping a person to build up his courage and renounce his self-pity, it allows him to surrender to the paternalism of the confessor.

The good confessor must help the pilgrim to act courageously on his realization that God is not a tyrant but a gentle lover and a forgiving Father. The pilgrim has to learn to return to his view of confession as one of the great healing agents and channels of peace given us by our prodigal Father.

The suffering of scruples will not easily be laid to rest when it is brought on, not by particular sins, but by darkness and desolation as fallout of the newly awakened awareness of the distance between the holiness of God and the sinfulness of man. When this is the cause, the conscience is gradually refined, and the suffering transmuted into pure sorrow for sin and reverence for God.

Perhaps the most heartening news is the fact that many cases of scruples threaten to last for a lifetime, but actually pass rather quickly.

The experience of scrupulosity can further alienate the pilgrim from secular affairs. How can he take seriously the trivial events of his daily routine when he is fighting within the raging battle for eternity? In fact, however, healthy activity, especially self-giving activity such as serving the sick or needy, can take him out of himself and be a healing agent.

Directors of experience learn to respect the ways of God and of the spirit. Spiritual processes have their mysteries and their seasons and they must be suffered: "Let it be so now; for thus it is fitting for us to fulfil all righteousness" (Matthew 3:15). In due time the pilgrim will once again see the beauty of the days and the earth and the people, and he will esteem them more because he better understands that God gave the world His only Son, for love of that world.

During this conversion period it is not unknown for a pilgrim to experience bodily the sensation of holiness. It may happen in a quiet church before the Blessed Sacrament. Then it is as though every cell of the body is attracted forward in love, yet draws back in reverence. It is as though one long out in the cold of the spirit were drawing nearer with a delicious shiver to the blazing fire that warms the heart of man. The value of this body experience of entering into the Presence of the holy, and of all similar sensible spiritual experiences, is contained in the lesson even the body learns—that it too can delight in holiness, that the pursuit of God holds joys and ineffable promises of which food and drink and sex know nothing by comparison. The psalmist manifests this realization in his cry: "O God, thou art my God, I seek thee, my soul thirsts for thee; my flesh faints for thee, as in a dry and weary land where no water is" (Ps 63:1). Until the body *does* participate in experiences of the holy it is highly unlikely that anyone can catch fire with whole-hearted love of God.

There is the complication that some persons are able to induce pseudo experiences of the holy, and they seek out a religious atmosphere not to find God but to find gratification through their spurious religious experiences. The authentic experience, on the other hand, is not sought but given, and has the effect of inflaming the recipient with love of God and of drawing him to God, not to seeking repetitions of the experience.

When God makes His divine visitations to a pilgrim and gives him the taste of Himself which weans him from the things of earth, the pilgrim can in no time mount to a height of trust in God and a generous return of love which many years of ordinary ascetical efforts and practices would not enable him to match. One pilgrim who was given a taste of God's provident care and His deep love responded to Him in the following prayer:

> Sin has darkened my understanding and weakened my will. I am unable to refrain from evil; I am much less able to choose always the greatest good. I often choose a passing pleasure in place of greater love of God for all eternity. But Your understanding and Your will are infinite, Our Lord, and in Your wondrous love for me

You desire that I seek always the eternal joys . . . I surrender my will to You, O Lord, and seek Your will to guide me. Even if You would have me die today, dear Lord, I desire it, for what better thing is there for me than Your will? I would rather die this day, O Lord, if it be Your will, than live justly before Your face for many more years. I will never fear Your will, for You, Truth, have said: MY YOKE IS EASY AND MY BURDEN LIGHT.

This pilgrim used to repeat his prayer daily with devotion in an effort never to lose the realization which he had been given. The result was that he developed a remarkable readiness for whatever God asked.

If the pilgrim finds God in anything but prayer and the Mass and the sacraments during this period, it is likely to be in pure and simple things like the company of little children and unaffected adults. He may seek out the company of priests and Sisters of unaffected holiness. He may find rest and refreshment in classical music with its measure and grace and restraint.

He has little besides the promise of God, but like impotent old Abraham and barren Sarah he has trust and he has hope in God's goodness. His hunger for God is one of his dearest possessions, for he senses in his longing an unceasing prayer. He looks to the joy he awaits in faith, a joy he already tastes faintly as you can taste the salt spray on a windy day before you reach the ocean's shore. "For God alone my soul waits in silence; from him comes my salvation" (Ps. 62:1).

SPIRITUAL PROJECT TWO:
Searching for Interior Freedom

If you continue in my word, you are truly my disciples, and you will know the truth, and the truth will make you free" (John 8:31-32).

1. Do I believe personal experience of God is possible for me, or is my attitude: *The Saints, yes; me? No way!*
2. Do I really believe (act on the belief) that God has a Father's concern for me and my affairs, and a word to speak to me directly?
3. Do I wrongly conceive of "life in the Spirit" as awaiting a flash of light from heaven before I make any decision? Or am I aware that God can and does guide me by imperceptibly influencing my inner life, so that when I come to a decision in freedom, joy, and peace, it is God's work as well as my own?
4. Am I habitually ready to pursue God's way even before it is

discovered, or is my enthusiasm suspended until I know what it is?

5. Do I easily renounce everything but that to which God calls me?
6. Do I keep on the lookout for, pray and work against my every opinion, ideology and natural bent of temperament that prevents me from listening freely for the word of God?
7. Can I accept the fact that sometimes God may not want the humanly efficient way?
8. Am I aware of my scars from the past, my lack of freedom, my need for conversion?
9. Am I able to advert to, name, and own all my feelings and emotions, so that I may know I am a sinner in danger of self-deception?
10. Am I ready to find out what God wants and to do it, or am I a slave to fear of suffering, alienation, and human respect? Cf. Hebr. 12:1.

4.

The Kingdom of the World

Grows Manifest

The Holy Spirit has a most delicate task in this period of the pilgrim's development. Gently and gradually the Spirit will expose to His pupil the most terrible reason for his experience of the absence of God in the world. He will open the pilgrim's eyes in faith to see a world so evil it cannot be loved at all, and a world so good it cannot be loved too much. The task is delicate because once aroused against evil the pilgrim may give way to hatred not only for evil but for evildoers. It is more delicate still because he himself is infected with evil and is in real danger of rejecting even himself.

A word of caution to the reader is in order. What has just been said can be misconstrued as a disloyal attack on mankind and a blatant wholesale rejection of human efforts—that is, as alienation from human nature itself. No man wants to be alienated from man, and when the danger arises human passions rise with it. The inclination is to stop one's ears as did those who heard St. Stephen— judging the speaker a misguided traitor. Yet if we want the truth, we must heed the Scriptures, face the issue of the world's evil, and accept truthful accusations.

Scripture uses the word *world* in two senses. In the one sense it is the world of Babel, the world of those who claim to be their own masters. Scripture teaches that this world cannot be loved at all: "Do not love the world or the things in the world. If anyone loves the world, love for the Father is not in him. For all that is in the world, the lust of the flesh and the lust of the eyes and the pride of life, is not of the Father but is of the world. And the world passes away" (1 John 2:15-17). In the other sense, the world is the creation of God and cannot be loved too much, as God's own love shows: "For God so loved the world that he gave his only Son. . . ." (John 3: 16).

The pilgrim is now consciously caught up in the struggle between these two worlds and he is constantly beset by the struggle to set loyalties in order within his own life. Self-deceits which used to facilitate convenient false loyalty to friends, organizations and ideologies begin to be uncovered and renounced, and the consequences bravely endured. The Lord is purging the pilgrim's worldly attitudes as He purged those of His first followers. Jesus repeatedly censured their false loyalties and their collusion with a sinful world until they could accept the fact that the world resists, punishes, and persecutes the man who is for God first. In response to St. Peter's attack on His prediction that He would be killed by His persecutors Jesus retorted: "Get behind me, Satan! You are a hindrance to me; for you are not on the side of God, but of men" (Matthew 16:23).

The ordering of the pilgrim's loyalties, and the attacks on them, will begin in a small way. A layman who starts attending daily Mass may be treated as though he has lost good judgment and is no longer giving the world its due. One faithful and industrious housewife and mother found time to attend daily Mass—only to be attacked by a relative for neglecting her duties. One boy confided to his father his aspiration to the priesthood. He then wrote in shock to a priest that he was assailed like one planning a murder. Teenagers who live loosely are often treated indulgently by parents; yet these same parents view them with horror and even physically attack them when they join the Sodality of Mary. Many are alarmed when they see religion overstepping the bound which they have assigned to it.

Even in religious communities similar things happen. One group of religious disliked their superior and offered him passive resistance. A companion who refused to join in was persecuted.

Experiences similar to these multiply, so that the pilgrim begins to see what unjust demands men make upon one another. Each clique, organization, group and society has its unwritten laws, its party line. Each member must surrender and subscribe in return for the companionship, power, and prestige group identity bestows. The party line can be in matters of attitudes, policy, politics, or theology. Submission does harm always, since even if one does not cajole himself into being a believer, he stops giving witness to truth as he sees it. He no longer represents thought and conviction and faith, but only some predetermined party line often labeled conservative or liberal. Capitulation is a partial surrender of one's own mind and conscience, and it is therefore a betrayal of God.

Some pilgrims suffer much more than others under these pressures. One with an affable disposition, a charming personality, and wisdom in the ways of the world can take his stand subtly and firmly, with a good humor that minimizes alienation. This is the way of a St. Thomas More. Others lack these gifts, perhaps because they do not have the same vocation. Their witness is angular, obtrusive, openly prophetic, as was that of Jeremias and St. Stephen, and their persecution is certain. Even for the Thomas Mores there comes a time of inescapable confrontation.

The pilgrim who adheres to the guidance of the Spirit and braves dislike, ostracism, and rejection will find life difficult but by no means impossible. There are the joys of integrity, fidelity, and the consolations of God.

This problem is fated to grow worse before ever it abates. Initially the pilgrim is viewed as an eccentric or a maverick, and such are tolerated more than they are hated. It takes time for the world to realize with alarm that it is not dealing with an annoying but rather intriguing declaration of personal independence; it is confronted with the far more alarming event of a man who is transferring his first loyalty to God.

In the process, the pilgrim grows in all the virtues, for the virtues are the right ordering of love. When holiness becomes manifest in him, the world will understand what is really afoot. Then ostracism is compounded by jealousy, and jealousy by hostility, and hostility can lead to violence. Cain, we are told, was jealous of Abel because he was favored by God, and his jealousy led to violence. The violence the pilgrim is most likely to meet with is not physical but psychological violence.

The more the pilgrim discovers the world's evils, the more he feels responsible for witnessing against them, and the more he is punished in return. No one can denounce the world for its evasions, rejections, and abdications of responsibility, and escape hatred. Denounce racism, abortion, war-mongering, fornication, pornography, perversion, profiteering, international exploitation, political chicanery, petty pilfering and laziness on the job, parental irresponsibility, and lying interpretations of the faith, and enemies multiply on all sides. Denounce educational institutions which promote libertinism more than truth, health facilities more concerned with money than with mercy, nations which seek power rather than justice, national policy which promotes the impotence of religion rather than its free practice, religious orders more concerned with the things of men than the things of God, affluent Christians concerned with their own affairs and not those of Christ and His poor, militant groups selfishly disrupting the common good with tactics better calculated to gain revenge than lawful rights, and one will have few friends, for friends expect selective indignation and causes "discreetly" chosen. The pilgrim called by God to work in the world has a conscience stirred by the Spirit, and he can no longer be a party to selective justice—to hypocrisy.

So all-pervasive is disorder that the pilgrim is soon in conflict everywhere. "Go not forth into the field, nor walk on the road; for the enemy has a sword, terror is on every side" (Jer. 6:25).

The pilgrim faces the danger of taking this hostility too personally, and being destroyed by it. His hope lies in adhering to the truth that he is marked for rejection not because he is *not* a worthwhile person but because he *is*. Fulfilled in him now are those Gospel predictions which seem so exaggerated to tepid Christians: "If the world hates you, know that it has hated me before it hated you. If you were of the world, the world would love its own; but because you are not of the world, but I chose you out of the world, therefore the world hates you" (John 15:18-19).

The pilgrim remains confused and hurt by the attitudes he faces daily. He cannot yet see to the cause of these experiences. He thinks he is dealing with minor misunderstandings which confrontation and reasonable discussion can end. The truth is he is facing something as deep as the heart of man and as perverse as his deviation from God. St. Augustine explains this terrible truth about the city of man in his *City of God*: "Each individual in this community is driven by his passions to pursue his private purposes. Unfortunately, the objects of these purposes are such that no one person (let alone the whole world community) can ever be wholly satisfied. The reason for this is that nothing but Absolute Being can satisfy human nature. The result is that the city of man remains in a chronic state of civil war" (XVIII, 2).

Unfortunately, the pilgrim is likely to return some of the world's hostility. In this he is meeting another crisis. The sin of the world is in him too. The unjust hatred directed at him stirs his own unregenerate passions. He resents ill treatment; he resents the hardships sinners cause, he resents the roadblocks they throw up against the kingdom of God; he resents the silence of good people who buy false peace at a great price. Hatred against him stirs hatred within him. He battles these disordered affections, but even when he succeeds in freeing his conscious motives and deliberate actions from hostility, deeper, more unregenerate currents remain. These insinuate themselves into the tone of his voice, a gesture, and other forms of "body language." The Spirit leads him to discern these disorders too, and labor against them, and be humbled by them, because they give witness that he too bears the guilt.

Here too he can learn from Scripture. Esau hated his brother Jacob and planned his murder, but Jacob himself is hardly free from blame. And by humility and generosity Jacob won reconciliation. In fact, Esau seems to have renounced his hatred even before Jacob did anything. Such changes in men's hearts are above all the work of God, as the pilgrim is finding out. He can subdue his own disordered affections with much effort, but he cannot uproot them. The only treatment powerful enough to remove them is repeated divine visitations within, and the intensely humbling and purging self-knowledge that accrues from them.

The pilgrim's regeneration will progress, but it will not save him from the world's hostility. The more innocent he becomes, the more consideration he shows, and the less militant he is, the more some will take umbrage. Even if he no longer judges others, they cannot believe it; and even if they believe it, his very presence judges them:

"He claims to have knowledge of God, and calls himself a son of the Lord. Before us he stands, a reproof to our way of thinking, the very sight of him weighs our spirits down" (Wis. 2:13-14 JB).

He is an offense to others because men who come to a sure knowledge of God by faith are scorned for their arrogance. The world loves ignorance of definitive truth as a license to hold what it wishes and do what it pleases. The pilgrim is a thorn in the world's side because he holds doggedly to the knowledge that God's way is holy and not man's, and that true loyalty to man is founded on loyalty to God.

He sees men insist on negotiating even with God to make their own judgments prevail concerning what is true and false, what is right and wrong, what is righteousness and what is sin. Man judges even God's word, but he knows that this is a judgment on oneself, as the Spirit is making evident: "And when he comes he will show the world how wrong it was, about sin, and about who was in the right, and about judgment" (John 16:8 JB).

One other cruel temptation is almost certain. Like Adam tempted to choose his beloved over God he will be tempted. And Tamar's half-brother tempted her to sin, and even though she resisted she was dishonored. All who truly love are sooner or later tried and tortured by such requests.

To endure hostility and hatred without growing embittered is one of the greatest problems in the growth of an apostolic contemplative. One pilgrim who wrestled with this problem gives his solution:

> Sometimes I deserve this rejection for my own sins and sometimes I do not, and sometimes I do not know, and that is bitterest of all. After praying over it, I offered God my willingness to accept it to the extent I deserve it, and beyond that to embrace it with joy as a share in the injustice Jesus bore. So I no longer worry my head about whether I deserve it or not, except that I stay on the lookout to weed out my own sins. I also have to meditate on the Passion of Jesus, and to remember that even though He was "the most beautiful of the sons of men," he was rejected with a kiss.

These experiences cause grief, suffering, and even bodily sickness. Endurance will issue in a gentler, more understanding and compassionate love for others. The pilgrim is coming to know this sick and sinful world for what it really is, and he is coming to know his own sinfulness in the process. This knowledge is crucial to the work God has sent him to do in the world. It must continue to grow, for it is not yet adequate. Once he was blind to much of the evil in the world, for a time he is blind to much that is good, but there will come a time when he will see both clearly. That time will not come swiftly, for it is no work of a moment to grow into a love like that of the Father who "sent the Son into the world, not to condemn the world, but that the world might be saved through him" (John 3:16-17).

When the pilgrim's faith convictions meet the onslaught of the world's hostile forces of unbelief, his surest source of steadfastness is his unconditional trust in the goodness and holiness of God: *Our Father . . . hallowed be they name!* God alone is holy, God's ways alone are unfailingly good.

The pilgrim needs iron faith to keep a grip on his belief in the goodness of the world while that goodness is so obscured by these trials. For the present that goodness bursts through only rarely, whether it be in the sight of a face aglow with innocence passing on the street, or in seeing unsung acts of human heroism, or in a kind favor received, and moments of unaffected love given and received. Above all, the divine visitations which give him a taste of God speak so compellingly of goodness that he cannot help but believe in the goodness of what God created. Each of His handiworks must be good beyond understanding, must have in it something as incorruptible as the law of gravity, some force of goodness as tireless as the winds and waves and rains, which never cease to wash away defilements and restore pristine splendor, though eons pass before defilement ceases, and eons more before restoration is accomplished.

One day his faith will become more luminous and he will see with his eyes this glory deep down in things. Until then he must think on his sins and the sins of the world, mindful that Christ said not to judge harshly, and indeed not to judge at all, for the Evil One is more responsible for men's sins than they know. Untold good is left undone because the good intentions of others are blocked by the same rejections he has met. What better course can he take than to plead for himself and for all sinners in the words of the pioneer Sent Contemplative who, seeing to the roots and causes of all things, cried: "Father, forgive them; for they know not what they do" (Luke 23:34).

SPIRITUAL PROJECT THREE:
Attitudes Toward the World

1. Have you experienced the pressures, rejection and alienation

that Jesus and other biblical figures suffered for God and conscience?

2. Can you distinguish these objective persecutions from deserved censures, and persecutions imagined because of your own over-sensitiveness and other psychological faults?

3. Do you succumb to bitterness, self-pity and self-rejection, or do you search out faith-aids to help you endure trials, and even come to joy in being found worthy to share Jesus' burdens?

4. Do you face up to the Scriptural teaching that there is a "world" which cannot be loved or fraternized with?

5. Do you realize God's creation must be loved into health by you?

6. Do you obey Jesus in refusing to judge another's guilt since you can know only actions, not motives, weaknesses, and Satan's influence?

7. Do you have a habitual optimism or pessimism that is a trait of character rather than a response to ambient reality? Or have you met the world of evil, and yet held by faith to the knowledge of its potential goodness, and the sureness of God's redeeming power?

Part Two

AWAKENING TO THE KINGDOM OF GOD

1.

The Experience of Love

This chapter and the one that follows must be verbally bracketed, for it is not known what proportion of contemplative apostles are led by the path described in these two chapters. Those who do not identify with them might do well at this point to read instead "Experiences of the Incarnation" (Part Three, Chapter One), for that account should put them in contact with their own "Experience of Love." Still, this present chapter cannot be omitted from the treatise because what is described here is for some a wellspring of first graces and an unforgettable spiritual adventure. Furthermore, it is an experience too central to the whole Christian dispensation to be omitted.

To avoid literary complexity, it seems best simply to ascribe the experiences of these chapters to "the pilgrim"; but here especially the real meaning will be "the pilgrim who comes this way," without settling the question of whether he represents many or few. To some degree that is the attitude with which the whole treatise should be approached. The reader is the final authority on whether or not a given experience represents his own.

Those who, a long time before, have come the way described in this chapter, may not recognize themselves as they should unless they are adept at "returning to the springs of first graces," a practice which will be described in the course of the chapter.

With the dramatic swiftness of sunrise in a mountainous land, the Kingdom of God bursts into the life of the pilgrim, in a way he had not anticipated, from a quarter he did not expect—nor does he recognize it as the advent of the Kingdom when it comes. Only years later, when he makes a mental pilgrimage back to this spring of his first graces, and drinks of it anew, does it begin to dawn on him that this joyful grace was the beginning of God's answer to his long-repeated petition: *Thy kingdom come!*

This inability to grasp the deeper meaning of many spiritual developments in our lives calls for a digression. Certain events are the wellsprings of our future. It is most helpful to recognize them for what they are, yet often we cannot at the time they happen. Only when we look back much later do we see how, like a beckoning path nestled between unscalable peaks, they influenced the whole course of our journey, and gave rise to a long series of connected events which have determined the very shape of our lives. That is why it is so helpful to the pilgrim's understanding of his vocation for him to make frequent mental journeys back to the springs of his first graces. Many holy persons have done this, and because they did their lives lay like an arrow before them, carrying them always in the direction of God.

The Scriptures themselves enjoin on us the practice of returning to the springs of our collective and individual first graces. Moses recounts the wonders God has performed for His people, and concludes: "You shall therefore lay up these words of mine in your heart and in your soul; and you shall bind them as a sign upon your hand, and they shall be as frontlets between your eyes. And you shall teach them to your children, talking of them when you are sitting in your house, and when you are walking by the way, and when you lie down, and when you rise" (Deut. 11:18-19). The Pharisees followed this injunction literally. Mary fulfilled its spirit by pondering in her heart the works of God in her life and the lives of her forefathers.

The supreme example of this practice of returning to the springs of first graces is the Church's usage of returning daily to the springs of the Eucharist. Just as the Eucharist is meant for all time, so are the springs of a man's first graces. They never dry up, for the touch of God in His visitations has an eternal quality. It is perpetual nourishment the way a seed planted springs up into a fruit tree which nourishes the owner of the land each time it comes in season. Or just as a tree grows above its roots but never outgrows them, the pilgrim grows out of these first graces, but they continue to sustain him. The very first stirrings of an awakening call to marriage, to the religious life, to a deeper love of Jesus and Mary, have something about them as perpetual as the state of life to which they call. One neglects keeping in contact with those first stirrings at the peril of losing stability in his calling. Those first stirrings continue to give life, as roots give it to trees.

Thus it is that the apostolic contemplative must perpetually ponder the first experiences through which he began to perceive that he was being sent into the world as an "ambassador . . . for Christ Jesus" (Philemon 9). Even in the places where I write of the pilgrim recognizing a certain grace to be one he needs for his call to be a sent contemplative, I am writing anachronistically. Since in its early stages he cannot yet have identified his call so precisely, the most he actually recognizes is that some grace suits a felt need, and moves him in a direction he dimly senses as the right one. One day he should come to know the nature of his vocation consciously and with clarity, but whether he ever does may depend on pondering the great things God has done for him across the years.

To neglect such pondering can be to forfeit the joy of knowing who he is to the Lord and who he is in himself: a new creation of Christ, a man with a new identity and a new name: "I will give him a white stone, with a new name written on the stone which no one knows except him who receives it" (Apoc. 2:17). Upon the white stone of his unfolding vocation is written his new identity, but only he can read it. Should he fail to do so through prolonged meditation on his own life, he is inviting a spiritual identity problem. And then sometimes God calls him in his heart, calls him by his new name, calls him to the work he is sent to do, and he will not recognize he is being addressed because he does not know his own name. This is the same as saying the pilgrim will have been hindered in learning the spiritual art of the discernment of spirits. That art is at the heart of the life of a mature apostolic contemplative with the vocation being described in this book.

The experiences of one's earliest vocational graces serve a double purpose. First, they are a call from God that give personal instruction to a man concerning the use of his life on earth; and second, they are such lucid communications with God that they serve as a divine instruction in how to recognize God's inner influences and how to separate them from wayward impulses parading as divine calls. Meditation on these springs of first graces after they have proved their authenticity by their fruit gives a pilgrim a growing ability to tune out spurious impulses and tune in the communications of God. Just as a man who has once known true joy never again mistakes for true joy moments of mere giddy pleasure, so the man who has once heard, resonated, and responded joyfully to God's call no longer mistakes the too human impulses of his own nature for divine messages. He has the means of knowing when the same Lord is calling again.

I return to the Kingdom grace which may descend on the pilgrim at this time. In the desert lands water is scarce, hardly to be found at all. Yet a season comes when the skies burst open, a deluge descends, and in the desert where before there was not even a stream-bed, a mighty torrent rushes, a Niagara of abundance, a miracle of plenty for every creature. The desert is the pilgrim's soul, thirsting for love, and the sudden torrent is Mary. *Hail Mary, full of grace!* At once there is love in abundance and superabundance flowing through him in a river and a million streams.

This is a love the world does not know, the love of a mother and son before the fall, the love of brother and sister in Eden, the love of a man and a maid in an age without sin. No one can tell of it, he can only use words to call it to the mind of those who have experienced it. It is an influx of that grace of God which is given without measure, that deluge of tears which washes away bitterness, that reconciliation which begins to bridge every alienation, that immersion in love which makes a man begin to understand what heaven is.

Christ has inducted the pilgrim contemplative deeper into the Kingdom by that same portal through which He brought it. The Mother of fair love has come with her invitation to awaken to love: "Like a vine I caused loveliness to bud, and my blossoms became glorious and abundant fruit. 'Come to me, you who desire me, and eat your fill of my produce. For the remembrance of me is sweeter than honey, and my inheritance sweeter than the honeycomb. Those who eat me will hunger for more, and those who drink me will thirst for more. Whoever obeys me will not be put to shame, and those who work with my help will not sin" (Sir. 24:17-22).

The pilgrim experiences the fulfillment of these promises. Graces flood his prayer. Mary answers his petitions almost before he makes them. He learns the true power of prayer, and its delight. It is the manna with every good taste. He delights in Mary in and out of prayer, and honors her with many practices. He speaks of her with touching words. He speaks to her with unfeigned love, and gives her everything, above all himself.

Even for those who do not have such an intense experience of Mary, her entrance into their lives in a less marked way is not only a great grace in itself, it is often a harbinger of some special grace which is just surfacing or just about to surface. The testimonial of one pilgrim illustrates this:

> I felt an attraction to the religious life, but also an attraction to

pursue a meaningful career in the world, and to get married. I was thinking about what I should do when Mary came into my thoughts, and in my mind I had a kind of dialogue with her. In her presence, as it were, I thought of my indecision, and in my imaginary dialogue Mary said: "Do you love me?" And I said, "Well, sure I love you." I suppose that somehow I knew what that interchange meant as regards my vocation. That night I awoke from sleep, got up, knelt down and said the rosary, as I often did. When I finished, I looked up. Mary was standing there . . . I looked down, not being worthy to look at her. But that was no good, I had to look. She was smiling at me. I smiled back. Then I went to bed and fell asleep. Not long after I entered the religious life.

Was this vision a true mystical experience? That question can rarely be answered with certitude, and need not be in most cases (as will be explained in the sequel to this book, which will treat of the mature years of the sent contemplative). Still, a reasonably good judgment about its authenticity can be made by an informed spiritual director who considers the structure of the experience, the condition of the pilgrim who experienced it, and its meaning for him, as well as his subsequent religious history. In this case, the author's personal contact over many years with the pilgrim concerned leads him to believe this was a genuine, transforming religious experience. True, elements of the vision may have been provided, not by infused species and suchlike, but by the pilgrim's own psyche striving spontaneously to clothe an ineffable experience of Mary in suitable imagery the way the inspired writers of Scripture clothed the revelation they received from God in words and figures which they had a role in choosing. In any case, this and other religious experiences recounted in this work are presented simply as deeply religious experiences of imperfect but sensible and authentically religious pilgrims on their pilgrimage.

Let us return to the pilgrim of our treatise. At this time he is too absorbed in Mary to recognize that she is the approach to the Kingdom, the morning star, the dawn, the harbinger of still greater glories to come. Mary is the lesser light of Genesis, which illumines the night in which the pilgrim still dwells. Yet to him the night seems gone. He is cheered by the warmth and the light as of a summer day. There is a long road still ahead, but the pilgrim cannot know this. He has reached a way station on his journey which is so lovely a place that he can almost forget he is still a pilgrim.

SPIRITUAL PROJECT FOUR:

The Practice of Personal Anamnesis

Objective: To return to the springs of personal first graces, just as the Church returns daily to the Last Supper to drink at the springs of the Eucharist.

Orientation: *Anamnesis* means *memory* or *recall*. In biblical usage, however, the recall involves not just a memory but a real presence: of God to His people, or of the people returning to God. In the latter sense, the believer prays or offers sacrifice, asking God to remember him, to see and pay attention to *his* presence before God (Lev. 2:2; 2:9; 2:16; Ps. 38:1; 70:1). In the former case, God enjoins the believer to remember Him, His deeds, His perpetual presence (Ps. 46:1) and His past deeds which have an effect on our present (Deut. 7:18; 6:6ff), as in His promise to be Eucharistically present when we practice the *anamnesis* of the Mass (Luke 22:1). Thus biblical anamnesis is a recalling or *reenacting* of earlier divine actions ritually to experience them anew, in power, in the present, in their continuing effects. It is a way of keeping in contact with the God of Abraham, Isaac, and Jacob, and of one's own personal religious experiences.

Practicing Personal Anamnesis. Jogging the memory with the help of times, places, religious practices and fateful decisions, try to locate those deep artesian wells of grace in your soul which sprang up in the past, one for each of your deepest religious experiences. Locate any one of those experiences, and allow it to flow into the present with its whole complex of feelings, moods, thoughts, convictions, commitments, peace and joy. Discover how *alive* and *present* those experiences still are. What follows are suggestions to be used only if they are needed to help make this contact:

1. My first passage from *belief* in God's love to the realization: *God loves me!*
2. My deepest, most peace-giving experience that *God forgives me!*
3. The day You let me know *You are calling me to follow You!*
4. The hour when not fear but love led me to the great victory of chastity for Your sake.
5. My most cherished prayer-experience of You.
6. My most loving experience of You in the Eucharist.
7. The day and hour I learned You really are my personal Savior.
8. The season I came to know You as God my Beloved.
9. My most profound discovery of You in another.

10. My most wonderful finding of You in nature.
11. How I learned You have called me and sent me into Kingdom service.
12. The season Mary really came into my life.
13. The most vivid religious dream I've ever had.
14. The time I at last gave in to Your wishes.
15. Other experiences too personal to easily categorize.

Note: To do this project well, choose one spiritual experience, and spend an hour of meditation on it. Use paper and pencil to jot down all the related and recurrent experiences of the same form.

2.

Transformation in Mary

The pilgrim's communion with Mary reaches a new intensity. His affections are awakened in a manner that leads to rich and complex growth which, if it could be traced at all, would require a treatise of its own. Here I will only highlight a few of the most far-reaching influences of Mary on the pilgrim's developing personality and spirituality.

Absorption in Mary takes the form of prolonged contemplation of *her* growth experiences. The pilgrim contemplative re-lives in prayer the Gospel accounts of Mary, sometimes with the help of the rosary, sometimes in other ways. Mary is so close to him in these days that these imaginative contemplations of her are a living companionship.

He is engrossed by Mary's absorption in God. She acts, observes, and ponders. She observes Jesus, ponders, and acts. She misses nothing, finds inexhaustible meaning in the coming of the angel messenger, the conception of the Child in her womb, His birth, and the remarkable speed with which the shepherds find their way to her and Him. "Mary kept all these things, pondering them in her heart" (Luke 2:19). He must do likewise. He finds he is learning too, and swiftly, like the shepherds. He finds Mary so taken up with God in everything that he begins to see at least dimly that she finds Him not only in prayer, not only in Jesus, but in all things. She does not have to turn inward to find God. "The Lord is with you" (Luke 1: 28). These words take on new meaning. They not only mean Mary is a temple of God, they mean that God walks with Mary in the practical affairs of her life, just as He walked with Enoch, Abraham, Moses, and with His whole people. The pilgrim senses that He is called to this same intimacy, he too is invited to walk with God, to have God with him in power. With Mary's help (which he finds unfailing), and in view of what has already been done for him, he has secure confidence that he can be faithful.

The nature of Mary's holiness changes before his eyes. Brought up in the Catholic faith, he has always reverenced Mary's exalted holiness. It had towered over him inaccessibly: "Blessed are you among women!" (Luke 1:42). What is happening now is changing that. The change can be illustrated by an episode in the life of one pilgrim. This man used to frequent a certain church with a heroic size statue of the Virgin near the main altar. For a long time only mildly devoted to the Mother of God, he used to look at her from a distance. She was gazing down, as though fully absorbed in her own holy reflections. One day need and love drove him to make an advance, to overcome the distance between them and kneel at her feet. When he looked up into her face, he discovered that she was wholly absorbed in him. She had been waiting all the while.

It is in such things that the pilgrim is finding out about Mary at this time. He is discovering a simple young girl from a small town who marvels at what is happening to her. Even though she is becoming the intimate of God, even as she is discovering she is the woman of glory, the new creation's first woman, the Mother of God's only Son, she remains the lowly, warm and tender friend of her neighbors she always was.

His own affections are taken into hers, are made more pure and vital, and at least begin to reach out to all as do hers. He is discovering that her holiness was never unapproachable, just not approached. Known close up, she is irresistibly appealing because she is utterly human yet much more than that. She is like a lovely, simple little cottage which, once entered, is found to have secret stairs leading down into the mysteries of the earth, and up into the mysteries of the heavens.

She is no doubt as exaltedly holy as he thought her, yet she is in no way inaccessible. Without ceasing to think of himself as nothing, he begins to think of himself as like her. She has disarmed him, dissolved the diffidence which had made him keep his distance. He is undergoing an amnesia which has erased the memory of the gulf between them. With boldness, with the very madness of love, he begins to expect and to plan his own complete transformation. It is quite consciously also the madness of faith, for he is holding stubbornly to the truth that "with God nothing will be impossible" (Luke 1:37). He is holding to the revelation that "with faith nothing will be impossible" to him (Matthew 17:21). Innocence *can* be restored, the world *can* be transcended. It is the Father's own word that He has "blessed us in Christ with every spiritual blessing in the heavenly places, even as he chose us in him before the foundation of the world, that we should be holy and blameless before him" (Eph. 1: 3-4). If he cannot believe God's word, take it at face value, whom can he believe? Now that he is responding with love, his rebirth in Christ, with Mary's sure help, is more than possible—it is assured.

Another change has taken place in his life which makes this hope quite realistic, not an emotional flight of fancy. He has taken to heart Mary's own attitude toward God: *He is the Lord.* His will is more hers than her own will: "Behold, I am the handmaid of the Lord; let it be to me according to your word" (Luke 1:38). Everything about Mary is contagious now, and the pilgrim is convinced that she has bequeathed this submission of hers to him in her last recorded words, her last will and testament: "Do whatever he tells you" (John 2:5). Surely, he *can* do whatever God tells him. It is not hard. He can do even what the Saints did, if God calls him to that. And, in fact, he is already doing much. The devotion building up in his prayer is speeding him through his day's work, human interchanges, and ascetical practices without strain, and with a keen desire to do more.

His spiritual appetite is keen. He devours books on the spiritual life, on the following of Christ, and especially on Mary. He is blessed if at this time he comes on such tender and ardent writings as *The Glories of Mary*, by St. Alphonsus Liguori. An opportunity to make a retreat at this time is a godsend.

The pilgrim finds with delight and consolation that he would be willing to do more than the little fasting, good works, and penance that his responsibility to his duties, his spiritual director, and his own judgment permit. It is a joy to know that his desire to give has outdistanced his ability to give. It means that he is giving himself, and this is what the Lord and Mary want, as he wants the Lord and Mary.

His apostolic spirit has been awakened by Mary. He is taken with her conduct. How it impresses him that, almost the moment she conceived Jesus, when she would so desire to remain with Him in prayerful repose, "Mary arose and went with haste into the hill country" to be of service to Elizabeth (Luke 1:39 f). Pilgrims in this stage feel in themselves the same strong impulse to serve, and each does it in his own way. One began visiting lonely sick people in a hospital. Another made regular visits to an orphanage. A third sought out the destitute, and collected clothes for them. Another promoted the First Saturday devotion to the Immaculate Heart of Mary for the sake of world peace. He prevailed on the leaders of the devotion in a certain college to keep up the practice during the summer recess when it was customarily discontinued. One (and there are many like him) felt called to the priesthood and religious life where he could be fully at her service.

These are only beginnings, firstfruits, a period of training. It takes time for a pilgrim to become an effective "ambassador . . . for Christ" (Philemon 9) in service to the world. A pilgrim needs spiritual direction at this time so that he does not disperse himself too thinly and harm his potential for greater future contributions. If he is a student, he should not neglect his studies; if he is married, he should not neglect his family; if he is in professional work, he should not neglect it for lesser good works, since through wise planning he can often make his greatest contribution to the Kingdom through his own area of expertise. With purified motives and awakened Christian purpose, the pilgrim contemplative can generally transform his career into a significant Christian activity. It is thus, *from within each field,* that the Kingdom of God must come: "Let everyone lead the life which the Lord assigned to him, and in which God has called him. . . . Everyone should remain in the state in which he was called" (1 Cor. 7:17, 20).

The pilgrim in this stage is readily led by his new fervor to overdraw from his energy bank and experience fatigue and exhaustion, but this can even enhance his devotion at this time; Mary is so near in everything. She has become so much a part of his prayer that even when he receives Holy Communion he invites Mary to enter and claim what is hers.

The pilgrim has advanced to the dawn of unlimited hope. It is still only a hope of holiness, not possession, though the hope is so great it consoles him as though it were possession. Outside the time of prayer, old patterns of anxiety persist. Old habits of being concerned about many things still plague him, but at least he recognizes them as disorders, resists them, and makes progress against them. He learns to use like a weapon against each trouble some appropriate saying of the Lord.

In Mary's company, the pilgrim is already making forays out of the fertile lowlands of contemplation into the hill country of action. Mary is sharing everything with him. All she has and has experienced are his, and he is hers. "All mind are thine, and thine are mine" (John 17:10). To live thus, on the heights of love, is almost too much for weak human nature to sustain.

3.

The Mother of All the Living

It should prove valuable to complement the forgoing account of the pilgrim's experience of Mary with a reflection on its broader meaning. God Himself revealed to us that He "created man in his own image, in the image of God he created him; male and female he created them" (Gen. 1:27). This is to reveal nothing less than that man and woman in their interplay are a great revelation of God. To observe or experience these interplays is to gain a bountiful knowledge of God.

Marriage is, therefore, a revelation of God, *but we too readily stop there.* Man and woman are related in other ways too. Mother and son, father and daughter, brother and sister, men and women friends, all are part of the one pattern of revelation. And all of these are complemented and enhanced by the Christian experience of Mary.

Following an ancient tradition, the *Constitution on the Church* calls Mary "the new Eve" (# 63). She is *Woman* as God meant her, she is *tainted nature's solitary boast*, so that only with her do we experience (as much as our own sinfulness does not prevent it) what God meant relationship with woman to reveal. This fact intimates the graces that can pour into our lives through union with Mary.

In her virginal marriage to Joseph, and in her virginal relationship to us, Mary also reveals to us the more spiritual aspects of marriage, and this is important because Scripture holds up marriage as an image not only of the Divinity, but also of the union between God and man; and Paul sees marriage as a reflection of the sublime union of the Son of God with His people: "This is a great mystery, and I mean in reference to Christ and the Church" (Eph. 5:32).

For all these reasons, the contemplative in action, whose vocation requires a knowledge both of things divine and things human, will find his relationship to Mary a true gift of grace, and one truly suited to his needs.

That man and woman together form a central source of divine revelation can be seen above all in the relationship of Jesus and Mary. Where they interact the Incarnation comes about, Christ the Savior is brought into the light of day, the Church buds forth, woman's true nobility is exalted, and the power of Christ grows manifest.

The pilgrim called to be God's apostolic workman in the world needs Mary to warm and vitalize his work. No one who enters into relationship with Mary can fail to become more fecund spiritually. She is "the mother of all the living" (Gen. 3:20) in the spiritual order. Without her, something is awry, there is something missing, there is some lifelessness. The *Constitution on the Church* states that "In her life the Virgin has been a model of that motherly love with which all who join in the Church's apostolic mission for the regeneration of mankind should be animated" (# 65).

Mary is the woman of faith, and it is especially in her faith role that the pilgrim of this treatise needs Mary and her pioneering example. As one who must learn that he is being sent by means of contemplative communication with God, the pilgrim has to discover that his whole mission is supernatural, as was Mary's invitation to motherhood. The pilgrim needs faith like hers to say as Jesus did to the doubters: "You know where I come from? But I have not come of my own accord; he who sent me is true . . . I know him, for I come from him, and he sent me" (John 7:28-9). And as one sent to do a work that is divine, the pilgrim needs to learn that the supernatural enters his life not only in the *way* he comes to know his mission but in the *power* he needs to carry it out. And here again Mary is model. Through faith she cooperated with God to transcend all human possibilities and conceive a son virginally. So too, to bring Christ to the world in his actions, the sent contemplative must work works impossible to human powers. There are times when he will falter or give up unless he shares Mary's faith that "with God nothing will be impossible" (Luke 1:37).

It is not that Mary is indispensable to God, but rather that she is Christ's chosen helper and His wonderful gift to us. The *Constitution on the Church* is careful to put these truths in perspective:

> In the words of the apostle there is but one mediator: "for there is but one God and one mediator of God and men, the man Christ Jesus, who gave himself a redemption for all" (1 Tim. 2:5-6). But Mary's function as mother of men in no way obscures or diminishes this unique mediation of Christ, but rather shows its power. But the Blessed Virgin's salutary influence on men originates not in any inner necessity but in the disposition of God. It flows forth from the superabundance of the merits of Christ, rests on his meditation, depends entirely on it and draws all its power from it. It does not hinder in any way the immediate union of the faithful with Christ but on the contrary fosters it (#60).

Each pilgrim must come to Christ in the best way he knows, and he should give witness to others about that same best way. It is in this spirit that this chapter is written. "Do not fear . . . Mary" (Matthew 1:20).

4.

Practices of Perseverance

The pilgrim has transferred his loyalty to God, but he must yet develop the virtues and practices necessary for perseverance. He continues to find consolations of God in prayer, but little of God in the world. It might be expected that fidelity to his daily secular responsibilities would prove very difficult; it might be supposed that the pilgrim would use prayer as an escape rather than as a foundation and a stronghold. The fact is that for a pilgrim contemplative with a true heart and a genuine love for God and His kingdom, these are only human imaginings which leave out of account the guidance of the Spirit. If in the beginning some such disorders prevailed, they prevail no longer, especially after the meeting with Mary.

The Spirit is teaching the pilgrim growing fidelity to everything he is called to do. The first springs of love which issued from his prayer have become a stream, and the stream a river of devotion to God's will. The very consolations of God have weaned him from consolation and disposed him to seek the will of God in all things, for that is God's will. The tasteless works of the day have the one good taste of God's will.

The first sturdy sprouts of apostolic zeal continue to surface. The pilgrim begins to seek outlets for his zeal. One pilgrim in this stage saw in the magazine *Maryknoll* a picture of a priest giving Holy Communion to a girl on some far-flung mission. He conceived a desire to carry the Body of Christ to those in distant lands who might otherwise never taste the Bread of Life. He applied for entrance to the Maryknoll society.

This new zeal continues to need guidance to keep the pilgrim from channeling it into by-ways which lead to the neglect of the duties of his state of life. Married persons in particular must not neglect their families, and breadwinners the work which supports the family. Zeal is a powerful force which needs wise guidance if serious errors are to be avoided: "It is a snare for a man to say rashly, 'It is holy' " (Prov. 20:25).

Perhaps the hardest things, and the most fruitful for the majority of pilgrims, is to find the Kingdom and the way to make it grow hidden within their own activities. In most cases the new zeal is not meant to uproot them from their normal activities, but to find ways of making those activities better serve the coming of God's Kingdom. The *Pastoral Constitution on the Church in the Modern World* points out that the divine plan is that man should "subdue the earth and perfect the work of creation, and at the same time improve his own person" (# 57). To that end, the same document declares: "The Council exhorts Christians, as citizens of both cities, to perform their duties faithfully in the spirit of the gospel. It is a mistake to think that, because we have here no lasting city, but seek the city which is to come, we are entitled to shirk our earthly responsibilities; this is to forget that by our faith we are bound all the more to fulfill these responsibilities according to the vocation of each one" (# 13).

Among the world's greatest needs are a more human and Christian family life, and families imbued with orthodox Christian purpose. The members of such families will infuse Christian values into those aspects of human life which they help to shape by their careers. Self-evident as these things can become after sufficient reflection, they are not evident to a newly-awakened pilgrim. Nor are the ways of being effective within the confines of one's own work. Zeal tends to be indiscreet and drive a man impatiently from one thing to another. A good spiritual director will help a pilgrim contemplative direct his zeal in accord with his God-given responsibilities and his best long-range service to the Kingdom.

The Catholic hope of transforming the world relies on its seven hundred million laymen. Pilgrims in the stage here being described can be helped immensely by all the documents of the Second Vatican Council, but especially by the one just referred to, and by the *Decree on the Apostolate of the Laity*.

As the zeal of these lay people is awakened, it must be channeled with the greatest care. It is hard to distinguish the impulse of the Spirit from one's own raw zeal. That zeal is only too often yanked headlong into the service of a man's own ambitions. A pilgrim should submit his subjective impulses to the scrutiny of an objective observer and spiritual guide, as the Scriptures make evident: "The way of a fool is right in his own eyes, but a wise man listens to advice" (Prov. 12:15).

If the pilgrim's zeal is to be more than a passing burst of enthusiasm, he needs to use the means of growing in prayer. Prayer growth requires nourishment from many sources. Prayer is a spiritual crop. It needs not only the good soil of an open heart, but the seedings of spiritual reading, the rains of grace, the fertilizer of good works, the weeding of self-denial, and the sun of consolation in its seasons. It even needs the drying winds of desolation to keep it from decaying into selfishness.

The pilgrim needs daily prayer to commune with God, to meditate on the life of Christ and Mary, and to reflect on the events of his own life. He needs scriptural reading to feed his faith and provide the substance of his meditations. He needs lives of the Saints to interpret Christ's life for him in ways sanctioned by the Spirit and the Church. He needs prayerful examination of his conscience and his activities, to reinforce fidelity and expose any drifting away from God's purposes.

To find time for these spiritual exercises is no easy thing for most pilgrims. Here surfaces one of the life-long problems of contemplatives in action—the problem of effectively balancing and blending prayer and activities. Only the most committed pilgrim will ever take adequate means to keep action from taking over in his life.

In this planting and germinating season, it is urgent that the pilgrim cultivate growth in prayer. Prayer will never be easier. Some find the influx of grace so great that in this stage they eagerly sacrifice periods of recreation and cut back on their sleep to give more time to the Lord. These rich graces should be corresponded with in their season. They are laying the foundations of a deep life of prayer that will survive lean days when apostolic burdens are heavy, and abundant prayer time is rare.

It must be admitted as a possibility that even in this early stage of growth in the fusion of prayer and action, some pilgrims may be led by another way—one involving fewer periods of formal prayer —but it should not be readily believed that it is so. The life of Christ, the precedent of the Saints, and the pastoral prudence of the Church give little support to the idea. There is a season of growth for everything in this life, and cutting it short stunts and kills. Theoretically, God could free people from the need for bodily food too, but He rarely does so. Yet, if a pilgrim is led another way, he and a discerning spiritual director will know if they listen to the Spirit of God, and observe over a long period whether service and contemplation are both flourishing.

Prayer can generate such ardor at this time that even privation and mortification can be easy. Privation is rarely easy. To sacrifice hours of recreation for spiritual reading, to cut into sleep for prayer, to answer the neighbor's needs and forget one's own, to respond to other inspirations of service generously, can never be easy over a long period. But for a time now it can be so easy as to be overdone and harm the pilgrim's health. That is why a sound spiritual director is needed. To renounce one's own fervor of inclination and moderate everything under a director's guidance is difficult, for every man loves his own inclinations. Yet even if the director is over-cautious, the act of submission itself makes for rich growth; and if he is not being over-cautious, the pilgrim will be saved from a break-down which would bring his apostolic activities to a halt and perhaps even destroy his ability to carry on the duties of his state of life. And so during this time God teaches the pilgrim how to grow in many ways.

It is time to turn to the one thing which is not easy now, and is never easy: enduring the slurs and rejection of the world. Rejection is never easy, for mankind was made one. Rejection is separation, and separation is an experience of dying, and it is never easy to do all the dying one must do to live only in Christ. It was not easy for Christ Himself to be rejected, to be betrayed, to be abandoned, and to die. Even when there is rejection in little things only, it is not easy. The pilgrim finds it hard to remain gently loving toward those who reject him, or pressure him to renounce what he believes and change what he does, though he feels he must do it. He will surely fail to endure it all patiently at this time, for his new fortitude is as yet untamed by long usage, and too unsure of itself to forego all counterattacks.

To see how great a victory he is winning, and how one more massive obstacle to fidelity is beginning—but only beginning—to give way before his advance and topple like the false idols of old, we must look back a bit. Until now, even if the pilgrim has been faithful to each thing God has called him to do, he has sometimes feared the judgments, remarks, and secret thoughts he knows or imagines acquaintances and even friends to entertain in his regard. He has tried to carry out God's purposes, but sometimes he has done it sheepishly, and sometimes secretively, like Nicodemus furtively coming to Jesus at night. Spiritual writers call this undue fear of the judgments of others *human respect.*

All the while the pilgrim has trembled before this specter, he has been gazing on Jesus. Jesus always proceeded boldly, and came through such confrontations manfully, as even his adversaries testified: "It is evident you do not act out of human respect" (Mark 12: 14). The words and actions of Jesus have now shown him that there is a shame that it is right to feel, and a shame that is itself shameful: "Whoever is ashamed of me and of my words in this adulterous and sinful generation, of him will the Son of man also be ashamed, when he comes in the glory of his Father with the holy angels" (Mark 8: 38).

He is now becoming indignant at the false shame which the world cleverly induces in himself and all the men, women and children who dare to adhere to God's values and not the world's. He grows angry with a world which makes young men and women ashamed of their virginity, and the unclean proud of their depredations. He becomes ashamed of his false shame of the past, and angry with all who promoted it. Human respect begins to look as ridiculous as the idols of old. Now he can stand against the mocking judgments of the world, such strength does he take from the judgments of God, such conviction does he have in the rightness of what he is sent to do. He stands against the arrogance of the world and rejects its rejections. He feels something of the assurance given Jeremias: "But you, gird up your loins; arise, and say to them everything that I command you. Do not be dismayed by them, lest I dismay you before them. And I, behold, I make you this day a fortified city, an iron pillar, and bronze walls, against the whole land . . . they will fight against you; but they shall not prevail against you, for I am with you, says the Lord, to deliver you" (Jer. 1:17-19).

We should give more attention to the importance of this victory over human respect. All pilgrims need freedom from human respect, but one sent by God and guided by Him to break new ground in the building of the Kingdom needs this freedom with a special urgency. If he remains paralyzed by human respect he will often be a useless ambassador of Christ. He will be hiding out when his vocation calls him to be out confronting the world's euphemisms, pretensions, hidden injustices and open scorn of right values. He must be free as a feather to fly with the wind of the Spirit of God and the will of God. Human respect kills that freedom.

Human respect renders an ambassador of Christ worse than useless; it makes him a scandal. The representative of God who remains silent when denunciation is called for and leadership is needed takes the heart out of the listeners and affords them excuse for being derelict in their duties.

The pilgrim who remains in bondage to human respect is likely to find his growth constricted like those dwarf trees of bonsai culture, which are produced by repeatedly clipping the roots and confining their space of growth. Such trees remain so small that what God made to tower over men and houses has room enough in a flower pot. Pilgrims cultured by human respect are similarly constricted. They may appear attractive, but at their false maturity they remain frail and delicate miniatures unfit for those sturdy tasks God meant to lay on their shoulders. Conversely, the pilgrim who breaks free of this bondage will already be serving the world mightily by rejecting its immoral sophistications and its sham moral judgments and bringing it face to face with itself. "He who boldly reproves makes peace" (Prov. 10:10).

It might be helpful to take the care of distinguishing discretion from human respect. Those who overcome human respect can proceed too far and lose discretion and thoughtfulness. One pilgrim whose friends congratulated her for being bold and open found herself in troubled waters. With the help of a counselor she reexamined her conduct. She discovered she was open—but only in one direction. She was speaking out, but was no longer listening herself. There is a time to be speaking out, but also a time to be silent—and there is also a *way* to speak out: "Pleasant speech increases persuasiveness" (Prov. 16:21). The prophetic word is sometimes kind and sometimes severe. To be truly prophetic, however, it must be inspired by God, and to be open to God the sent contemplative must be always attuned to Him. God's gifts go deep, and they operate even below the conscious level, as the word of Scripture witnesses: "The plans of the mind belong to man, but the answer of the tongue is from the Lord" (Prov. 16:1).

There is one other problem arising from the effect to persevere which deserves treatment here. So intense is the pilgrim's desire to be faithful to God that he can become anxious about it. He wants to sin no more and do God's will in everything, but he is unpracticed in it and full of unvirtuous habits and so cannot count on himself. Certain pilgrims go on for years without finding a way to overcome anxiety. This fault wastes much energy and detracts from a pilgrim's witness value, for it gives others the impression that he has no confidence in God, whereas in truth he has no confidence in himself.

One pilgrim suffering from this fault early found a help that never deserted him. He came one day on the words of Jesus: "Can any of you for all his worrying, add a single cubit to his span of life? If the smallest things, therefore, are outside of your control, why worry about the rest? Think of the flowers; they never have to spin or weave. . . . Now if that is how God clothes the grass in the field which is there today and thrown into the furnace tomorrow, how much more will he look after you, you men of little faith! But you, you must not set your heart on things to eat and things to drink; *nor must you worry*" (Luke 12:26-29 JB). Since the Lord was forbidding him to worry, how could he any longer consider worry—even about doing God's will—a part of God's will? He kept these words before his eyes for weeks until they became a part of him, and day by day his anxieties lessened.

Can a time scale be provided for the growth process so far described? Let us take as our point of departure the visitation by the Lord which caused the pilgrim's conversion. We could say in a general way that this conversion is unlikely to occur before adulthood, and that it would take a minimum of several years thereafter to reach the present point of development. It could take much longer. There are too many variables such as age at the time of conversion, the richness of the graces involved, and degree of fidelity, the availability of guidance, to say more, or to insist on the accuracy of this estimate. After all, the Church has *canonized* youths who died in their teens, in accord with the words of Scripture: "Coming to perfection in so short a while, he achieved long life; his soul being pleasing to the Lord, he has taken him quickly from the wickedness around him. . . . The virtuous man who dies condemns the godless who survive, and youth's untimely end the protracted age of the wicked" (Wis. 4:13-16 JB) It is more accurate to read the state of a man's soul by the signs of his life than by the years he has spent on the spiritual road.

5.

The Cross of Love

Present developments in the pilgrim contemplative's life require that we look more closely at his relationship to creation. He is drawn to the world as the place where he hopes to find the Kingdom of God, and repelled by it as the place that rejects the Kingdom of God.

We have seen that the world of sin and petty pursuits began to lose its hold on him from the moment when God made His first visitation of the pilgrim. That visitation, however, did not by any means at once show forth the Kingdom of God within creation. And so he who had before felt very much at home in this world gradually came to discover that he was a pilgrim on pilgrimage to his true homeland.

Even the Kingdom grace of Mary's visitation did not immediately lift the darkness which hung over his contacts with the world. As already recorded, however, continuing prayerful entrance into the Gospels has at least intensified the pilgrim's sense of responsibility toward the whole human enterprise. He has willed to identify with Christ's plan for His followers, the plan which He put before the Father in prayer: "I do not pray that thou shouldst take them out of the world, but that thou shouldst keep them from the evil one. . . . As thou didst send me into the world, so I have sent them into the world" (John 17:15, 18).

Despite this commitment to the Lord's plan, there has been something too detached about the pilgrim's motives and manner. He has been laboring in secular affairs as an outsider, a benefactor, and not as one at work in his own house.

Now a subtle change is taking place that is giving the pilgrim a new identification with secular affairs and secular needs. The world of men is becoming identified once again with the sap of his own life. Less like a benefactor and more like a member of the human family—more like one who feels hunger with every hungry man and soiled with every sinful man—he is crying out to the Lord his rescuer and praying: *Thy kingdom come!* Let us trace the events which have produced this profound change of attitude and brought on this new identification with the world of men.

The pilgrim had for a while broken free of society's claims on him, and disdained them, and been wary of them. Had he not felt like the rope used in a tug-of-war, with Christ and the Saints straining at one end, and the world at the other? And had he not sometimes found the self-same friend and companion pulling sometimes at one end of the rope and sometimes at the other?

Now, however, he is guardedly re-identifying with the best of society's concerns because that is clearly God's plan and because he is developing a growing need to find God at hand in the world and the world in God. Why is it do difficult to be involved at the level of deep love with both God and the world? Is it not in fact necessary as well as desirable? Yet the moment he begins to do so, he is once again caught up in powerful divergent claims upon his loyalties, and resistance to those claims forces on him the very alienation he rejects. He is like the biblical infant claimed by two mothers, but there seems to be no Solomon on hand to render a wise decision. He yearns for peace without betrayal, but there is no peace. Life is warfare.

He is afraid of this new-sprouting love for the world. While it lay dormant he easily gave himself to God without taint of hypocrisy or fear of self-deceit. During that period of withdrawal and freedom from the world he observed like a watchful bystander the subtle power of the human heart to rationalize its own desires, especially the desire to escape conflict by promoting false reconciliations for the sake of an hour's peace. He began to see more clearly that the struggle between the Kingdom of God and the kingdom of the world is not a clear-cut war between outright good and evil, but rather a battle between men busy about the things of God and men busy about the things of the world.

What he has perceived only dimly St. Augustine had put lucidly: "This, in fact, is the difference between good men and bad men, that the former make use of the world in order to enjoy God, whereas the latter would like to make use of God in order to enjoy the world—if, of course, they believe in God and His providence over man, and are not so bad as those who deny even this" (*City of God* XV, 7). The conflict is subtle, and that is why the pilgrim's fear is not empty. Will this re-awakened loyalty to man and his affairs once again subvert his hard-won fidelity to God? Will conflicting loyalties erode his strength and elicit self-deceiving decisions? "Every way of a man is right in his own eyes, but the Lord weighs the heart" (Prov. 21:2).

Prolonged meditation on his accumulating experience has opened to him the depths of things, and he is stunned by the extent of human alienation. Man and woman are alienated from one another, and lover and beloved, parents from children, brother from brother, race from race, nation from nation, the born from the unborn, man from God. Sin has hewn the cords which bound humanity together. The severed cord which bound man to God is found to be the very cord which bound men together not only among themselves but within each self. The mystery of iniquity is not simply a dearth of love but a hatred of love. Love and hate are at war in man's heart. The good man hates the evil loves that infect him, and the evil man hates the good loves that persist in him. The evil in a man kills the things he most loves.

With painful slowness the pilgrim is renouncing, even in the depths of his own psyche, all of these alienations. He gives special attention to the alienation between those who govern and those who are governed, for he sees this is the root of all alienations: "I will not serve!" (Jer. 2:20). The depths of the soul in which this disorder hides can be reached and healed only by God's grace and deep prayer that goes on continually. The pilgrim renounces not only all his own rebellions, but all hostility toward rebels. He renounces a too-severe justice toward those who are hostile to justice. He knows that unless his heart reaches out to all, it cannot reach out freely even to God.

How can he proceed more swiftly? He turns to Christ for answers. Jesus saw and foresaw the alienations which he is experiencing: "Brother will deliver up brother to death, and the father his child, and children will rise against parents and have them put to death; and you will be hated by all for my name's sake" (Matthew 10:21-22). Undaunted by them, Jesus made them an opportunity for service: "But I say to you, Do not resist one who is evil. But if any one strikes you on the right cheek, turn to him the other also. . . . Love your enemies and pray for those who persecute you, so that you may be sons of your Father who is in heaven; for he makes his sun rise on the evil and the good, and sends rain on the just and the unjust. For if you love those who love you, what reward do you have? Do not even the tax collectors do the same?" (Matthew 5:39, 44-46). Here he finds the outline of a program that is clear and straightforward, but extremely difficult.

If only he could find not only the will of God but the presence of God in the world into which he is being sent to carry out this program, how much warmer, how much more attractive it would be! To that purpose, he returns repeatedly to another, more cryptic, saying of the Lord: "Truly, I say to you, as you did it to one of the least of these, my brethren, you did it to me" (Matthew 25:40). He pries at the gist of this mystical saying as at the meat of a nut impervious to cracking. In these words God and creation, Christ and humanity, are poured together so completely that surely here is all the light needed for a whole lifetime of finding God in all things.

Yet the light stubbornly refuses to flash out. What a contrast with that other saying of Jesus which has burst like a joyous sunrise over his life: "Behold, I stand at the door and knock; if any one hears my voice and opens the door, I will come in to him and eat with him, and he with me" (Apoc. 3:20). Is there a direct connection between the two sayings? Could it be that even the one that has burst like a sunrise of divine visitations has only begun to open up to him, and that when it fully opens the two sayings will be as one? Certainly, some new understanding is stirring to be born in him.

O God, he prays, *end this division of my loyalties. My own powers are powerless against it, for it arises through your command of love. Christify the world, bring your Kingdom, end the division, and the world will be mine as You are mine. Thy Kingdom come!* For a long time there is the stirring of a faint response. At last he is able to formulate the answer he hears in his heart: *You make it come!* That, then, is the divine plan. He is being sent by God to fulfill his own desire. There is to be no easy answer, no fast peace, no wringing of hands about God's "Absence." The Kingdom of God is coming and will come through himself and many like him. In hearts and lives like His own the Spirit is rejoining God and the world in one embrace. The cry of Christ and the Catholic is *I will serve!* With the pilgrim's hands the Spirit will minister in many ways to a troubled world. The strife goes on, but with his newly revived love of human affairs and his deeper understanding of his mission, he finds some peace. At least within his heart, and as far as the outreach of his activities, there is in him and in millions like him a movement toward the reunion of God and creation.

6.

Interrelations between

Prayer and Action

This account of the pilgrim's growth has so far reported on his prayer life primarily as it directly related to his secular experiences. The reason we took this approach is that it is the *interconnectedness* of religious and secular experience which is the distinguishing mark of his vocation to contemplation in action.

Now, however, it is time to bring into our account another tradition of prayer in the Church, the one which is characterized more by withdrawal into contemplation than by association with secular action. This tradition does not deal with the complexities of a prayer life interwoven with the secular world. It spells out the growth of prayer in its pure state, with little reference to external activities. It is to cloistered contemplatives that we owe thanks for the best accounts of the growth in interior prayer. Here ought to be mentioned the work of St. Teresa of Avila and St. John of the Cross. Even they, of course, insist that prayer must issue in external service—though for cloistered contemplatives that service is generally confined to serving the members of their own community. St. Teresa, for instance, warns that contemplation without service of neighbor produces only spiritual dwarfs.

Why bring this purely interior prayer into our account of the growth of a sent contemplative? There is a compelling reason for doing so. *The growth in purely interior prayer does not belong to cloistered contemplatives alone.* They have best described it for us, but they would be the first to say that some degree of it should have a part in the life of all Catholics. And I insist that it must have a place in the life of a contemplative in action. Certainly, without growth in interior prayer no sent contemplative can grow to maturity; for at the very heart of his vocation throbs the need of being in on-going contact with God—of receiving continuous orders and directions from Him. Jesus Himself sets the norm. He often rose early to pray, as Luke recounts. And when He was about to decide who the Twelve were to be, He spent the night in prayer. In harmony with this conduct of Jesus and its imitation by His Saints, let it be said here that development of interior prayer relies on going apart alone for prayer daily, for a half-hour, an hour, or more.

Since interior prayer is a part of the life of the pilgrim, we ought to examine it briefly, and take account of its influence on the shaping of his external experiences. Let us do so by surveying the first several stages in the growth of purely interior prayer, and then trying to find the connections between it and the progress of the pilgrim.

The first stage of interior prayer is simply called *meditation*, because it consists in prayerfully meditating, pondering, probing, and inter-connecting the mysteries of our Catholic faith. In all of this, the central focus is Jesus and His life.

Meditation builds up a developing vision of Christian reality which gradually awakens religious feelings and emotions. A certain amount of progress in this direction awakens and nourishes a wealth of affectivity. When this takes place, it signals that interior prayer has developed into a deeper prayer called the *prayer of affection*.

The prayer of affection consists initially in affections that come and go rather quickly and with much diversity in the course of a meditation. This is not because they are the emergence of suppressed and conflicted psychological energies, as some might think; it is because they are stirred by the still characteristically quick-moving train of thoughts and exciting discoveries which constitute the activity of the intellect in this stage. They are the awakenings of the affectivity that follow on the spiritual awakening which is taking place. Proof enough of this is their gradual development into steady states of love, peace, and joy in response to reflection on the Lord and divine revelation.

The onset of deeper, more settled reflections in prayer, together with the more steady, calm and lasting affections which they generate, signals further advance in interior prayer. This new state is called, appropriately enough, the *prayer of simplicity*. It consists in the now-developed capacity to gaze at one spiritual truth in a prolonged way, the way one gazes at a beautiful sunset or a human work of art.

To this point, the initial vigor of the wide-ranging meditation on religious truth has been slowly subsiding; or better, it has been gradually transmuted into a more settled, more affectionate gazing at truth and reality. This transmutation is nothing else than the *onset of contemplation*. Since the habit of contemplation, once it is developed, tends to spread from the time of formal interior prayer and diffuse itself over all the activities of a person, one can see readily how significant this interior growth is for the life of a contemplative in action.

From the prayer of simplicity on, the decline in meditative activity during formal prayer will continue (it should be added, however, that there are commonly currents of regression to meditation brought about by various life circumstances such as a lack of opportunity for prayer). Eventually, if progress continues, the rich sensible affections in prayer will begin to decline as well. When the twin peaks of meditation and affectivity have been left well behind, one is entering the *prayer of faith*.

The prayer of faith, like the act of faith, reaches out, not to an idea of God, not to an image of God, but to the living God, unseen though He be. God cannot be adequately represented by any idea or image, but even if He could, love is not satisfied with the image of the beloved but only with the beloved. Love itself drives prayer on to this stage. Predominant in prayer now is not thought of God but God. This is not easy to explain, but let us try to understand. Prayer has developed beyond the flurry of sensible affections because while sensible religious affections are good, they are not good enough. They are driven out by the need for a deeper, more spiritual response of the soul to God in which thoughts about Him are replaced with a more direct, habitual communion with Him. The prayer of faith is the beginning of this habitual communion. More will be said about it shortly because it has great importance for the contemplative in action.

Now let us see how these insights into interior prayer cast light on the trek of our pilgrim. Little has been done in pertinent literature to trace the relationship between these purely interior states of prayer and the growth of contemplatives in action. *Is* there any fixed relationship between the one and the other? There seems to be. I will attempt to show an interconnection only where it truly promises to clarify the growth of the pilgrim whose development we are attending. To try to do more would over-complicate this rudimentary account of the growth of a sent contemplative. It would also confuse those readers who grow in interior prayer without any formal awareness of the stages of their growth; and furthermore, the interconnection between interior states of prayer and contemplation in action is not yet well enough known to be fully described.

If we now extract the essence of the nature of growth in interior prayer, we will see how it sheds light on the experiences of the pilgrim which have already been described; and how it promises to shed light on future developments. Interior prayer develops along a line from meditation to contemplation. Pure interior contemplation is communication, communion, and union with God in faith. This contemplative growth proceeds through purification, darkness and negation more than through tangible positive experiences (with the important exception of the experience of love). This fact sheds much light on what has so far been described of the pilgrim's growth. He too has often been traveling along the way of God's *absence.*

It seems to this writer that it has been widely assumed without warrant that the way of a contemplative in action in the world is a VIA POSITIVA, a POSITIVE FINDING of God in His creatures by virtue of their likeness to Him. Experience, however, speaks otherwise. It shows that in some stages of growth, at least, contemplation in action is a VIA NEGATIVA, a disappointing and painful discovery of how UNLIKE God His creatures are. Instead of delighting by their likeness, they disappoint by their unlikeness. Psychologically and experientially, the pilgrim is finding God ABSENT from them.

A partial explanation for this failure to find God in creatures is as follows: Since the day the pilgrim first experienced God in that simple and seemingly inconsequential prayer event recounted at the beginning of this treatise, he has been developing a sense of the *transcendence of God.* He listens with open ears now when Scripture tells him that God is above us and our ways as the heavens are above the earth. Now the earthly beauty which once captivated him only reminds him of the absence of Beauty. Creatures once viewed as powerful remind him of the absence of Power. Lonely, the pilgrim traverses the earth, seeking but not finding. "Have you seen him whom my soul loves?" (Song of Songs 3:3).

This experience of God's absence together with a second reason for it, is witnessed to by a mature, aged, and highly apostolic sent contemplative:

> I do not see God in His present creatures, I see Him in His absence. I see the need of God, the want of God, the thirst for God, in the hungry, the shabby, the cold, the outcast. These persons are not meant to live in that want. They are meant to be cared for, provided for, and loved. Only God can awaken this care and sustain this love and reward this attention. And the human misery present is a cry and plea to God, and a scream to one's fellow men to fulfill their family role and distribute to the needy their inheritance and so witness to the love of Christ for the beggar Lazarus, and for Jairus' daughter and the penniless widow.

This pilgrim sees God's absence above all in man, God's prime likeness—and he sees the cause of it in man, and he sees the corrective for it in man: not through a prayer that will discover His presence, but through an action that will incarnate it.

What can the pilgrim do—besides apostolic work—to restore a more positive finding of God in the things of earth? *The answer is that only through further meetings with God within, in faith, apart from the world, can he be aided to find God in the world.* On the face of it, that postulate seems to contravene the evidence. Was it not the meeting with God in the first place that turned earth to dust? Yes, but the dynamics of that meeting involve a subtle interplay of many elements which move more like dancers than like arrows toward the final destination and purpose of the meeting.

Let us examine those elements. Firstly, there was the loving meeting with God that lit up and exposed the dark and terrible loveless state of human affairs. Secondly, the soul fell in love with God. Thirdly, the soul grew love-sick and weak—*but not as a result of the meeting with God*, but of His subsequent *absence.* If only God would return to stay, the pilgrim would stop languishing with desire for Him, and the pilgrim would once again turn with vitality and zeal to help human beings, who could be like God, to actually become like God.

Thus the pilgrim would not feel God's absence so burdensome in the exterior world if only he found Him present in the interior world of his own soul. Even more subtly, however, the pilgrim must not find God *too* present within. If he finds God too fully present within, he will be interested in nothing else; if he finds Him too little present, he will be interested in nothing at all. His love-sickness will go on. In brief, a contemplative in action finds his purpose and his driving force through just the right degree of yoking to God, which God alone knows and controls. This brings us back to the prayer of faith.

The prayer of faith is the beginning of a habitual living with God, who is present in a veiled way. It is this habitual character of His presence, and even this veiling of His presence, which suits it to the pilgrim's present need, and makes it differ from the earlier momentary experiences of God which first awakened him.

We find here then, an interesting parallel and interconnection between what is just now happening in the pilgrim's interior prayer experience, and what has long since happened in his external world experience. For as he reaches the prayer of faith, meditation and the prayer of affection seem to become within what the world outside has long been: useless for finding God. And so, just as he has long since had to find God in the world *by faith*, he must in addition, at this stage of interior prayer, find God within by the *prayer of faith*.

What the pilgrim who reaches this austere stage of prayer must come to realize is that he will no longer find God adequately through his thoughts and feelings any more than he can presently find Him in the things of the world. Both the inner and outer failure to find God in the old ways stem from the same root: *Knowing things about God can no longer satisfy his hunger*; he yearns to "understand fully, even as I have been fully understood" (1 Cor. 13:12). He must give up the illusion that words and thoughts and created things will satisfy the union with God for which his now-great love longs. He must descend deeper within his deepest spiritual self and find God in pure faith.

Many spiritual passages which never revealed their meaning to him before now sparkle and shine and light his way to this realization. As though he had never heard it or read it before he understands what Jesus is saying when He promises: "If a man loves me, he will keep my word, and my Father will love him, and we will come to him and make our home with him" (John 14:23). And he finds promise of meeting God in the world in the words of Paul: "God chose to make known . . . this mystery, which is Christ in you" (Col. 1:27).

The pilgrim takes these revelations at their word. If he cannot see God yet, he can know by faith that God is with him. By faith he can enjoy God's presence always. During prayer, he can even take his rest in God's presence by faith. This realization becomes the source of the prayer of faith. Habitually now, in prayer, he calls to mind one of these scriptural promises of presence, and then rests in that presence which is not felt but known by faith. He neither thinks about it nor grasps at it with his mind, but with his mind as it were vacant, he rests in God. This arid prayer brings satisfaction and peace both in and outside of formal prayer. His yearning for God softens in this assurance of God's presence in work and play and prayer. The Lord is with him.

7.

The Meaning of the Presence of God

The man of prayer whose interior journey into the prayer of faith I described in the last chapter was the pilgrim contemplative whom we have been following from the outset of this treatise. Although destined to be sent into action as God's apostolic contemplative in the world, he arrived at the prayer of faith through years of fidelity to long hours set apart for deep interior prayer. Unfortunately, however, not all who are called to his vocation have the opportunity for long periods of mental prayer every day.

Are there other routes to the prayer of faith? It would seem that there are, just as there are other ways of experiencing God. All of these ways of experiencing God depend in some sense on the "presence of God." In this chapter, therefore, we will consider the meaning of *the presence of God*; in the next chapter, *the ways of experiencing God*; and in the subsequent chapter I will provide a set of practices for *cultivating God's presence in the course of action*. The cultivation of God's presence would seem to be crucial to all sent contemplatives, but critical for those who do not practice formal daily mental prayer.

To enhance clarity, we will consider the meaning of "the presence of God" from two vantage points: from God's own, as He looks down upon creation; and from our own, as we look up to Him from within creation.

God's presence from His vantage point is described in terms of His *essence*, His *power*, and His *presence*. God's *essence* and substantial reality is present wherever He acts, for to everything that exists He is present as its creative Source, somewhat as the spring is present to the stream it originates. In *power* God is everywhere since "with God all things are possible" (Matthew 19:26). In personal *presence* God is everywhere, for He sees and knows all that takes place everywhere. His omniscience is beautifully detailed in Psalm 139, and is expressly revealed in the Letter to the Hebrews: "Before him no creature is hidden, but all are open and laid bare to the eyes of him with whom we have to do" (4:13).

Our more immediate purpose here is to consider the "presence of God" from the second vantage point. We want to consider the looking to God, the experiencing of the presence of God from our own centers of consciousness, the interacting of our consciousness with His.

God's presence through His *essence* becomes known to us when we ponder the reality all about us: "Ever since the creation of the world, his invisible nature, namely, his power and deity, has been clearly perceived in the things that have been made" (Rom. 1:20). God's presence in *power* and *omniscience* become known to us by meditation on His acts of creating, and conserving what He created; and by experience of His providence; but also by His own testimony, that is, by revelation.

To the presences already mentioned we must add the most meaningful presence of all: that presence to His most favored creatures by which He lets them know Him personally through the friendship called *grace*. By grace God makes His home in the graced one, and lives there "as the loved one in the lover and the known one in the knower." St. Paul thus asks: "Do you not know that you are God's temple and that God's Spirit dwells in you?" (1 Cor. 3:16). The believer should to some degree taste this presence of Father, Brother, Lover. This way of knowing God contrasts with the other ways as intimate personal friendship contrasts with a set of ideas.

This grace-presence of God is the primary focus of prayer and of the practice of the presence of God. Ordinary prayer is a *grace-communication* with God personally present and responding. This communication at times flames into a communion, and then we call it a *divine visitation*. That expression is valid, but can be misleading. The presence of God, on His part, does not change. In these visitations, He who is present does not come to us, we come to Him. We come to Him by a change in ourselves. This change gives us at least a moment of awareness of God who has always been present. St. Augustine writes of this in his Confessions: "You alone are always present even to those who have put themselves furthest from you. . . . And where was I when I was seeking you? You were there, in front of me; but I had gone away even from myself. I could not even find myself, much less you" (V, 2). Since this change in ourselves that produces the experience of God cannot be made without God's help, we are justified in saying that God "comes" or makes a "divine visitation".

The value of the foregoing reflection is that it can free the contemplative in action from misleading spatial images and underscore his own potential for entering more fully into the presence of God.

One important consideration remains: If God is omnipresent, why do we have to *change* to see Him? And why do we need His help to make that change? A look at purely natural relationships which evoke similar questions will suggest the answers to these questions.

Why does the eye fail to see the radio waves which pass right through it? The reason is the eye does not have enough in common with radio waves to detect them. Ability to know is based on some likeness between the knower and the known. Animals have senses and can know sensible objects; they cannot know God because He is not a sensible object. Man has senses, but he also has a mind which transcends and senses and "sees" what the senses know nothing of. Man contacts sensible things with his senses, reflects on their causes, and comes to "see" that he can see no explanation for anything except in a Supreme Being who exists in such a transcendent way that His Being is sufficient to explain both itself and the being of everything else.

Man, an embodied spirit, comes to know material things directly; and being spiritual as well, he comes to know spiritual things both directly and indirectly. But God's spiritual being is so beyond the nature of our own that though we have sufficient natural kinship with Him to know *that* He exists, we lack enough kinship to understand His divine nature. God's gift of grace comes to our rescue by transforming our souls into His likeness, so we can know Him and have fellowship with Him. Spiritual growth is further assimilation to God. It depends on God, for it is not within our power to lift ourselves above ourselves into His likeness, as Jesus taught: "Truly, truly, I say to you, unless one is born from above, he cannot see the kingdom of God" (John 3:3).

This consideration on the need to be like God to meet God has added the final touch to our reflection on the presence of God. In the end, presence in spiritual matters is a question of likeness—even as bodies are present to one another when they have a *like* location. Even in eternal life we will see God not because He will change but because He will change us: "Beloved, we are God's children now; it does not yet appear what we shall be, but we know that when he appears we shall be like him, for we shall see him as he is" (1 John 3: 2). When we have become sufficiently *like to* God we will by that fact enjoy always the presence of God.

8.

Ways of Experiencing God

We have just looked at the gap between God's omnipresence and our experience of His presence. What can the contemplative in action do to close that gap? He can make increasing use of the God-given helps of *revelation* and *faith*. Here we will examine those helps.

Revelation is God's self-communication to us. *Faith* is our free, self-communicating response.

Here we are interested in God's self-revelation as something we *experience*. Such revelation cannot be summed up in a set of propositions, since it is God's self-communication. It includes ways we can experience God's self-manifestation with our whole being, body and soul as well as mind. Neither can our *faith*, which is our response, be a mere cold act of the intellect and an emotionless act of the will. Faith at its best is a living person-to-Person response that is *in itself* a rich experience of God. This means our look at God's revelation and divine faith will be a study of the ways of experiencing God.

The Dogmatic Constitution on Divine Revelation has condensed insights into God's self-communication. It tells us that "By divine revelation God wished to manifest and communicate both himself and the eternal decrees of his will concerning the salvation of mankind" (# 6). He does this "by deeds and words" and "in Christ . . . who is himself the sum total of revelation" (# 2). This is to say that we *experience* revelation. Christ is an *experience*. He was an experience for the apostles who learned "from the lips of Christ, from his way of life and his works"; they also learned through "the prompting of the Holy Spirit" (# 7). Peter could say to Jesus: "We have believed, and have come to know, that you are the Holy one of God" (John 6:69).

Christ is an experience for us too. We live with Him in mystery, but so did the apostles. The Church's faith, like Peter's, hinges on her *experience* of revelation. Her past experience of Jesus during His life on earth is, of course, unrepeatable. That is why it is carefully guarded in her *tradition*. That is why it is so esteemed that "both Scripture and Tradition must be accepted and honored with equal feelings of devotion and reverence" (# 9). Her experience continues today and tomorrow, but it is dependent in part on the past: "The Tradition that comes from the apostles makes progress in the Church, with the help of the Holy Spirit" (# 8).

We individual believers too come to *believe and to know*. The Spirit teaches us to read the Scriptures, to obey the successors of the apostles, to contemplate, study, and act, and to come to "the intimate sense of spiritual realities" we experience (# 8). Our faith is a complex of hearing, experiencing, knowing, and responding to God with such whole-hearted trust that we commit our ways of living to Him: "He who through faith is righteous shall live" (Rom. 1:17).

We come to a clearer knowledge of all this if we distinguish *the faith* from *faith*. *The faith* is the whole complex of our commitment to God in Christ in the Church. It encompasses our whole relationship to Him mystically, as well as in our creed, worship, and moral life. *Faith* as the abstract theological virtue is the power God gives our intellects by which they turn to Him as He is in Himself, but without yet being able to see *what* He is. Faith is our response to the revelation which sets us staring near-sightedly at God, believing He is there, but not so much seeing Him. St. Thomas Aquinas explains: "Faith is a kind of knowledge, inasmuch as the intellect is determined by faith to some knowable object. But this determination to one object does not proceed from the vision of the believer, but from the vision of Him who is believed" (Summa I, 12, a. 13, ad 3).

We train our consciousness directly on God by faith, but see Him only darkly through the reflections projected by the various propositions and experiences of faith. Even so, St. Thomas sees in the act of faith the beginning of the actual vision of God, for in eternity our myopic staring will suddenly become perfect vision by a new Divine gift of light to our minds. The psalmist speaks of this light: "With thee is the fountain of life; in thy light do we see light" (Ps. 36:9). Or, in the words of Paul: "Now we see in a mirror dimly, but then face to face" (1 Cor. 13:12).

What has so far been said is not the same as saying we can have no direct experiences of God in this life. We can, and we shall consider that fact later. For now let us simply say that to experience Jesus is to experience God, but it is not to see His divinity face to face as yet. Nor did the apostles during their life. That is why the apostle Thomas, when his faith was failing, could be healed by the sight of the risen Christ, but could not be relieved of the need of faith by that sight. No experience of God in this life relieves us of the need for faith.

Biblical faith, then, is not just the theological virtue of faith. It is the whole sweep of our relationship with God which we have called *the faith*. Biblical faith is communicated to us interiorly by the Holy Spirit and exteriorly by the Church, as Christ mandated: "Go into all the world and preach the gospel to the whole creation. He who believes and is baptized will be saved" (Mark 16:15-16).

Biblical faith, then, engrosses a man's whole intellectual and affective consciousness. As when the Scripture describes the marriage act by saying that "Adam knew Eve his wife" (Gen. 4:1), so does it treat the knowledge of God that comes through faith as an ardent relationship to God.

This intimate and ardent knowledge of God is impossible to man unless momentous changes be worked in his nature to transform him to godlikeness. It is just such changes that the Church works through Scripture and the sacraments. We are "born anew, not of perishable seed but of imperishable, through the living and abiding word of God" (1 Peter 1:23). Through this new birth we are brought into the presence of God, and given possession of God. Paul tells us this when he writes: "God's love has been poured into our hearts through the Holy Spirit who has been given to us" (Rom. 5:5). This presence to God is not a mere juxtaposition, but a love-union, for "he who is united to the Lord becomes one spirit with him" (1 Cor. 6:17).

This gift of God as love and this gift of loving as God loves are what extend our *power* to know God even during earth's exile. Divinized by this power, we can know about God by knowing ourselves in our new life; and exercising this divinization in prayer, we come to know God in Himself. The mystics affirm this, and St. Thomas Aquinas taught it: "This sympathy or connaturality for Divine things is the result of charity, which unites us to God, according to 1 Cor. 6:17, *He who is joined to the Lord is one spirit*. Consequently wisdom, which is a gift, has its cause in the will, which cause is charity, but it has its essence in the intellect, whose act is to judge aright" (Summa I II, 45, a. 2). In other words, the baptized man is united directly to God in the union of love, and this union is a high source of knowledge whenever it comes to be known by faith, or by experience, or both.

This brings us back to faith, that inexhaustible concept. Faith's lowest level is to believe *that* God exists. The second, the crucial level, is to know and believe in him through acceptance of His self-witnessing word and deed—to become saturated with feelings of warmth, tenderness, intimacy, *trust.* This *trust* leads to the third level of faith, which is to believe everything God promises, because His word is an extension of Himself. This third and final level puts direction in our lives and gives content to our meditations. It also makes us know that to experience God is to experience love, for God has revealed that "God is love" (1 John 4:8).

The foregoing thoughts on the revelation and the faith do, like flashes of lightning, light up the paths and byways of our pilgrim's travels. All his paths to the experience of God are the pathways of the revelation and the faith. Let us conclude this chapter with a reflection on some of those paths.

When the pilgrim ponders the Scriptures the Spirit gives him insight into God's plan; when he ponders contemporary events the

Spirit, at work in history, reveals to him how the prophecies are coming to fulfillment in the events of which he is a part. When the pilgrim's affections well up in prayer and even overflow into the senses, the Spirit is giving him a taste of Himself.

When the pilgrim's belief in God's promise of abiding presence grows so stalwart it takes on the worth of experience, it means the Spirit has led him up into the mountains of the *prayer of faith*. Now God's *promise* of enduring presence is more meaningful than actual but fleeting *experiences* of His presence. The pilgrim is so *convinced* of God's presence that he is able to enjoy God's companionship by faith almost as much as though he were experiencing it in more tangible ways.

In the Eucharist many pilgrims commonly have deep intimations of Jesus' presence, and of His love, and of union, and of strength gained from Him. This is to be expected, for the distance between man and God is must fully bridged and closed when the God-man is bodily present—even though His body is already glorified. Let it be said that these experiences need not involve visions and raptures, for Christ can give tastes of union with Himself in more subtle and more divine ways.

When the pilgrim subdues distractions, puts off excessive activity, and subsides into deep prayer, the ever-present God sometimes kindles touching experiences of His love in accord with the promise of Jesus: "Behold, I stand at the door and knock; if any one hears my voice and opens the door, I will come in to him and eat with him, and he with me" (Apoc. 3:20). The mystics and the Church affirm the reality of these direct experiences of God. "These lofty manifestations of knowledge can come only to the soul that attains to union with God, for they are themselves that union; and to receive them is equivalent to a certain contact with the divinity which the soul experiences, and thus it is God Himself who is perceived and tasted therein. And although He cannot be experienced manifestly and clearly, as in glory, this touch of knowledge and delight is nevertheless so sublime and profound that it penetrates the substance of the soul, and the devil cannot meddle with it or produce manifestations like to it" (*Ascent of Mount Carmel*, II, c. 26).

Even here, it is only by faith in the living God that the pilgrim knows these incomparable experiences of love can come only from God, the greatest Lover. St. Paul confirms the occurrence of such profound religious experiences when he writes: "I know a man in Christ who fourteen years ago was caught up to the third heaven— whether in the body or out of the body I do not know, God knows.

And I know that this man was caught up into Paradise" (2 Cor. 12:2-3).

When the pilgrim carries on his ordinary works with selfless love, and especially when he serves another directly, God may suddenly come bursting in on him like a dear and familiar presence. A needy person's smile of gratitude may suddenly so tear away the veil it is the smile of God. This experience is probably less rare between pilgrims banded together as brothers or sisters in service to Christ. These experiences rank among the most cherished experiences of God, for the expression of mutual human love out of which they burst sets a special seal of confirmation on them, for "He who does not love does not know God; for God is love" (1 John 4:8).

A professional athlete who is a devoted spiritual pilgrim and apostle describes his experience of finding Christ through another:

> One of the Christian activities with which I am involved is the Fellowship of Christian Athletes (FCA). This organization challenges teachers and athletes to strengthen their prayer life and to serve as missionaries to others seeking a meaningful relationship with Christ. Athletics is our contact with these others who are looking for direction and perhaps a nudge toward Christian commitment. One thing I do is tell young people what Christ has meant to me in my life as father, husband, business man and athlete. I approach my various missions with the knowledge that I, as servant of Christ, am nothing without the direction and guidance of Christ in all I do.
>
> I visit one FCA member, a high school boy permanently paralyzed from the neck down by a football injury. He feels guilty about being a great financial burden to his family, all of whom are suffering in various ways through the strain brought on by his condition. The truly amazing thing is that N. has kept his faith and believes strongly that Christ is in control and will deliver him from this tragedy—though doctors give him no hope.
>
> I have made up my mind to visit him regularly. I have grown close to him and now feel some of the pain that he is experiencing. I dread the visits that I make because they drain me emotionally. I want so much to help him and can do so little. No FCA activity has been more difficult or more rewarding than these visits. I feel closest to Christ in this blending of agony and joy.

As we conclude this reflection on the ways of experiencing God and His presence, we may well decide that it is all very mysterious. All experience is mysterious, but the experience of God is most mysterious and most incomplete. The Scripture itself tells us that with the exception of Jesus Christ "No one has ever seen God" (John 1: 18). Yet the same Scripture confirms the fact that many men have had extraordinary experiences of God, and that He is eager to commune with all who desire to commune with Him. Many people right among our acquaintances have had both ordinary and extraordinary experiences of God, or this treatise could not have been written.

To experience God in this life is not to see Him openly as He really is; it is rather to taste a taste of Him which earth cannot match, and it is to be drawn to Him as words cannot describe. To see something of how this can be so that in our own lives we may pursue the God-experiences of other contemplatives in action, has been the purpose of this chapter.

9.

The Practice of the Presence of God

We have reflected on a theology of divine presence to help us understand and make our own the pilgrim's growing ability to find the presence of God in his prayer and his life. This ease in finding God seems a necessary part of the vocation I describe in this treatise.

Every vocation has its own way of imitating the inexhaustibly rich life of Christ. The quality of Christ's life which the vocation of the sent contemplative calls him to have a particular share in is His charism of *carrying out a mission perpetually directed by the Father.* Our pilgrim needs the grace of living in communion with the Father as Jesus did. That Jesus had this charism is clear from His own words: ". . . I do nothing on my own authority but speak thus as the Father taught me. And he who sent me is with me; he has not left me alone, for I always do what is pleasing to him" (John 8:28-29). This passage specifies the grace the pilgrim must cultivate. Note that Jesus connects the Father's abiding presence with fidelity to the Father's will. The Presence is not simply a reward for doing His will, but a means of knowing it and a strength for executing it.

Many pilgrims feel a growing hunger to live with God more continuously, but do not know how to bring it about. In the last several chapters I described how our pilgrim grew into the faith-realization of God's presence through many years of fidelity to a long period of daily mental prayer. His realization of God's presence grew so powerful that at length God became a true companion of his life.

Many contemplatives in action cannot imitate the pilgrim's long periods of daily prayer. Their daily responsibilities are too heavy. What are they to do to nourish their sense of God's presence? The Spirit, surely, has many answers to that question. In this context, I have but *one*: They should cultivate *the practice of the Presence of God*. I believe that by this practice many who try to live the call to contemplation in action can turn failure into success.

Let us note in passing that the practice of the Presence of God is invaluable for all who love God, no matter what their vocation or their work. The reason it has special value for the contemplative in action is that his work is often so intellectually engrossing it seems to admit of no possibility of a prayer that will not interfere with that work. But by practice, such a pilgrim can cultivate the habit of injecting brief bursts of this Prayer of God's Presence in moments of relaxation, or at a time when he stops for a drink of water, or stoops over to pick up a pen. In other words, if used skilfully enough, it is compatible with the most engrossing activities. I will devote the rest of this chapter to a detailed instruction on cultivating the practice of the Presence of God.

The practice of the Presence of God consists in turning repeatedly during the day not just to God but to His *Presence*. The motive is the love which hungers to pass beyond communication with God to companionship with Him, and union with Him. Acting on the faith-knowledge that God is present, the pilgrim turns to God in brief bursts of loving attention in the course of work, meals, recreation, and waking moments in the night.

What does one do during this moment of communion? He does what is most useful to *promote the practice itself, the presence of God found through the practice, and fidelity to God at all times.* The promotion of these three different purposes may at times come into conflict, and in that case the purpose more important at the moment should be served. Let us look at each of these three purposes.

When a pilgrim first adopts this practice, his immediate objective will be to turn it into a habit by overcoming the obstacles. To begin with, when he turns his attention to God he may experience a sense of God's absence, not His presence. He can help himself greatly in developing a psychological sense of the Presence of God by repeating in faith one of God's many revelations and promises of personal presence. Many pilgrims find familiarity with Psalm 139 very helpful. On turning to God, just repeat an appropriate phrase: "If I take the wings of the morning and dwell in the uttermost parts of the sea, even there thy hand shall lead me, and thy right hand shall hold me" (139:9-10). Jesus' personal promise may be more effective: "Lo, I am with you always" (Matthew 28:20). When the pilgrim is in need of God's assistance, a different passage may prove more suitable: "God is . . . a very present help in trouble" (Ps. 46:1).

After the practice has become a firm habit, the pilgrim will want to use the form of it which most enhances his finding of the Presence of God. He may find that a moment of completely wordless attention is best, in keeping with the Scriptural invitation: "Be still, and know that I am God" (Ps. 46:10). The use of the Name may be best: *God*, or *Jesus*, or *Father*, or *Beloved*. He should do what brings him the most peace and joy.

The third purpose of the practice is to find in renewed contact with God a revitalized sense of fidelity to His will. The practice will generally expose immediately any straying from God's purposes and invite spontaneous amendment in faithful love. That is why this practice can be such a powerful agent of growth. This rhythm of moments of *loving attention to God and renewed intention* to do His will penetrates to the heart of the spiritual life.

An apostolic contemplative who is further along the way of development will find these moments helpful to clear mind and heart, find deeper union with the Lord of creation, and receive illumination concerning God's will even in very complex circumstances. This is to use the moment of attention as a discernment of spirits. Used in this way, the practice will make of a pilgrim a more perfect and reliable ambassador of God. It inserts him into the authentic tradition of salvation history wherein God is an Acting Presence influencing and shaping events through the person of His human agents: "Now therefore go, and I will be with your mouth and teach you what you shall speak" (Exod. 4:12). And to suppress the error that only a chosen few are God's agents, the First Letter of Peter says: "As good stewards of God's varied grace, employ it for one another: whoever speaks, as one who utters oracles of God; whoever renders service, as one who renders it by the strength which God supplies" (4:10-11).

How frequently should one turn to God? With the frequency suited to the pilgrim's type of work and compatible with his supply of mental energy. If the practice interferes with his work, he is going about it wrongly, or with too great a frequency; or it is not for him, at least not at this time. If the practice tends to exhaust him, the same is to be said. To find the right usage is a matter of experiment. Does the practice bring him devotion, peace, and joy, without overtaxing him? They are signs enough of its efficacy. Consultation with the spiritual director is also advisable if one wants to be more sure of finding his own authentic path.

When the Spirit wishes to introduce a pilgrim to this simple yet sublime practice, He will personally teach it to him, or lead him to someone who will. One pilgrim recounts his discovery of the practice:

> I was longing for the Lord but did not know how to find Him. I came on a chapter on "the practice of the presence of God" in Rodriguez' *Principles and Practice of Christian Perfection*. I began practice at once, but did not remember to do it very often. I began carrying a pebble in my hand, and each time I adverted to this "nuisance," it reminded me to turn to God. Soon the practice was a habit that brought me much joy. Not long after, while I stood by the roadside alone and lonely on a long journey, God suddenly made me conscious of His presence without any act on my part. My surprised reaction was: "I'll never be lonely again!" The sense of God's presence soon faded, but the old loneliness has never returned, or at most very rarely. "He who sent me is with me" (cf. John 8:29).

Another pilgrim, an old farmer, always carried an acorn in his hand. This idiosyncracy amused his family. On his deathbed he revealed his secret: *An acorn is a living thing. Where there is life, God is.* A young Sister adopted the practice of turning to the Presence of God just before falling asleep. Several months later, when she awoke one night, God made her feel His Presence.

When the Practice of the Presence of God is used over a long period, words, phrases and thoughts are inclined to drop from its usage, and then it tends to become a subtle and almost continuous form of the *prayer of faith*.

It seems, therefore, that pilgrims who do not have the opportunity for many hours of formal prayer *can* be led by this practice, which is so suited to their vocation, to the same *prayer of faith* which pure contemplatives reach through a path of more prayer and less action. Both arrive at the peace and consolation of living by faith with God, who is "a very present help."

Part Three

THE KINGDOM OF GOD COMES IN POWER

1.

Experiences of the Incarnation

More and more our pilgrim contemplative has been feeling the desire "to know Christ and the power of his resurrection" (Phil. 3: 10). Now Jesus comes. It is love's Mount Tabor. The advent of Jesus, like the advent of Mary, and even more than the advent of Mary, cannot be described, only reported. Jesus is an experience, not a set of ideas that lends itself to recounting in words. The experience of Jesus is a richness of affections, of feelings, of emotions, ardent searchings, joyous findings, passionate commitments. "The love of Jesus, what it is, none but His loved ones know." Love descends with the power of a summer storm, with the tenderness of a nightingale's song.

Prayer to God is no longer the former longing, praising, searching, sorrowing. It is no faint and shadowy companionship. It is the ardent presence of Jesus. Now the pilgrim's prayer is nothing if Jesus is not in it.

The pilgrim is, of course, not discovering Jesus for the first time. As far back as memory goes he has known Jesus, believed in Him and loved Him, and on occasion had deep experiences of Jesus' love for him. But generally his belief in the greatness of Jesus' love for him had about it something of the paleness of sheer propositional faith, whereas now it has the healthy glow of almost continuous personal experience. Think of a man climbing a mountain. After a time he looks back, and finds himself on a promontory contemplating the lakes and valleys far below. He goes on and up. When he looks down from his new pinnacle, he is among the clouds, and far below, hardly distinguishable from the valley floor, is the promontory on which he stood before. That far below now is the pilgrim's former experiences of the love of Jesus. Never before could he fully believe that Jesus loves him as much as he now knows that Jesus loves him.

He is discovering the Incarnation with new intensity, at a new height, where it is putting forth a new branch, which he is. Until now he had never known the Incarnation was continuing, but now he experiences that progress in himself, into himself: "I am the true vine, and my Father is the vinedresser. . . you are the branches" (John 15:1, 5).

Those who earlier experienced the advent of Mary are keenly aware how Mary, who once prepared herself for Jesus, has now prepared them. The heart of the Hail Mary becomes a new song of praise and thanksgiving: *Blessed is the fruit of thy womb, Jesus!* Their gratitude to Mary is inexpressible: "How to praise you, O holy Virgin, I know not!"

At last, in Jesus, the contemplative in action begins to catch glimmers of the real possibility of the union of heaven and earth for which he has been searching. Jesus is the "key of the house of David" (Is. 22:22) who will open for him all the secrets of the universe, with God at their center and heart.

No longer is the pilgrim searching for God, he is finding Him in the presence of Jesus. His prayer now is not for presence but for union. Its expressions are as rich as a symphony, but its theme does not falter.

The advent of Jesus changes everything in his life, for the coming of Jesus really does make all things new. The sacrifice of the Mass has long since dominated his life, but only now is he discovering how really he possesses Jesus to offer to the Father, and how he should offer himself with Him, and how to offer both for the world's salvation. The Mass is, too, that banquet of the wise king which, even in its prefigurement, left the Queen of Sheba breathless (1 Kings 10:5). For this banquet he would, if he could, sacrifice all other food, so much sweetness, delight, and strength does he find in it. In this stage some pilgrims spend hours before the Blessed Sacrament praying, reading, resting, speaking not a word.

In Jesus whom he has always known he only now finds the Kingdom of God palpably on earth. Jesus is everything that God is and everything that he is. Jesus is God and man, God and the dust of the earth made perfectly one, perpetually one. Heaven and earth *have* been fused. In Jesus at least the Father's Kingdom is already perfect.

In prayer and the Mass, then, the pilgrim finds Jesus easily. The rest of the day is spent longing for Jesus. It is a tender longing, for Jesus is not really absent, He is just not fully present. The very name of Jesus evokes His presence. He never tires of speaking The Name, forming it on his lips and embedding it in his heart. This preoccupation with Jesus can "interfere" with his work—if that is the right word. The pilgrim has still to learn how to bring the power of Jesus to bear upon his activity in the world for the sake of the Kingdom. Wise spiritual direction can help him here. The Spirit who is constantly recalling him to Jesus is also sending him to his work. He must continue to learn how to integrate the two inspirations which constitute his vocation to prayer and apostolic service, to prayer in the course of service, to prayer that guides his service. He can be helped by the practice of the Presence of God, which was presented earlier with norms for appropriate usage. Now, however, it will be the *practice of the Presence of Jesus.*

His day is becoming a living expression of that day's Eucharist, and a preparation for the morrow's. Not his prayer but the Eucharist is the headquarters of his day. Prayer is a deep experience of Jesus, but the Eucharist is the certainty of union with Him, for the God-man has said so, and the pilgrim measures the value of things not primarily by experience but by the revealed word of God, as understood in the Church. Should all experience of Jesus in the Eucharist cease he would, he feels, hold to the same hierarchy of values.

He tries to lose no opportunity to make prayer and life a preparation for the Eucharist. In his prayer he calls upon many of the Saints whom he knows most intimately to prepare him for Holy Communion. Above all, he relies on Mary's help. What will she not gladly do to make him go more worthily to Jesus in the Eucharist? The Queen will send him as her son to meet her Son. Her prayers will make him a very son of God to meet the Son of God. With one or other such spiritual stratagem a pilgrim in this stage will wisely meet the exigencies of love. He will become acutely conscious also of the interplay between the way he works and lives and the way he receives the Eucharist. To whom can he refuse love and service during the day, and not refuse it to Christ? This felt interplay becomes a powerful incentive to growth in the ability to accomplish the mission on which he has been sent.

Jesus has risen like the morning sun over the landscape of the pilgrim's life. The pilgrim who also enjoys the presence of Mary the morning star finds it easy at this time to blend his love with the love of Jesus and Mary into a symphony of three loves. The following traditional hymn tells of the experience of such pilgrims:

Mary the dawn, Christ the perfect day!
Mary the gate, Christ the heavenly way!
Mary the root, Christ the mystic vine!
Mary the grapes, Christ the sacred wine!

2.

Effects of the Advent of Jesus

If the nature of the advent of Jesus is not susceptible to description, at least the context of the meeting with Jesus can be reported. The context is often a Gospel episode, and therefore accessible to all. The pilgrim is now regularly poring over the Gospel accounts of Jesus. By prayer he enters deeply into the experiences of Jesus through imaginative contemplation. Thus he approaches as closely as he can to sharing with the apostles the privilege of living with Jesus.

The experience of Jesus is likely to produce many effects in the pilgrim. An account will be given of those effects which make manifest the rapid spiritual and psychological growth now going on in him.

One of the first of these effects is an experience of unworthiness. The experience is peaceful, but deep beyond words. The pilgrim feels a kinship with St. Peter in that moment when he expostulated with Jesus: "Depart from me, for I am a sinful man O Lord" (Luke

5:8). What, the pilgrim asks Jesus, has sin to do with Innocence? What companionship can rebellion have with the Father's true Son? What partnership can death have with Life? Instinct with the Spirit, his protestations are in reality the *one claim* he has on Jesus. Jesus is the Savior and he is the one in need of salvation. The love with which Jesus responds to the pilgrim is as dramatic a reassurance as the words with which He answered Peter: "Do not be afraid; henceforth you will be catching men" (Luke 5:10). The pilgrim is being confirmed in his realization that everything is gift, and this makes his joy greater because it makes it the more secure.

Not all pilgrims see at once that God's favor is unearned. One pilgrim who was being swept away by God's love kept asking her spiritual director: *What have I done to deserve this?* He would keep answering: *Nothing!*

The pilgrim's confidence in Jesus is all the more secure because by meditation he has come to know Jesus' passion to do the Father's will; and he knows the Father's will for His Son: "I will give you as a light to the nations, that my salvation may reach to the end of the earth" (Is. 49:6).

Now lowliness exerts a powerful attraction that draws the pilgrim into its orbit. He knows instinctively that heartfelt lowliness is both the way of truth and the most eloquent plea to God to feed his hunger for holiness. He wants Jesus to accomplish great things in him, and he knows unerringly that his part is to dig as deep as he can the foundations of humility. Then Christ can build as tall as He wills.

With the same instinct he knows that lowliness and love are inseparable, two sides of the same coin. He discerns this passion for lowliness in the lives of both Jesus and Mary, and understands why it must be so. No person who has genuinely approached and experienced God can escape by more than a hairsbreadth from total annihilation. One who has seen the mountains and understood the galactic spaces where stars burn like little candles can no longer think of himself as tall. Even excessively, even at the seeming cost of reducing their apostolic effectiveness, many pilgrims feel impelled to cultivate a retiring modesty. While such cultivation may in fact hinder their suitability for certain works (and this may be why all are not inspired to it), it will greatly promote their general effectiveness when they are sent on mission by God. The reason is that all men hate pride in others, and they hate it most in a man of God, and rightly. The man of God is commissioned to communicate another than himself; the proud man of God comes in the name of another and communicates himself.

It is well that the pilgrim is drawn to humility at this time, for sudden growth in holiness is a heady gift. Spiritual insight easily leads to pride and an authoritarianism that presumes to correct and dictate to others. Few who grow rapidly seem to escape these faults, which harm both the pilgrim and his mission. Involved here is a difficult problem. The pilgrim with the gift of knowledge needs also the gift of discernment, to know when to speak out boldly in the name of God, and when to remain silent lest he be speaking only in his own name.

As the pilgrim draws closer to Jesus, he also draws nearer to the front lines of the war against sin, the enemy of the Kingdom. He finds Jesus uncompromising in this warfare: "If your hand causes you to sin, cut it off . . . if your eye causes you to sin, pluck it out!" (Mark 9:43, 47). This war against sin is no peripheral concern, but the first step in the pilgrim's mandate to labor for the coming of God's Kingdom. And the place he must begin is within himself. He hurls himself into the battle against temptation with renewed severity. Austerity of life, penance and fasting are easy for him at this time—they will never be easier—because the purification of the senses which they bring reward him at once by deepening his devotion to Jesus and increasing the ease of finding Him.

The sacrament of forgiveness and reconciliation glows with new significance. It heals at once his recurrent wounds, and he feels the way it brings him closer to God and all his companions. He is incapable of avoiding all sin, but the Lord has provided this remedy which leaves nothing behind but the scars of the sin of Adam and of his own past sins. Scrupulosity can launch itself against some, but in the presence of the felt love of Jesus it is a weak adversary. Given the spiritual director's wise advice that it is not from God, they will boldly thrust it aside.

Just as the search for a sensitive conscience can occasion an attack of scruples, the promotion of a sense of unworthiness can degenerate into a sense of worthlessness. One pilgrim was assailed by this temptation for a whole year, and for a year he fought back doggedly with the scriptural logic of St. Paul. Is it possible that "he who did not spare his own Son but gave him up for us all, will not also give us all things with him?" (Rom. 8:32). The pilgrim had already experienced the Father's gift of His Son. How could he be duped into believing that the Father will not also readily provide him with the qualities of personal worth? What he did not yet have, what he had not yet become, he would in due time be given and become.

Making no headway against this weapon of God's word, the diabolical temptation at last left him for a while.

The advent of Jesus promotes growth in many ways. It orders and simplifies life, it simplifies values, it simplifies prayer. It intensifies the desire to serve. One young man who had recently entered the religious life felt very strongly the call to service which the advent of Jesus brings, and he found a practical way to serve that was in accord with the limited opportunities his novitiate life provided:

> I awakened to the desire to be like Jesus—to give myself to others and for others. To be a servant became extremely important and my life became very simple: "I have given you an example: if I have washed your feet so you also must wash one another's feet." Serving my brothers became a way of life: with great desire and willingness I began to serve by doing ordinary chores. Washing windows, mopping floors, cleaning and setting up the refectory, doing the dishes, scrubbing pots and pans—all these became concrete expressions of "washing the feet of the brethren"—of serving them whether I felt like it or not. I looked upon serving at table as a great privilege. I did things I did not feel like doing—and that others did not want to do: inspiring a baseball game, putting bats and balls in a protected place, etc. All of these were tiny ways of being a servant and produced deep personal satisfaction. It was costing me something, but it was a great joy just being like Jesus, being obedient to His command: "Love one another as I have loved you."

This inspiration to service inevitably grows into an aspiration to do great things for Christ, and the growth brings troubles of its own. To begin with, when a pilgrim contemplative responds with magnanimity of soul to the inspirations of faith, he is liable to be criticized and treated as arrogant by companions who have not experienced such an inspiration, or who lack the courage to respond to it. True, some pilgrims are justly criticized because they leave off doing what is possible for them, and without true guidance of the Spirit aspire to something unrealistic. Or again their aspirations may be mixed with ambition and lead to frustration.

The latter difficulties arise from one of the root problems of human life: the failure to see and order values properly. While there are great projects on all sides crying out for apostles with the training, natural endowments, and expertise to accomplish them, there are also humbler tasks with their own greatness which also need doing. One pilgrim of great desires who felt constricted by circumstances pondered the matter:

In his early twenties Michelangelo carved out works of undying beauty; Einstein was laying the foundations of his untrammeled thought; Thomas Aquinas was recording his perennial philosophy. What have I to offer you, Lord God? Thinking thus in the past, I have almost despaired, but today you have renewed the realization of my true worth, and of the worth of every man. . . . What is true human value, what is it that brings men peace, and joy, and abiding happiness? It is loving you and being loved by you, God my Jesus; it is possessing you and being possessed by you. If all else has to be sacrificed for this, it is as a little dung. . . . Have I loved the Lord my God with my whole heart and soul and strength and mind? In this is creativity and herculean labor and challenge enough for the most favored men. Help me to remember this and I will not be bitter any more.

This is the scale of values the pilgrim must have if he is to make the sacrifices necessary to his own growth, and if he is to be effective in his work as one sent by God. Only when he has learned that aspirations must be tempered by one's commitments, state of life, and natural endowments, and the *true purposes of God* for himself as they are manifested in these conditions—only then will he walk contentedly. Only then will he walk reverently among those he is called to serve, and find it possible to see what a great work it can be to do lowly works for those people whom this world considers of no account.

It takes no magnificent insight for even contemporaries or confreres to recognize the stature of a Thomas Aquinas or an Augustine, but it is a great gift when contemporaries have the insight to see in the Little Flower a spiritual giant, long before the Church bestows its honors upon her. This is the kind of insight the pilgrim needs if he is not to overlook the sometimes lowly people who will most profit by his help and make it pay the greatest dividends for the Church and the whole Kingdom of God. And conversely, a pilgrim who wins plaudits for some prestigious accomplishment needs the same insight so he will take no false pride in his achievements, and so he will know where true greatness lies, and so never forget that no human achievement is comparable in value to God's gift of holiness. When values are set in order according to the word and the work of God, covetousness and ambition topple, and God's purposes alone become important.

As the days pass, the closeness of Jesus waxes and wanes, in accord with the mysterious rhythms of spiritual realities. When desolation persists, pilgrims should look to their faults in their labors, or to negligence in their spiritual activities. One universal remedy for desolation is meditation on the Passion of Jesus. When all other experiences of the love Jesus has for him forsake a pilgrim, he cannot doubt the meaning of the Passion. The Son of God has loved him, delivered Himself up for him, and showed him the way he too must travel. One pilgrim in darkness used to make the Stations of the Cross with one simple plea at each station: *Take me with you.* That had become the meaning of his life, as it is the meaning of the life of every pilgrim who has come this far, and is beginning to experience for himself what St. Paul set down as his experience: "I have been crucified with Christ; it is no longer I who live, but Christ who lives in me; and the life I now live in the flesh I live by faith in the Son of God, who loved me and gave himself for me" (Gal. 2:19-20).

Meditation on the Passion of Christ reminds the pilgrim that desolation and suffering need not be his fault at all; they are signs of the weakness to which he is *subject,* and of the little power he has to control the shape of his spiritual experiences. All is in the power of God, and His good pleasure must be not only accepted but adored.

The pilgrim's readiness to endure all for the love of Jesus is no delusion. It is evident in the way he lives and speaks, and in his love for others. For the present his life and its hardships are easy to endure because so frequently the love of God is tangibly pouring into his spirit and heart and mind and body. Jesus has let Himself be experienced as Savior and Companion, Guide and Light, "a lamp to my feet" (Ps. 119:105).

3.

Further Effects of the Advent of Jesus

There are certain other less common effects of prayer at this time which ought to be considered. Let us take the lesser ones first, with the note that we are attending to them not because they are important but because trouble can be warded off by giving guidelines which underscore their unimportance.

Of the many pilgrims who experience a deep love of Jesus in prayer at this time, there are some whose bodies emanate "the sweet odor of Christ" during prayer, and even afterwards. There are also phenomena of touch. At times, while deep in meditation, a pilgrim may notice an unusual sensation on the top of the head, as though a finger were lightly pressing on the hair. Other pilgrims report that in the course of their activities they occasionally experience a tap on the shoulder or something similar which calls their attention to some matter, or recalls them to fidelity when they are even slightly wayward. There are also phenomena of taste. One pilgrim who had been conversing spiritedly about Jesus suddenly experienced a strange, rich taste in his mouth which he had never known before and has never known again.

The first thing that should be said about these phenomena is that they are not important and are not to be desired, for that would be a diversion from Jesus. The history of spirituality shows that they are not even a proof of holiness. Their meaning in the providence of God may be their use in converting even the senses to the Lord, assuring even the body of man in a way it can understand that the Lord is its fulfillment too in the age to come: "O taste and see that the Lord is good!" (Ps. 34:8). In that sense they serve a prophetic role.

Experience teaches, however, that when pilgrims become fascinated with these trifles they draw the whole man away from God. Catholic religious tradition warns of this danger. There is another phenomenon which can be more upsetting. When a person is deeply affected by the love of Jesus, as in receiving Holy Communion, his joy and happiness can overflow into the sensible affections, and this is good, but it can at times go further and stir the whole body to sensual and erotic feelings. In *The Dark Night of the Soul*, St. John of the Cross calls this "spiritual luxury," not because it is spiritual but because it begins with the spiritual (I, 4). The effect originates from the fundamental unity of soul and body, but its more immediate causes are spiritual imperfections, an over-excitable temperament, or the temptation of the devil. It frightens some people away from prayer either because they are badly instructed or because they let their fear of sin hinder their love of God.

The error on the other extreme is to think it is all right to indulge such eroticism. Experience teaches that what is needed here is the counsel and calming assurances of a knowledgeable spiritual director. Probably the best advice which he can tender is that which St. Teresa of Avila offered in a letter to her brother, who was thus troubled: "I am quite clear that they are of no account, so the best thing is to make no account of them" (letter 168). Spiritual growth can be retarded if one fears to mention them to a spiritual director and consequently remains plagued by scruples and indecision regarding right conduct. Bringing the problem into the open may end it outright, for fear and anxiety aggravate it. Such openness is especially necessary if the devil does have any part in it, for one of his chief weapons is secrecy, as St. Ignatius indicates in his *Spiritual Exercises* (#326). This problem could have been mentioned earlier, especially when we were treating of Mary's advent in the pilgrim's life. Human affectivity easily takes wrong turns in fallen man, but there can be no sin where there is neither evil intent nor irresponsibility in obeying God's law.

Let us turn now to two other effects of more importance which eventuate in some pilgrims at this time: the gift of tears, and the conflict of loves.

The gift of tears may be given through the advent of Jesus, for His advent touches the deepest wellsprings of human affection. The affections rise up and overflow the vessel of the soul, and gentle tears flow. They flow in moments of feeling sensibly the overwhelming pity of God, and in moments when the pilgrim experiences the tenderness and sweetness of God's presence and simultaneously recalls the terrible ordeal of His absence. They flow when the pilgrim's longing for God is suddenly relieved by His presence, and when in the presence of God the pilgrim is reminded of his own pitiful state and the pitiable state of all men, brothers all. Sometimes the tears become a storm of weeping and sobbing. Sometimes in prayer they flow without any conscious emotions at all, but even then they bring an other-worldly sweetness and peace, and their aftermath is a light-hearted joy.

The gift of tears should not be slighted as a mere external thing. That is to misunderstand it completely and may lead to shunning the gift as runaway emotions, and resisting it if it is offered. What rain is to terrestrial ecology, so the gift of tears can be to the inmost part of man. It is a work of God, and it is not empty. The advent of Jesus (or earlier, of Mary, and earlier still of God in the first divine visitations) awakens pure affections because it heals the very roots of human affectivity. The gift of tears is one of the means to that healing. It cleans and purifies the channels of the affections. It washes away the hard barriers to spontaneous affections which sin builds up over the years. It ends aridity and purges harshness and warms coldness. It tempers justice and all forms of sternness. A season of the gift of tears leaves a pilgrim's affectivity rich with new growth and sparkling with the freshness of clean air after a summer rain.

The magnitude of the value of these changes is hidden, so it will help to recall that human affectivity is at the heart of religion, and its purification and growth are the advance of religion. Purifying the affections is the work of the Spirit: it is a sharing in the love and compassion of Jesus. His affectivity exemplifies in such a consummate way St. Paul's encomium of the affections that where St. Paul used the word *love* we can substitute the word *Jesus*: "Jesus is patient, Jesus is kind, Jesus is not jealous or boastful . . . arrogant or rude" (1 Cor. 13:4). Contrast this with Paul's description of irreligious men and men who have corrupted true religion: "God gave them up to a base mind and to improper conduct. They were filled with all manner of wickedness" (Rom. 1:28-29).

Even the foregoing consideration does not make sufficiently manifest the great value of this growth and purification of the affections. It is necessary to recall that affections must be deemed among the truest, deepest forms of human communication: "If I have all the eloquence of men or angels, but speak without love, I am simply a gong booming or a cymbal clashing" (1 Cor. 13:1 JB). Love without the rich array of affections and emotions which best express it is truncated and imprisoned, as even the philosophers teach, and as psychiatrists know so well.

Even to this point the whole significance of this growth in affectivity, which is so facilitated by the gift of tears, has not yet appeared. It cannot appear until we consider the importance of awakening and directing to God our whole potential for affectivity. The human dynamism and capacity for giving and acting is not wholly under the aegis of the will, but is greatly subject to the passions. The passions are by nature such that they await an awakening by another than their owner. Only when the passions are awakened to love of God and enlisted in the cause of God is a man's full potential for service marshalled. Not until a pilgrim's love for God becomes a passion can he speed along the way of the Saints. What else is Scripture teaching than this when it commands: "You shall love the Lord your God with all your heart, and with all your soul, and with all your mind, and with all your strength" (Mark 12:30).

Spiritual affections and tears have another significance which is connected with the fact that they are a gift of God's *consolation.* God communicates with man by evoking ideas and realizations, but He also communicates with man through affectivity states. A pilgrim must often find the way in which God is leading him by discerning the course of action which best promotes *deep peace and joy,* since man was made for happiness in God. This process of finding God's will for oneself is called the discernment of spirits. Facility in its use depends on an affectivity that is rightly ordered, purified and mature, integral and spontaneous.

Not only do Scripture and tradition teach this, but it is verified by reflection on our own religious experiences. Our interior life does not consist in a face-to-face communication with God. It consists in communication with Him through the revealed doctrine and through a developed contact with one's own religious affectivity states, thoughts, experiences, intuitions, and motives as these reflect God acting on one. This means that these subjective experiences can be experiences of God and His will for me personally. We must therefore cultivate our interior life not only in the sense of being attentive to God, but in the sense of being attentive to our own affectivity states, and of learning to interpret their meaning regarding our relationship with God and His purposes. This is of double significance for the apostolic contemplative who is sent by God to accomplish God's work. He must try to establish constant communication with God to receive the guidance necessary in the fluid circumstances of many apostolic works.

In connection with discernment of spirits, the pilgrim's experiences of spiritual affections and tears are teaching him the "feel" of the things of God, teaching him to know and recognize the state of soul of one who lives for God, who chooses "always . . .what is pleasing to him" (John 8:29). Through this schooling the pilgrim is being given a feeling for the state of soul which he should always try to maintain by making only the choices and doing only the things which promote sweetness, peace and joy. He is being trained to find consolation in everything, not primarily for the sake of the consolation, but for the faithful service of God, who gives this consolation as the sign of the right way. Decline in this consolation is a sign the pilgrim should reassess his conduct. If he finds no cause in himself, he may conclude that its source is not fault on his part but rather the necessity of sharing the sufferings of Christ.

These considerations help to explain why that renowned contemplative in action and expert discerner of spirits, St. Ignatius of Loyola, was also a man who valued affectivity so highly that he urged those who made his *Spiritual Exercises* to ask for the gift of tears (#55) and even to labor for it (#195).

The pilgrim need not understand these matters clearly to benefit by his growing affectivity and the gift of tears. The experience of them introduces him to a state of soul so attractive and so full of other-worldly peace that once he has known it he will seek it and conduct himself in a way that will promote it. As he progresses he will learn more about the discernment of spirits through experience and trial and error. If he comes upon an opportunity for formal training in this art in accord with the experiences of the Saints and the formulations of wise theologians, he will do well to take advantage of it.

The final effect of the advent of Jesus which we will consider here is the conflict which can arise between the love given to Jesus and to Mary. The conflict may be nonsense in theory, but it can be agony in fact. What is being referred to is not some silly jealousy or a divided heart, but the problem of attention. The pilgrim's whole attention is now drawn to the Lord, but he feels that to ignore Mary would be a show of ingratitude at the least, and at the worst an offense against both. It is a true problem, originating in human finitude. It is the problem of the two and the many in love, a problem rooted in the fact that we are creatures at once spiritual and material, aspiring to union with all, and yet constricted in time, space, and attention by our materiality. It is a crisis of growth, and it is compounded by the selfishness still in the pilgrim's heart. Such is his imperfection still that he too often gravitates to that course which brings him the most satisfaction, rather than to that course which only true love can discern.

Only the most selfless responsiveness to the Spirit of love can be an adequate guide here. How many reach this far, and what remnant of those passes beyond it selflessly? How many are great-souled enough for two great loves at once?

This crisis of growth has far-reaching consequences, for it is a school of growth that can solve a much greater problem. It parallels the struggle to love both God and creation. If the pilgrim cannot continue to give his faithful attention even to Mary, who is so innocent, so lovable, and to whom he is so much in debt, what chance does a sinful world have to attract his love? But if the pilgrim triumphs over this crisis of growth, if he grows spiritual enough to embrace Jesus and Mary in one selfless love, he will be well on the way to embracing all other creatures as well.

I ask your forgiveness, Mary, for my failure in loving you, and for the failure of others who have travelled this way. Help us, Mary, knowing that you will be teaching us to love not only you, but all creation. Holy Mary, Mother of God, pray for us sinners.

4.

Experiences of the Lord of Nature

Love, stirred by meetings with Jesus and Mary, has awakened the pilgrim's sleeping sensibilities. He now finds himself responding to beauty and goodness in all unspoiled things. One pilgrim, a housewife, describes her experience of becoming sensitized to nature:

> Suddenly my senses came alive—as though for the first time my eyes could really see—the sky was really blue, not just sky but a beautiful blue wonder, filled with soft, drifting, puffy clouds. The grass was greener, the trees waved at me and beckoned me to come and play. The spring flowers and flowering trees almost gave me physical pain—their perfection became so vitally apparent. During this period (when I played a great deal of tennis), if I happened to be early for a game I would sit down on the ground and in losing myself become almost drunk with the glory of God's artistry. . . . Before, I would have been mad as HELL at everyone for being late and would have stood tapping my foot with impatience. Instead, I became happy to have a moment of solitude to revel in such splendor.

In this experience nature is beginning to confide to the pilgrim its secret: it is a messenger and a message from God. The hitherto concealed passage between creation and Creator has been disclosed to him through his intimate personal friendship with Jesus, the God-man, who is Himself that passage, that stairway of which Jacob dreamed as he slept with his head on the rock that symbolized God: "He dreamed that there was a ladder set upon the earth, and the top of it reached to heaven; and behold, the angels of God were ascending and descending on it" (Gen. 28:12).

100

The pilgrim is beginning to walk through God's world the way he might walk through an artist friend's studio, or the way a son might walk through his father's carpenter shop. In the unspoiled works of nature he is now able to find God readily.

The finding of God in nature at this time generally takes place through conscious reasoning and the use of the analogy of being. Religious men have found God in this way through the ages because it is of the nature of man to discover in created things the marks and likenesses to their Creator: "Yes, naturally stupid are all men who have not known God and who, from the good things that are seen, have not been able to discover Him-who-is, or, by studying the works, have failed to recognize the Artificer. Fire however, or wind, or the swift air, the spheres of the stars, impetuous water, heaven's lamps, are what they have held to be the gods who govern the world. If, charmed by their beauty, they have taken things for gods, let them know how much the Lord of these excels them, since the very Author of beauty has created them. And if they have been impressed by their power and energy, let them deduce from these how much mightier is he that has formed them, since through the grandeur and beauty of the creatures we may, by analogy, contemplate their Author" (Wis. 13:1-5 JB).

Jesus awakens this sensitivity in pilgrims in several ways. The first is simply through the delicate sensibilities which every deep love awakens. The second is through Jesus' own use of the analogy of being. Every parable of His makes use of it. Probably no other man in history gives such evidence that his active life is shot through with the finding of God in everything. So simply through reading the Gospels, the pilgrim catches on. And then some pilgrims are able to discover a connection between their imaginative contemplation of the life of Jesus and this awakening. One pilgrim reflected on this in a letter to her spiritual director:

> Mysteriously, focusing in on a visual Christ seems to be producing its benefits outside the period of prayer as such. I can sense within myself a growing awareness and a deeper sensitivity to the presence of God in all creatures and all creation. It is as though this exercise has stimulated a spiritual aesthetic awareness wherein God is experienced. . . . I am conscious of a desire to relate to creation in its true essence—to go beyond the externals—to contemplate and love that "Something" which gives it its true value. I seek to penetrate the surface and find my God. It is causing me also to become more delicately aware of the weakness and imperfections within myself as God can be seen only by the "pure of heart." At

times, however, I find myself giving in to feelings of discouragement—my own surface is so poor a reflection of His image.

The more the pilgrim fills his mind with the revealed knowledge of God through Scriptural reading and meditation and through
habitual contact with the psalmist, who finds God in everything, the
richer this nature period will be—especially if he sets himself to
make a conscious effort to recognize natural things as messengers of
God. He rests before a fountain, and as he watches its eternal out-
pouring, he sees the Father who is the source of all, the One who has
given His Son, and poured out His Spirit upon the earth. He walks
through a summer field of golden wheat, he crosses a sunlit vine-
yard where the grapes already smell of wine, he strides across an
autumn landscape laden with orange pumpkins, and he is warmed
by the fruitfulness and the providence and the nearness of God. In
the night he gazes up at the star-filled heavens, and the silent im-
mensity tells him of God. He walks and mounts a rising slope which
conceals and invites to all that lies hidden beyond, and he is reminded of the limits of his own life, and its promise of pilgrim passage to the new land of eternity. He gazes at uncultivated fields
wild with a riot of colors, some slender and graceful and ephemeral,
restless in the wind, some stalwart and unmoving in ancient gar-
ments of bark, clad for winter and summer alike, and he marvels at
the God who likes these things, the God who thought them all up,
the God who converses with him through them, and he feels a great
kinship for Him, for he too likes them beyond telling. He drives
alone through the mountains, breathes in the chill rich air of the
peaks, stops and drinks from an icy artesian well, strips and plunges
into a cratered lake—and finds himself with his Maker at the prime-
val moments of creation.

The pilgrim also finds in nature similitudes of the life of Jesus.
He walks in the early morning, and sees the dewdrops which have
gathered virginally in the chill of the night to remind him of another
Virgin Birth. He walks in the evening light, and the crimson of dying
day speaks to him of the Beloved's Blood draining from Calvary's
sky. It is all there. Nature is recounting the story after it all happened, as it predicted it before it all took place. And so he finds affection for the God of creation. How could he have been so blind,
thinking the Beloved was far away, when he knew all the while how
impossible it is that a lover should willingly absent himself?

Humans and human things too speak of God to him. A man,
woman, and child pass, and he remembers the Trinity. A beautiful
face in a speeding car passes by, and he remembers the loveliness of

God. A lovesong meant for man and woman plays softly, and his heart is stirred for the Beloved of the beloveds. He spends an enjoyable evening with friends, and as he returns home he is close to the Friend of all friends.

Silence plays a special role in enabling creation to sing its Creator's love song and hint of His presence. Sometimes when he sits in silence and alone, enjoying the food which sustains his life, he finds Jesus in him, sharing and enjoying the repast with him. When he dines with others in the silent gatherings of retreats, he finds his companions and the very air surfeited with the divine presence.

These heightened experiences of God in nature are relatively rare. More commonly the pilgrim's efforts to find God through the analogy of being do not affect him deeply. Even so, the common and uncommon experiences together are enough to make him recognize in nature a kingdom of God, a garden where God walks.

5.

The Characteristics of Spiritual Growth

The discoveries of the God of nature which the pilgrim is making at this time stir sympathetic vibrations deep in his soul and bring to the surface the memory of similar experiences which came to pass long ago and had long since been forgotten. For each pilgrim these early experiences will be unique. He may remember a silver morning when the whole earth was a temple, or a golden twilight when the sun, setting in the west, seemed as sacred as a consecrated host. One pilgrim recalls his boyhood fishing expeditions in the night:

> There in the dark on the water I would listen to the chirping of the crickets and the croaking of the frogs. I would gaze up at the unblinking white stars and the flashing irridescent ones, and feel a quiet and a peace punctuated by the occasional splash of a leaping fish. I was vaguely aware of it even then, but now I realize more keenly why I was drawn to those nocturnal expeditions in the icy cold of night, and the sleeplessness. As I floated on the deep, under the vault of heaven, I was catching more than fish.

Scales may have formed over the pilgrim's eyes awhile, and his memory fallen into a torpor, but now once again he is in communion with the stream of his own life; he realizes that he has always been in contact with the personal Lord of the universe, his friend, his Beloved, his Father and Brother and Savior, who walks through His universe and camps there, even as once in the flesh He pitched His tent among a people and walked through our joys and sufferings and death to waken us to true life.

Once again it appears why, if the pilgrim does not habitually return to the springs of his first graces, he will be impoverished. Those springs are waters of grace which are not to be enjoyed for a moment, but used for a lifetime. It is out of those waters of grace that the roots of his present grew. He must not cut himself off from those roots by the amnesia of neglect, or the sap will not rise in its seasons to nourish the branches of his new growth. The first experiences of each kind, the virginal experiences, are eternal pools in the memory brought into being by the touch of God like the waters of Meribah in the desert. They are accessible by a journey of the mind. They are an ever-available source of renewal, they are light in darkness and hope in despair, as the psalmist knew: "I consider the days of old, I remember the years long ago. I commune with my heart in the night; I meditate and search my spirit" (Ps. 77:6).

This experience of the recall of forgotten graces illuminates the nature of spiritual growth. A reader forgetful of a caution given earlier in this account of the pilgrim's growth might wrongly think that each phase of growth so far described is a self-contained unit, inserted into the life of the pilgrim at the right time the way a generator is installed in a car on an assembly line. The truth is that the mystery of growth which we are trying to understand has little to do with such linear concepts. The Chinese have a phrase which catches the mystery of growth: *wu wei, non-action;* or even better *wei wu wei, action-without-action.*

These phrases distinguish the bustling external activity which assembles a non-living thing in linear stages from that internal action by which a living thing grows imperceptibly. Life develops immanently, quietly, non-linearly, with rich synergistic energies which never divide the whole. There is order, but no self-sufficient parts. There is process, but no commotion. No one ever saw a tree in action, yet in due time the leaves sprout, and later the fruit appears. Because the fruit ripens later, this does not mean that it was not growing even as the leaves grew.

The pilgrim's growth is a *wei wu wei* process. The baptized infant is already a child of God, he is already in possession of all he will ever be, as a seed contains the whole essence of what it will become. Christian growth is a developing of spiritual seeds, an intensification of early experiences, an overcoming of obstacles to the love already implanted in our hearts by the Holy Spirit, a learning to love with practical wisdom. The practice of returning assiduously to the springs of first graces reveals this to an amazing degree. We are capable of totally forgetting, and of never really recognizing even extraordinary spiritual experiences; and if we forget we will never see the unity of the whole of our growth.

Through all the years of the pilgrim's growth many developments go on hiddenly, simultaneously. Occasionally, early signs of a certain aspect of growth appear externally, the way a tree's blossoms appear long before they become fruit. We see a similar process in the natural growth of a child. He crawls, walks, runs, grows strong. He had some strength before we say he has grown strong, but there is a time when we can identify the *maturing* of his strength. And after his bodily strength has matured, his mental powers begin to reach their peak. It is in a similar way that I deal with the phases of growth of a sent contemplative. I sort out each type of growth and experience according to the relative order in which each peaks, and speak of it at its peak time.

I am aware that each and every pilgrim is unique, so that even the order in which each quality and experience peaks will vary somewhat, for there are these differences between individuals even in bodily growth. I am also aware that some qualities and experiences may not discernibly peak at all in certain individuals, whether it be an experience of Mary, or of Jesus, or of finding God in nature, or anything else. This too has its counterpart in natural growth. Some people never seem to develop an imagination, or an aesthetic sense, or a scientific sense. All spiritual graces come to us in our natural setting, and their growth can be retarded by our psychological formation, our circumstances, our wayward use of freedom, or some other factor. Grace itself varies, according to God's plan for us and His purposes in our lives.

Early in the spiritual life of some persons, all the best qualities they will ever have seem already in evidence: ardent love, zeal, generosity, deep experiences of God. Their growth consists to a great extent in persevering, and in promoting a fuller wedding of nature and grace. To have these qualities in the first fervor of spiritual awakening is one thing; to maintain them through all the temptations, trials, and apostolic activities of the spiritual life is another and much higher thing. To purify and integrate them in the ongoing wedding of body and soul, nature and grace, man and God, in a more and more spiritual and contemplative manner, is the highest of all. To have noble qualities initially is due to God's giving, but to retain them is due in some measure to one's own fidelity.

The whole process of an individual's spiritual growth seems akin to the growth of the Church. From the beginning the Church has possessed the whole *deposit of faith*, but through centuries of meditating on it, defending it against errors, and experiencing its meaning in history, the Church grows in understanding of its doctrine, and in living it out in ever more mature ways.

Temptation is an important operative in spiritual growth. The enemy which assails us is not nature but Satan, who is the enemy of both nature and grace. Having no hold on grace, he tries to subvert nature and make it tyrannize over grace. Grace should be the lordly part of us, but sinful nature, infected by Adam, is a rebellious bride: "Each person is tempted when he is lured and enticed by his own desire" (James 1:14). Only when "the flesh" (body and soul) is purged of sin and its wayward tendencies does it become "nature" as God made it to be, the bride of grace. The manner in which temptation can occasion growth will appear by drawing a comparison with the physical body. A child's body already possesses all the organs of maturity, but in the course of the years his body will be invaded by innumerable hostile organisms or antigens. Against each his defense system must produce a unique antibody. If it fails, his body will be weakened or destroyed. If it succeeds, his body will be more viable than ever.

So, too, temptation is not a wholly negative event, but an occasion for growth. A person is subject to temptation because he has loose ends, energies and passions which have not yet been sublimated, which have not yet found their meaning in Christ. Temptation is "a skid of the car," an opportunity to recognize and locate powerful energies which can be purified and enlisted in the love and service of God. God makes even temptation profitable: "We know that in everything God works for good with those who love him, who are called according to his purpose" (Rom. 8:28).

I would like to use another illustration to make it even clearer how I am reporting growth in this treatise. The complex processes of spiritual growth in the pilgrim can be looked at as starting out together, the way contestants do in a cross-country race. At each selected point along the course the announcer will mention only the man in the lead, together with the ones closest behind him. It is in a similar way that I attempt to report on the growth of the various aspects of contemplation in action. In the cross-country race, one runner may take the lead, fall back, regain the lead, and fall back again. So, too, some aspects of contemplation in action mature, recede, become prominent again at a new level of maturity, and so on. This can be due either to genuine growth, or to alternations of fidelity and unfaithfulness on the part of the pilgrim. He can, for instance, become apostolically zealous, and then grow discouraged, weary, tepid. He can lost and regain the same ground many times, just as happens in military campaigns. It would be impossible to report all these variations, even if one knew them all.

One final analogy. The view of the pilgrim's growth seen in this treatise resembles the view seen by a man ascending a spiral staircase. As the man spirals upward he gains a different view along each point of the rising circle; as he traverses the next level of the spiral, he sees the same things over again, but always from a new perspective, and with new things seen in the distance, for he is higher up. So too do growth processes have rhythms and repetitions, but always with a newness about them, a further movement, whether of maturation or decline. Just as in a man's natural growth his physical strength may already be on the wane before he peaks intellectually, so certain aspects of the pilgrim's development seem to peak and decline before others show any significant growth.

In this complex sweep of ascents and descents there are two qualities which mount ever upward in a faithful sent contemplative. He is ever seeing more deeply, more contemplatively, into everything around him, and into God Himself. And he is growing ever more skillful in his ability to discern and carry out God's purposes in his life. It is these two qualities together with a keen sense of mission which particularize his growth as a sent contemplative.

6.

God's Self-manifestation in

Nature and Event

It is time to return to the pilgrim's experience of meeting God in nature, to observe how it can develop into a second manner of meeting that is better than the first. In the first manner, it was the pilgrim who took the initiative, by consciously seeking similarities between the things of creation and the Creator. In the second manner, the Creator takes the initiative. He is the Lord of nature, and He makes His creatures sing His praises to the pilgrim and make themselves occasions of love-trysts with Him. The things of nature not only reveal their beauty and their glory, they open secret passages which lead the pilgrim directly to God.

One pilgrim who did a stint in the Merchant Marines was not able to attend Mass during his voyages, but he described to a friend how the play and power of the interminable sea around him fairly chanted to him of the glory of God.

A young nun who prayed and hungered for prayer entered upon a season when God rewarded her prayer by coming to her not in prayer but in field and stream. She writes:

> In my last year of novitiate, I gained a tremendous exhilaration in the outdoors. Everything reminded me of God. He treated me as a little child whom he loved dearly. Dandelions became a wonderful symbol for me of complete transformation in order to serve. And much to my companions' confusion I gained a great

love for rubber bands. It was silly but it was God's gift to his spoiled child to remind her of his presence and love. The circularity of the rubber band was a sign for me of God's omnipresence and ability to fit to me when I looked for him. I was delighted every time I found one and picked it up as a personal gift.

The genuinity of this adolescent's religious experience is vouched for by her later growth. A missionary Sister in the Far East wrote to a friend about her experience of the Lord of nature:

If we could walk in the ways I walk here, I'd show you a wonderful art exhibition—all the work is done by the same Artist and all have scriptural titles. There is one piece some one brought here as wood for cooking. It used to be part of a tree, but the touch of the Master's hand has entitled it: Jesus Embraces and Blesses His People even as His Dead Body is Taken Down. It's fantastic, one arm, the right is raised in blessing and the other bent towards his heart as He embraces His people. There is a big hole in the side and mud has caked there, almost coagulated. There are small scars all over it as if from scourging. It is not just my eyes that see it—I noticed and told Father to burn this one last. He has taken all the other logs from the pile and put them in a woodshed but this remains out for all to look at. Honestly, no imagination at all. There is a cactus in the shape of a heart, a big one—it is entitled: Love Grows Even When the Soil Seems Dry. This exhibition is different at different times of day—at 4:30 in the morning, the east wall of the museum is alight. Every few minutes a new view of dawn is presented—and the last star to leave the sky is in the far east . . . I'm not expecting anything to happen in Japan—I think it's that way just for me to continue to say to myself: I have seen His star in the East and that is why I come—to follow it, knowing full well that I will lose sight of it from time to time, but He'll always brighten it up a little more so as to attract my attention. In the evening the display is on the west wall and at night, directly overhead, the moon and stars which He did secure. On the road itself are many portraits—the Good Shepherd, my yoke is easy and my burden light. Branches bearing no fruit shall wither and die. Once you have put your hand to the plough, don't turn back. Endlessly, in the people coming and going to their fields the whole of the scriptures is painted.

Sometimes these experiences are like the experiences of a tracker hunting his quarry. They are imprints that tell the pilgrim that the Lord has passed this way. They are nature's way of answering his unceasing question: "Have you seen him whom my soul loves?" (Song of Songs 3:3). Sometimes the experiences are of the tracker suddenly becoming the tracked, and the hunter becoming the quarry as the Lord takes the initiative in seeking and pursuing, loving and tending. One pilgrim, a seminarian, recounts:

> One day I was walking with a companion in the heat of summer, my mind lying fallow. There was a sudden gust of wind—and at once I was aware of God catching my attention, playing with me by nearly tripping me in my furling cassock, and at the same time fanning my overheated body. It was as personal and intimate an experience as if God had laid a cool hand on my hot forehead. On another day, in almost the same spot, as by a premonition I suddenly looked up at the sky. I saw clouds scudding like galleons dashed by the wind. At once I was aware that my friend, God the Artist, had suddenly done these heroic paintings for me, to attract my attention, to entertain me, to exchange an intimacy as open as the sky and as hidden as the human heart. Such experiences happen rarely to me, but when they do they are unmistakeable and unforgettable.

These are not ways of finding God but of being found by God. They are passive experiences of God's visitations, and are deeply contemplative in nature, and yet occur in the course of activity. To those who have had no such experiences, the juxtaposition of event and the sudden awareness of God might seem explainable as a normal case of cause and effect, or of mere coincidence. But so then would the fact that the verse of Scripture which speaks to the pilgrim's need is repeatedly there in the liturgy of the day. So would a thousand other "accidents" like that which befell the retreat director who, in the course of conducting a very difficult retreat, found among the few books in his room a rare book of Chinese wisdom which helped him turn the retreat into a success. Or like that of the nun with limited wardrobe who had to rush off on a trip with a button dangling. She told Jesus her Lord that He had to care for her needs, and when she arrived in her hotel room, there on the bureau lay a threaded needle. What takes these events out of the realm of the accidental is that they are so frequent that they are a constant of the pilgrim's life.

There is another reason why the pilgrim seizes upon these events as neither accidents nor coincidences, but as the providence of God. The pilgrim's faith has grown so that he knows intuitively what the Scripture reveals and what scholastic theologians teach, that from God's vantage point there are no accidents. The word *accident* is used to describe an event in which man has not yet traced all the causes. The word is not in God's vocabulary because He is the Cause of all courses, and the Knower of all knowledge. The word is not in the pilgrim's vocabulary at this stage of development because his experiences of God have already led him to sing with the psalmist: "Even before a word is on my tongue, lo, O Lord, thou knowest it altogether. . . . Such knowledge is too wonderful for me; it is high, I cannot attain it. . . . Even the darkness is not dark to thee, the night is bright as the day" (Ps. 139:4-5, 12).

Such experiences inspire the pilgrim with new confidence in the Lord of history. Trying new circumstances are met with greater security and less anxiety. One nun who had to live outside her religious community to undertake some arduous university studies wrote to a friend of the experience:

> My school work has my head spinning. . . . At first the insecurity of being alone in a new situation had me running scared. Now, my prayer is that God, who is faithful, keep me faithful—not safe and secure amid all the new experiences but faithful to Him and His Spirit who bids me to grow in Christ.

These experiences of God in nature may seem to withdraw the pilgrim from the world of men, but it is not so. The next chapter will take up the reason for this—though it can be said here that if we respond rightly to God's gifts, none of them can do anything but join us more to men in the long run. One young pilgrim provides a spontaneous testimonial of how a hierophany led her directly to a more loving response to another human being:

> While I was contemplating nature and praising God for it there came to me the saying that goes, "you are more than the blessedness of sunshine. . . ." I realized that I was more beautiful than the mighty mountains and lovely trees and the delicate flower and this amazed me. . . . I understood that each and every one of my Sisters, each and every person, even those who had the ugliest appearance or habits was more beautiful than all this which I had been admiring. I was even more amazed and new vistas opened up to me. On the way back to the house I met a perennial beggar to the house who could be considered a nuisance especially since he had begun to lose some of his mental abilities. But I stood there and talked to him and listened to him with great joy and really wished I could tell him how great he was and hoped that he got some of the message by my concern. I felt sorry that he might not know and I was even sad when our conversation had to end.

I will conclude this chapter with a housewife's description of how she has made her finding of God in nature the source of a touching Christian ministry: the ministry of training her children too to come to familiarity with the Lord of nature:

The dirty dishes will be with us always, and can be washed another time, but to teach a child about God cannot always be done another time. A child is a child only a little while.

I find great joy in teaching my child to be aware of God. The lessons are simple and very easy. I take the time to take my child, even now at nine years, for a walk. Not necessarily a long walk, but one unhurried. Together we see how beautiful things are after a rain, the reflection of water is God's mirror reflecting the remaining clouds. The rainbow is God's colorful ribbon tying together all the gifts beneath it. Sometimes we watch the busyness of an ant hill, the tiny ant pulling and tugging at pieces many times larger than himself. There is the listening to the birds, each song clear and belonging to their own species. The white cloud formation like huge puffs of cotton in which there is a whole world of dreams. The brilliant sunsets in orange and red streaking out above us. The special rocks and "things" we find are saved in pockets for his collections. We feel the breezes from the cars that go whizzing by. These precious times are really great to tell a child about God and let him see all that God gives.

I felt great joy when my child came running indoors with, "Mom! come see, quick! See what God has painted." But even a greater reward came when my 23 year old daughter told me that she now takes her little girl for walks. At three years, she too is gently learning about God and His great gifts.

7.

The Effects of God's

Self-manifestation in Nature and Event

The hierophanies and theophanies considered in the last chapter are elemental experiences of the holy. They pervade the whole history of religion. They are of the very essence of contemplation in action, and this is made evident by comparing the notion of *hierophany* with the nature of *contemplation in action*. A *hierophany* is an event in which a profane reality suddenly reveals in itself something other than itself, something holy and transcendent, the way a blackened, smoldering log in a fire suddenly breaks open to reveal the vermillion loveliness hidden within. A hierophany is a paradox of intimacy between the Highest and the lowest, nothingness and Allness, the everyday and the Eternal, the relative and the Absolute. It suddenly reveals that what appears evident is really hidden, and that the most hidden things can suddenly become evident. A hierophany is an opening to transcendence, and so it involves a moment of contemplation, for a contemplative is one who is in contact with transcendence. A hierophany is, furthermore, an opening to transcendence from the starting point, not of withdrawn contemplation, but of contact with the external world. It is, therefore, an experience of contemplation in action, for the contemplative in action is precisely one who finds contact with the Divine through the instrumentality of action and creatures.

The significance of these divine self-manifestations for the contemplative in action should not be overlooked. He is one who fuses in himself a passion for God and a passion for action in the world. His danger is always that the tension between these two passions will degenerate from a healthy dialectic to a schizoid Jekyl and Hyde syndrome, wherein all integration is lost and the would-be contemplative in action gyrates uncontrollably between periods of cloistered contemplation and periods of dissipated activism. This degeneration is highly likely unless the pilgrim really develops the ability to find God in the world and the world in God. These divine self-manifestations are providing the pilgrim with that ability, not by giving him the power to produce these experiences at will, but by filling his memory with them so that if they pass memory itself will serve as an integrating factor.

There hierophanies also help open the pilgrim up to an expanding awareness of the scope of the kingdom of God. It is in this opening-up that the genuine contemplative act manifests its superiority over mere introspection. Introspection tends to lock the thinker into the prison of his own insufficient self, while contemplation opens him to unlimited horizons.

Contemplation has the practical effect of integrating the pilgrim *affectively* into the ambit of his daily existence. It transforms him from an operator on his world to a participant in his world. The non-contemplative activist experiences himself as a discrete unit, while the contemplative finds himself a part of the collectivity. No longer is he a mere agent or a helpless victim, but both a contributor to and a passive sharer of the destiny of the whole. This makes for patience, lowliness, brotherliness, integratedness.

Through these passive experiences of hierophany, the sent contemplative is slowly learning that he is recipient as well as agent, and that because he is of the body of Christ he is more than ever a part of the mystical body of mankind and of the cosmos. He learns, only slowly, to operate upon his environment not disturbingly, like an alien force, but more interiorly and spiritually, as harmoniously as an organ operates within a living body. He becomes sensitive to rhythms and seasons, attuned to serve in one act both the self and the whole, no longer a benefactor serving others but an identity acting upon itself. This is the way of love: "They become one flesh" (Gen. 2:24).

The dissipated activist is shorn of this sympathy, and since dissipated activism is probably the most common destroyer of contemplatives in action, it can well be considered here. The traditional term for dissipated activism is the Latin phrase *effusio ad exteriora*, dispersed in externals. The dissipated activist loses the balance and fusion of contemplation and action. He progressively converts more and more of his energy from interior to wholly exterior activity. He dissipates himself by undertaking more and more projects, and he works on them at a higher and higher pitch. Projects which he began freely from genuine inner-directedness have now taken control of him. He is passion-bound to go on and on. He is no longer attuned to the controlling inspiration either of the Holy Spirit or of his own soul. Thus this evil strikes at the heart of the vocation of the pilgrim contemplative. What may have begun as an authentic service in the kingdom becomes an unintegrated activism, becomes to some degree a slave-service to creatures, carried on by a sense-bound activist.

Dissipated activism abounds like the common cold, and in its lesser forms it is perhaps no more serious, but it can progress until it becomes spiritually death-dealing. Jesus Himself implied in one parable that even the more malignant form of the disease is very widespread: "A man once gave a great banquet, and invited many. . . . But they all alike began to make excuses. The first said to him, 'I have bought a field and I must go out and see it; I pray you, have me excused.' Another said, 'I have bought five yoke of oxen, and I go to examine them; I pray you, have me excused.' And another said, 'I have married a wife, and therefore I cannot come.' So the servant came and reported this to his master. Then the householder in anger said to his servant, 'Go out quickly to the streets and lanes of the city, and bring in the poor and maimed and blind and lame.' And the servant said, 'Sir, what you commanded has been done, and still there is room.' And the master said to the servant, 'Go out to the highways and hedges, and compel people to come in, that my house may be filled. For I tell you, none of those men who were invited shall taste my banquet' " (Luke 14:16-24).

In the later stages of dissipated activism a pilgrim shows signs of losing his interior freedom and his ability to find communion with God. Though he began as an agent of God, he gradually put off the yoke and became the agent of his own ambitions; and finally he becomes the slave of his own passion for action.

It may help to attempt a diagnosis of the causes of this disease, and to prescribe certain remedies. In spiritual beginners, the cause can be simply *a lack of interior life*. The beginner is absorbed in things of sense and in exterior activity because he has never learned to commune with his own interior; and since deep listening to God takes place through the medium of one's own deepest psychic and spiritual life, the beginner has not yet learned how to listen to God day in and day out. The remedy is a sound program of spiritual exercises, with firm adherence to daily mental prayer. To get a hold on himself, the pilgrim may have to withdraw entirely from his normal activities for a while, to seclude himself in prayer, and perhaps engage in a retreat. More advanced pilgrims can also lose their interiority and require the same remedy. There are many retreat houses and houses of prayer to serve their needs.

A second cause of dissipated activism is the *open-options syndrome*. This is the disease of personalities so attached to freedom of options that they seldom *use* their freedom to make a firm choice of *one* option. It is a common personality defect in today's world, wherein options so abound that they stun the human capacity to make choices. The pilgrim in the grip of this syndrome disperses his efforts over too many projects, or passes quickly from one project to another without rational assessment of what he is doing. The remedy is long, patient meditation on his own limitations and on the most promising long-term conjunction of his own best talents with the available opportunities for service.

The open-options syndrome can derive from the misguided aspirations of a generous, zealous soul, but it has the same sad result as dilettantism. The root of this disease is a non-contemplative approach to life. Impulses to action are originating at too shallow a level. The root of the syndrome is, therefore, a vice contrary to every form of contemplation in action, which demands that life be lived from out of the depths. In addition, the clinging to open options is a vice directly contrary to the sent contemplative's vocation in particular. His commitment requires him to sacrifice all his other options to become a "slave of God" (Rom. 6:22) subject to His Spirit, whose guiding impulses will send him to do the needed work of love in each circumstance. When he fails to make use of contemplation and total surrender as the means of being joined to the Spirit, he loses guidance and control and finds himself soon enslaved to many pursuits.

A third source of dissipated activism is ambition. Many pilgrims begin a work in perfect freedom, for the love of God and the Kingdom, but self seeks to interpenetrate such a pure motive as insistently as air rushes into a vacuum. As long as a pilgrim is working for the Lord, his work proceeds from him freely (to the degree he has *found* spiritual freedom). The first sign, therefore, of the taint of ambition, is a passion for work that begins to suppress spiritual practices, closes the pilgrim's ears to the counsel of others, and organizes his life around "the project" instead of around God. The remedy for ambition is not easily found, for ambition is the mark of the man who has turned from promoting the glory of God to promoting his own glory.

Probably the best remedy is prayer face-to-face with Jesus. To bring it about may require renewal of one's favorite forms of personal devotion to Jesus, supported by at least a partial withdrawal from work for the sake of intensified prayer where God can be heard again: "I will allure her, and bring her into the wilderness, and speak tenderly to her" (Osee 2:14). Within prayer the pilgrim may find additional causes of the activism, such as a drive to accomplishment motivated by his confreres' failure to esteem him as they ought. The pilgrim must then find a way to defuse such an explosive and dangerous self-defensive ambition.

A fourth source of dissipated activism is slavery to a will other than God's. Over-attachment to the flock one serves or the human leader one follows is a subtle transfer of allegiance from God to man, just as ambition is a transfer of allegiance from God to self. The remedy is like that for ambition.

A fifth and more subtle form of dissipated activism springs from various rationalizations which will here be treated as a complex of motives (both for the sake of brevity and because they are likely to occur together). The sent contemplative's call to transform creation into the Kingdom of God super-sensitizes him to the lot of all who suffer because of the present condition of human society. If, however, he becomes so empathetic with one class of sufferers that he can barely endure the pain of it himself, the whole fabric of his faith will be strained.

If it gives way in any respect, a number of things can happen. He may become scandalized at God's permissive will, and subtly discard his role as God's agent to pursue what he considers his own more God-like morality. Since he is a finite creature who has now taken on his shoulders the work of God (usually still "in God's name"), the load is inevitably too great for him, and so he accelerates to a higher and higher pitch of activism, which may continue to escalate until he collapses, or turns cynical and gives up. Alternatively, the strain on his faith may activate latent defects in his confidence in divine providence, so that he is driven passionately to provide what God has "neglected." Or again, the strain may show forth his imperfect submission to God's will. His humanism may defeat his obedience, so that he admits the superiority of God's way in theory, but does not follow it in practice.

The remedy for these errors is greater faith—which can be had by praying for it—and greater sympathy with God's way, which can be gained by pondering God's final purposes. St. Peter wrote: "The heavens and earth that now exist have been stored up for fire, being kept until the day of judgment and destruction of ungodly men. But do not ignore this one fact, beloved . . . the Lord is not slow about his promise as some count slowness, but is forbearing toward you, not wishing that any should perish, but that all should reach repentance" (2 Peter 3:8-9). The pilgrim unbalanced by the plight of the oppressed turns to unchristian means to save them, even when God is asking them to endure injustice in the likeness of Christ so that not only they but their oppressors too may be saved. By meditating on this final outcome of God's plan, the wayward agent can be saved from his own plan, which is bound to fail.

The effort to escape the burdens of contemplation is probably the most common source of dissipated activism. Like the seasons of the year, contemplative prayer has its pleasant times and its times of cold, of aridity, of storm. In such times the pilgrim's temptation is to manufacture excuses for burying himself in his work and leaving little energy or opportunity for prayer. The remedy for this temptation is better understanding of one's vocation, and greater fidelity to it. The sent contemplative must be generous enough to imitate Christ in doing hard work in the world, but to follow Christ he must also travel the arduous inner highways and byways of the soul. Readings and instructions in the nature of the inner pilgrimage can be a powerful weapon against discouragement when prayer seems useless. An able spiritual director is even more valuable, for he can provide this and other helps as well.

It can also happen that in the course of meditation and introspection, one pilgrim or other will unearth psychological problems deep within himself. Hardly recognizing what is happening, he finds himself developing a resistance to prayer. The reason is not that he does not want to commune with God, but that he cannot handle what he has unearthed. At this point the help of a spiritual director may be the only solution. And he, in turn, may have to recommend psychological counseling so that the pilgrim can find healing for the old but still unhealed wounds he has stumbled on in the psychic depths he has laid bare.

Dissipated activism is self-perpetuating because it leads to exhaustion, which is one of the great enemies of prayer. The exhausted man will far more readily do exterior things than enter upon the concentrated superactivity of the interior life.

Perhaps the most inescapable cause of *effusio ad exteriora* is genuine zeal driven beyond moderation by the needs of those served, and leading inevitably to exhaustion and the spiritual malaise and dispersion which follow upon too much work, too little prayer, and too little rest. This seeming excess *can* come about not through ignoring the Spirit but by the inspiration of the Spirit, for in extreme conditions it is what love must do. On one occasion Jesus saw that His disciples needed a respite and He said: "Come away by yourselves to a lonely place, and rest a while." But people crowded them in their new location and neither Jesus nor His disciples got a rest because "He had compassion on them, because they were like sheep without a shepherd" (Mark 6:31, 34). There is a special providence governing such circumstances, and it is sometimes manifested by miracles.

The only effective remedy for this sometimes inescapable overburdening of the zealous contemplative in action is to imitate Jesus. Though He overworked, there is no evidence He abandoned His times of prayer. In fact, the Gospel of St. Luke intimates in several places that He did not. Flexible, but reasonable fidelity to prayer is a good norm for judging whether the excess of effort is God's will or simply a giving-way to an indiscreet and ill-judged impulse of the agent. If the times of prayer and, especially, the sense of peaceful and harmonious relationship with God in the course of action begin to disappear, it is time to recognize the fault of overwork, and correct it.

One other norm for judging the health of the sent contemplative (when activist dissipation is suspected) is the state of his longing for prayer. Since he is both a contemplative and a man of action, the yearning for the desert and the drive to action are in constant tension and interplay within him. When he is healthy, this dialectic issues in the fusion that produces *the sent contemplative*, the man who continues his communication with God in the course of his interplay with the world. When he is spiritually healthy he will feel an impulse to such times of withdrawal and pure contemplation, just as in his times of withdrawal he feels concern for the world and impulses of service. This dipolar tension is the "first principle" of the sent contemplative's vocation, and therefore a sign of good health. When either impulse declines, there is trouble. When the impulse to prayer declines, dissipated activism should be suspected.

To priests harrassed and psychologically dispersed by the activist demands made upon them, *The Decree on the Ministry and Life of Priests of Vatican II* provides the following guidance: "Priests who are perplexed and distracted by the very many obligations of their position may be anxiously enquiring how they can reduce to unity their interior life and their program of external activity. This unity of life cannot be brought about merely by an outward arrangement of the works of the ministry nor by the practice of spiritual exercises alone, though this may help to foster such unity. Priests can however achieve it by following in the fulfillment of their ministry the example of Christ the Lord, whose meat was to do the will of him who sent him that he might perfect His work" (# 14). This call to imitate Jesus whom the Father sent to contemplatively find and carry out His will in all things is not only a sure remedy for dissipated activism but also an illuminating word to priests concerning their vocation to be sent contemplatives.

Further aspects of the spiritual disease of *effusio ad exteriora* will surface in the course of this treatise. Let us conclude the present treatment by considering one other cause which ought to be suspected *only after all other remedies have been tried and have failed.* This cause is that the pilgrim is being called by God into a more deeply contemplative form of the vocation to contemplation in action. Until he hears and responds, his soul will feel troubled and *poured out like water.* An actual case history will illustrate the experience:

> I was ordained in May of 1961 and worked in [my] diocese for eight years. I asked the bishop to allow me to "retool" at a local Trappist Abbey while I taught at the College of _____, i.e., I would live and pray at the Abbey and come out a few times a week to teach. He did not allow it. I felt the need for a deeper prayer life. Then I asked him to allow me to teach in the seminary where I could live the common life, teach and have a deeper prayer life. He gave me the O.K. for this. I trained in grad school for a year, taught for a year, but my prayer life was so shallow that I refused the offer to stay on teaching. . . . I felt [the congregation with which I was staying] lacked something—did not demand enough. . . . I wanted more . . . my life did not demand enough of me. . . . **Priesthood, especially the intellectual ministry, was too lonely and fraught with too many temptations without a hard and fast framework of vows and common life to support me. I needed to be loved in community, I needed a deep prayer life. I was becoming too intellectual, and shallowing myself with books.** I tried pastoral life *cum* thesis-writing. Nothing worked. . . . I applied to the Society [of Jesus] after much soul-searching.
>
> I have spent the happiest year of my life with the Society. I did not enter with my eyes closed . . . I knew the Society was full of problems. Dr. Johnson said to Boswell when the latter married at

an advanced age: "It is the triumph of hope over experience." I
feel the same. It is God's work. . . . I want and have received a
fuller life in prayer here. My life in _____ [former diocese] was a
very active one—teacher, pastor, canon lawyer, civil right's activist, college professor, chaplain of a Motherhouse of Religious
women, ecumenist coupled with a life of meditation and verbal
prayer. But nothing was enough. My soul itched constantly. The
Society would impinge itself on my affections and imagination
and always make a deep impact. It just never seemed the right
move—the canon was 'you are here. That must be God's will for
you. Put the Jesuits out of your mind.' Finally, my path crossed, in
England and Campion Hall of all places, with that of the Society.
They were a world apart from the men I had known in the States
—aristocratic, somewhat diffident (if not cold). Still the grace of
God worked into my soul in an atmosphere which began very cold
and lonely and grew into one of warmth and friendship with the
English Jesuits.

My novitiate has been one in which my prayer life has felt fulfilled. The call to contemplation was a true call and I have enjoyed
a remarkable simplification of soul and prayer life.

8.

Experiences with the Lord of History

One of the most crucial effects of God's self-manifestation in
nature and event is that they introduce the pilgrim *experimentally* to
the Lord of on-going creation, the Lord of history. They intensify
his awareness that *God is in charge*. God is active everywhere, what

need he fear? God's providence extends to everything. If God is for him, what can stand against him? What can happen that God does not will? And if God wills it, the pilgrim wants it. In theory at least, he no longer fears God's will, only his own. With courage in the face of resistance and opposition he speaks the word of God and acts on it.

Gradually he learns to detect God communicating with him in new ways. The Lord of history speaks to him in power, through *events*, and through the context and circumstances of his life. His faith must hereafter perceive this, his reason discern the patterns, and his affectivity intuitively single out the appropriate way of interrelating with the persons and events around him. Only thus can he cooperate with the plans of the Lord of the Kingdom.

This sensitivity to the action of the Lord of history attunes the pilgrim to read God's plans for him without the need for palpably numinous events. One apostle who has spent decades in the social apostolate recalls how he recognized his call through the crying need before his eyes:

> Working with black people never occurred to me until I was assigned to teaching Sunday School to black children. There were no whites because they could go to the parish school. This discrimination and deprivation began to strike me forcibly . . . but I went along with it as part of the system of the world. After my ordination I wrote my highest Superior (in Rome) telling him I would be willing to go to the foreign missions, but I felt the black people in this country needed help: they were deprived and nearly helpless, they had almost nothing, they were left out. A local superior, an old veteran of Negro work, said to me: "Don't send the letter, you are going to the blacks anyhow." This is what I wanted and have done all the years since, thanks to God and our Lady. After a brief experience of the Blacks I was drawn to them, not only by their need and the injustices they suffered, but also by their personal qualities. I found them thoroughly human, intelligent, dignified, beautiful, friendly, eager and generous. I thought it foolish and dull to try to make them like white people (as had been suggested). I thought the only worthwhile and inspiring purpose was to make them like Christ Jesus our Lord. Thus they could make their own distinctive contribution to the human race and the Church. Our Lord in them called out to me to help them in their development, maturity, and full inheritance in His Father's Kingdom.

A seminarian recounts the experiences in which he felt the call to commit himself to the purely spiritual work of conducting the *Spir-*

itual Exercises of St. Ignatius to help in the formation of young lay
apostles:

> A Jesuit brother . . . invited me to go with him on a weekend
> apostolic work which he had gotten involved in among high
> school kids in the area. I remember struggling somewhat with the
> idea of giving up a precious weekend of study. Anyway I went
> with him and offered some reflections on "Ecology and Religion"
> . . . . These young people were really interested in religion and the
> Church. They turned me on. The general principles of their organ-
> ization called CHRISTIAN LIFE COMMUNITY spoke more
> fully of the renewed sense of Church which I saw coming out of
> these young men and women. By committing myself during the
> religious experiences of the following months, just as the young
> people were being asked to do, I realized, though vaguely, that I
> was being called to help these people—leaders and all—and be-
> ginning with myself, come to understand and appreciate Christ as
> He is mediated through the "Spiritual Exercises of St. Ignatius."
> Events began to take shape to carry out this commitment.

Since all things human are subject to corruption, even experiences of the holy can be subverted by subtle temptations to self-
sufficiency, and by erroneous discernment of the meaning of meeting God in His self-manifestations through nature and event. It is
important, therefore, to expose these negative effects for what they
are.

Some Catholics who begin to find God in nature are tempted to
abandon the Church and adopt a God-and-I spirituality. Yet the
whole sweep of biblical teaching insists that God calls man to religious community, and that a man must not stand alone in his relationship to God, or his interpretation of God's word and His doings.
Even St. Paul, in the very vision in which he met Jesus, was sent by
Jesus to be *directed by a man.* Every major religion seems to follow
this policy of advising the individual to get help in discerning God's
intention, or at least in *confirming* it. There is always the need for
the guru, the roshi, the starets, the spiritual director.

A man who strays from the Catholic Church because he has met
God in nature and thinks the Church is now irrelevant is like the
referee of a cross-country race who disqualifies all the runners but
the man in the lead at the first mile marker. That man may not even
have the strength to finish the race, just as the experience of God in
nature may die out long before the pilgrim has run his race. It is certain to die out if not sustained by the Church which brought him to
it. Even if it perdured, it is not a spiritual diet which can sustain true
religion.

One pilgrim who met God at sea found the experience more moving than his experience at Mass. He consulted a spiritual guide, who told him that God comes to man in many ways, each in its season. He explained that the worth of a religious experience is to be gauged by the revelation, which gives us God's assessment, far more than by the degree of emotional experience it provides. Judged by the criterion of the revelation, the Mass and the Eucharist outweigh all other religious events. This clarified the matter for the young seaman, as it should for every genuine Christian, for all events must be discerned and judged by *faith*, which is the first principle of Christian life: "For in the Gospel the righteousness of God is revealed through faith for faith; as it is written, 'He who through faith is righteous shall live' " (Rom. 1:17).

Unfortunately, faith can be corrupted by a naive excess as well as by atrophy, and experiences of God in nature and event swiftly lead some to this excess. Certain pilgrims at this stage begin to see miracles everywhere, and to expect them in everything. They wait for miracles instead of calling the repairman or the doctor. Their unbiblical conduct, with its lack of good judgment concerning the proper use of natural means, destroys the faith of others instead of building it up. They do not understand that God's self-manifestations in nature and event are often not strictly miracles at all, because their causes do not transcend nature; but they are not accidents either, because they proceed from the providence of God, who sees and arranges all things. Sound faith sees God in everything, but it sees miracles only where they really occur. Poor judgment never praises God, but intelligence wisely used in faith always does.

Deep love of God awoke in the pilgrim mysteriously, and the Kingdom of God entered his life through Mary, and he experienced its joys through the coming of Jesus. Now he has found the domain of nature and event shot through with manifestations of the presence and power of the Lord of history, and trust in His providence reaches a peak. He still searches to find, and works to bring, the Kingdom of God into the domain of man. That he does not find it there is his suffering, and that he will is his hope.

9.

Recourse to the Word of God

As the months and years pass, a new austerity creeps of its own accord into the prayer, world and work of the pilgrim contemplative. The former visual, tactile, affectionate ways of finding God in prayer to which he won with such struggle diminish and fade. Past experiences of God—those springs of first grace which quenched his burning thirst—refuse even to come keenly into memory's focus. They take on the character of a mirage, a half-remembered dream.

The world through which he passes increases his burden. He walks through it the way a man walks the site of a carnival the morning after it closes. The night before, it was a lovely world of colored lights and beauty, of life and laughter and fun and music. In the morning light there are only the honky tonk remains, the papier mache, the tin and tinsel of a cheap make-believe world lifeless and rattling in the wind.

His work is likely to take on the same austere character and meaninglessness. What does his work have to do with the Kingdom of God? If he is not troubled by the thought that he is in the wrong work, he is troubled by the impotence of his efforts. He goes through the motion of his work, because God wills it—but what can he accomplish, what can man accomplish? Has he not found out by strenuous years of prayer and work? Nothing! "Thus says the Lord: Cursed is the man who trusts in man" (Jer. 17:5). What did even the human actions of Jesus accomplish? Only divinity made them effective.

What are these alarming doldrums? Doubtless it is a new crisis, but is it one of growth or decay? If of growth, how helpful it would be to know it, to know why, and to know what to do!

At this point the pilgrim's dynamic fusion of the virtues of hope and humility is under attack. Hope and aspiration to great things in the Lord tend to appear like presumption, and humility tends to corrupt into despair. Is he deluding himself in believing he is called to greater and greater union with God. Some pilgrims may feel trapped in a neurotic no-win dialectic between presumption and despair.

The knowledge and guidance of a spiritual director is needed now. Those who already have a good one are blessed. Those who want to look for one will likely hear the mocking words: *Who do you think you are, dreamer? A saint? What does your likes need a spiritual director for?* It is a common error to think that spiritual directors are the preserve of mystics and Saints, but the truth is that they are helpful to all who are serious about their spiritual life, as has been said. There will be needless suffering now for those who refuse to believe this, as well as for those who lack the courage to act on it, and for those who make only a half-hearted search for a director in the conviction that "They are not worth a director's time, and anyway a good director is hard to find." The truth is that anyone hungry for God is well worth a director's time; and while good directors *are* hard to find, so too is gold—but that never deterred an avid gold digger.

The pilgrim ponders the meaning of this new state of affairs. He does not really believe God has abandoned him, and he is still altogether willing to abandon himself to God. Why is it, then, that the old pleasures of prayer, when they recur at all, are now only cloying and oppressive, so that he even resents them, the way a little boy resents too much hugging and kissing?

One day illumination comes. He recognizes the source of the crisis. Up to this time his spiritual food has consisted in enriching thoughts about God nourishing his intellect, appealing truths about God drawing his will, and imaginative imagery filling him with warm feelings and affections for God. Now he no longer wants his prayer and his world to give him mere thoughts and images of God. They are so many false idols! He does not want these things! *He wants God.* Thoughts, feelings and emotions are not so much abandoning him—he is abandoning them. As a mountain climber leaves lovely fields and streams and gentle climes behind and below him, and mounts to barren and frigid heights to reach the very peak, so the pilgrim leaves these thoughts and images behind. They are a canoe which has carried him to the base of the mountain of God, but must now be abandoned as excess baggage.

This realization helps him cooperate willingly with changes which invade his life whether he wills them or not. It helps him understand past experiences, and enigmatic passages of Scripture, and certain advice he had been given without understanding its meaning.

He remembers the many things and places in which he could find nothing of God, and how, suddenly, he did find Him in those very things—in thoughts, in images, in nature, in events. Was it that God had not been there? No, it was that he himself had never before really penetrated those things where God had always been. When finally he did penetrate them to their depths, he met God there. Now he is moving on once again from the things and places where he has found God. Are there not many more realms to discover and enter, to enter more spiritually and there find God more in Himself? Memories of the past illumine the future, dispel the diffidence, and urge him on.

So far he has found God mainly in thoughts, in creatures, in imagination. The sad thing is that these are mere traces of God, not God Himself. Why has he not reached more to the Divinity directly, inwardly, through himself, made to God's image and likeness? The Scriptures and the Saints and the teaching Church give him the answer: he has blocked the way himself. He has heard God's invitation, but not clearly; his mind is open, but only partially. His earthy faith and failings are a clouded glass obscuring his inner vision. Even his spiritual feelings and affections are a wind riling the surface of his soul, reflecting the light back to heaven. Only when a lake is calm and pure does heaven's light penetrate its depths. Has he not heard the Scriptures advise him to go beyond thoughts and searchings to let God enter? *Be still, and know that I am God* (Ps. 46: 10).

What is actually happening is that the pilgrim is being enriched by the Holy Spirit with the gift of knowledge. This gift reveals to him the "nothingness" of creatures by communicating to him the beginnings of a profound knowledge of God. This knowledge is so secret the pilgrim is not formally conscious of it, and so profound that it cannot be verbalized or even conceptualized. But the inner light of it shines down to the very roots of creatures and exposes their frailty and pitiable mortality. What are even the greatest men of history but fleeting actors on the stage of time, which sees oceans come and go, mountains rise and fall, and stars come to birth, grow weary and die? God alone is the Eternal One who stands outside this panorama of matter in motion.

It is this new light of God and eternity that has been flashing into his own life and work, revealing its real nature: its transience and circumscription and relative impotence. To continue to find real purpose he must more and more look to God's purpose and will, however mysterious these remain for him.

The pilgrim hungers for God, and once again cannot find Him in creation, but this time he knows how to go on in the darkness. God has provided the light of faith. If he cannot see God nakedly, he can hear Him speak about Himself. If he cannot lay his eyes on the Word of God, he can read the word God has spoken. And so he turns to the Scriptures.

10.

The Word of God in the Life of the

Pilgrim Contemplative

The preceding explanation of why the pilgrim now turns earnestly to the Scriptures is probably fairly accurate, but it is also abstract and oversimplified. It needs to be supplemented here with concrete experiences of the discovery of Scripture.

From their infancy Catholics are put and kept in contact with the Scriptures through the Mass. But for many, the Scriptures sound stilted, foreign, of another time; they are both confusing and enigmatic. Weak faith and tepid hearts find these obstacles sufficient excuse for neglecting the Bible.

The pilgrim contemplative who is growing begins to have a different experience of the Scriptures. Even before the priest at Mass gives his homily on the readings from Scripture, the pilgrim is stirred by them. They flash like sparklers, lighting up things he never before understood. Passages come to mind during the day to support his fidelity. When he prays, Scripture comes spontaneously to mind. This development takes place gradually until finally a tiny interest has grown to a great one.

Some pilgrims awaken suddenly to the marvel of Scriptures. For one the occasion is a college Scripture course; for another, an experience of shared prayer in which one participant after another speaks and makes manifest the hidden meanings; for some, the Pentecostal prayer group has awakened deep faith in the word of God, and given witness to its power in lives. Many learn of the richness of Scripture when they are introduced to daily prayer over a scriptural passage. But the awakening is not occasioned by these events unless there is the hunger for God within. The soil must be right for the seed to sprout.

Whatever the external event that causes the awakening to Scripture, the internal preparation is the work of the Spirit. He disposes the pilgrim by the gift of understanding. The gift gives him new spiritual taste buds, as it were, so that he can now taste directly the deliciousness of the divine things of revelation without sensual help from beautiful creatures of nature.

And so the pilgrim turns in hunger to the Scriptures. He marvels to discover that, like the Eucharist, Scriptures are "manna . . . the bread of the angels" (Ps. 78:24-25), full of every good taste. Now the bread of the divine Eucharist is supplemented through the day by the bread of the Scriptures. Even Jesus, when He promised the Eucharist, intimated it should be so, for He mingled and joined His talk of the Eucharist with His talk about the power of His Word (John 6). And as a man Jesus Himself was nourished by the word of God. When the devil tempted Jesus to turn stones to bread, He said: "It is written: 'Man shall not live by bread alone, but by every word that proceeds from the mouth of God' " (Matthew 4:4).

It is almost impossible to exaggerate the impact of the Scriptures upon the pilgrim at this time. They fill his prayer with consolation and confirmation, so that he can say: "How sweet are thy words to my taste, sweeter than honey to my mouth" (Ps. 119:103). But they also fill his life with light, and direct his choices with wisdom: "Through thy precepts I get understanding; therefore I hate every false way. Thy word is a lamp to my feet and a light to my path" (Ps. 119:104-5).

Nor is this light and guidance restricted to purely spiritual matters, for the word of God encompasses all creation. The word of God makes the pilgrim spurt in growing not only as a contemplative, but also as an *agent*, capable of discerning and executing God's will for him in practical apostolic affairs. St. Paul, out of his own vast apostolic experience, gives witness of this to Timothy: "All Scripture is inspired by God and profitable for teaching, for reproof, for correction, and for training in righteousness, that the man of God may be complete, equipped for every good work" (2 Tim. 3:16-17).

Instinctively, the pilgrim supplements his reading of Scripture with its exposition by the Saints and the teaching Church and its authentic spokesmen and orthodox scriptural exegetes. Thus he gains a great additional good and avoids a great evil. He gains the good of sharing in the wisdom which the Spirit has imparted to the faithful who have pondered the Scriptures over the centuries. He avoids the evil of falling into fad interpretations resulting from ignorance of Scriptures as a whole, and of falling into misinterpretations through arrogating to himself the right to ignore tradition and appoint himself as the master of God's word. The word of God itself teaches him this wisdom: "In an abundance of counselors there is safety" (Prov. 11:14). The Ethiopian of the Acts illustrates the necessity of an interpreter of God's word. He was reading the Scriptures, but when he was asked if he understood he answered: "How can I, unless some one guides me?" (Acts 8:31). It was to provide an interpreter that the Holy Spirit, who inspired this humility in him, brought Philip to his help by the message of an angel. The Second Letter of Peter, too, warns against cavalier interpretations of St. Paul and of all Scripture: "There are some things in them hard to understand, which the ignorant and unstable twist to their own destruction, as they do the other scriptures" (2 Pet. 3:16).

Within the authoritative exposition of the Scriptures by the Church, the pilgrim finds that God speaks to him personally through the Scriptures. He makes His revelation come alive, He makes it understandable and meaningful and thrilling, He makes it personal and spoken afresh within the hour to him in his present need. This is the marvel of God's word, that it can suddenly become as fresh as a breeze after a storm, as vibrant as a stroke of lightning, as powerful as a tornado: "The word of God is living and active, sharper than any two-edged sword, piercing to the division of soul and spirit, of joints and marrow, and discerning the thoughts and intentions of the heart" (Hebr. 4:12). For the pilgrim, these texts of Scripture on Scripture are so representative of what is taking place in his life that he can take these words in his own mouth and use them as testimonials of his own experience.

The pilgrim at this stage finds that the word of God provides him with practical help in every need. Is he desolate? It consoles him. Does he feel worthless? It condemns these feelings as a neurotic lie. Is he proud and arrogant? It humbles him. The help from Scriptures is inexhaustible. As white light contains every color, the Scriptures contain every kind of help. They never fail him. They are also self-authenticating—*he constantly experiences the truth of what they say, to the point of amazement.* They are one of God's wonders.

If the pilgrim is still young and not fully matured psychologically or spiritually when he is awakened to the power of Scriptures and faith in the greatness of God which they communicate, he can feel oppressed. One pilgrim tells of such an experience. She was engaged in shared prayer over the text, "O Lord, thou hast searched me and known me . . . and art acquainted with all my ways. Even before a word is on my tongue, lo, O Lord, thou knowest it altogether" (Ps. 139:1, 3-4). She recounts her experience:

> Psalm 139 tore me apart. After hearing the others tell of the peace and comfort engendered in their hearts by this psalm, I was very embarrassed. I told them that my feelings were directly the opposite. I was very upset and also angry with God. I felt that he was intruding into the secret places of my heart which I hadn't even let myself examine or face up to yet and I didn't think that it was fair. My pride couldn't stand the thought that God could know me as I really was . . . I really didn't trust his love or believe in it completely. And God wanted me to know that this was his message to me, because everything that day was in tune with Psalm 139 and night prayers started with Psalm 139. It took almost a year for me to be able to read this psalm restfully and thank God for his presence, concern, and love.

This testimonial is an illustration of a God-given scriptural message received in faith. It is an experience truly grace-filled and truly human; it has its legitimate place in the Christian tradition. But there is another practice in which the person does not await such messages, but as it were demands them miraculously. He "cracks the Bible," and expects a special message for himself from the first lines on which his eyes fall. The defect in this approach—at least if used habitually—is that though it has a show of faith, it lacks faith in the intimate inner relationship between God and the human spirit. Within the heart, without the need of books and external signs, God can give His guidance; He can also call to mind the Scripture He pleases, if the pilgrim nourishes himself with scriptural reading. The habitual practice of *Bible roulette* seems frowned upon if not condemned by the very Bible it uses: "Unless you see signs and wonders you will not believe" (John 4:48).

The *angelism* implicit in such practices is the typical fault of pilgrims who have recently awakened or re-awakened to great faith and fervor, and have been spoiled by God's kindness, and grown presumptive. The Lord has His own ways of discouraging the practice, as the following experience shows. A missionary Sister in India was living in a small village. She volunteered to travel to the city of Patna to do a certain favor. She describes what happened:

> Secretly, I was, I think, quite happy to come, probably all the way savoring the things which are unavailable in the village or strictly forbidden by our vegetarian diet which means no eggs, no (no point in listing the no nos, it means only vegetables.) and only two kinds are available so the change was to be looked forward to, a kind of hundredfold from the Lord.
>
> His ways are definitely not mine—I arrived to find that an effort to say something about famine had prompted many of our sisters and employees to declare 48 hours total fast—nothing but water. All are not participating, and they urged me to be a nonparticipant. Each day . . . I open the Scriptures just to see if the Lord has a kind of spontaneous message. Yesterday what hit my eyes was Jeremias 49:12, "If those who did not deserve to drink the cup must drink it, . . . you too must drink." The message seemed clear so my hundredfold is the grace to participate in two days of fast—the 48 hours ends just about the time I reach the village again.
>
> And it's my birthday, too!! Wow.

Subsequently, this pilgrim seemed to lose enthusiasm for Bible roulette.

Whether for prayer or for work, the pilgrim finds in Scripture the help and guidance he needs. As to prayer, he nourishes it by reading Scripture and meditating on it spontaneously through the day when his work permits. Even if his period set aside for daily mental prayer is spent now in a prayer so austere and rarefied that it rarely makes use of words, even scriptural words, still Scripture read daily and meditated in snatches through the day seems to be an essential preparation for such prayer.

The very stages of growth in prayer, such as this one, are cryptically expressed and authenticated by the word of God. One pilgrim recounts an experience of this authentication by Scripture:

> For years in my prayer, I had found Jesus frequently in His many Gospel-recounted experiences, through imaginative representation to myself of the events given there. Then gradually these richly affective meetings with Him grew rare, and I wanted and needed a less imaginative, more direct meeting with God, beyond and above meeting Him in these sensible ways in His humanity. I was concerned about this. Was I going astray? I spoke to my spiritual director, a truly wise guide. He assured me I was on the right track, and quoted the words of Jesus to His Apostles at the Last Supper: "I tell you the truth: it is to your advantage that I go away, for if I do not go away, the Counselor will not come to you. . . . When the Spirit of truth comes, he will guide you into all the truth" (John 16:7, 13). I was amazed how well these words applied to me. I had sensed my need to pass beyond sensible realities to the world of God who is Spirit, but until my director quoted these words of Christ to me, I lacked assurance I was not deluded. From then on I had no more serious doubts and continued to grow in prayer.

Like Jesus' first Apostles, this pilgrim had reached the point where he had to pass beyond the more sensible experiences of Jesus, so that he could listen to His word more attentively, be guided by His Spirit more readily, and enter into deeper communion with divinity.

The prayer of the pilgrim in this stage is helped more than ever by that promise of Jesus: "If a man loves me, he will keep my word, and my Father will love him, and we will come to him and make our home with him" (John 14:23). The pilgrim now receives this promise with such deep faith that it seems to convey to him the very texture and substance of what it promises. By the secret ways of faith these words lead to the divinity. The pilgrim hears, sees, tastes, smells and feels nothing, but some experience beyond the senses makes him content to remind himself of these words, and then rest wordlessly with the Father and the Son. It is a prayer of nothing but faith, and yet his workday is punctuated with longing to return to it.

The pilgrim learns that the Scriptures are as helpful in his life and his work as they are in his prayer. They gradually open his eyes to the true nature of the Kingdom of God and the work that it requires. It is fitting to close this chapter with one pilgrim's account of this gradual awakening:

As my love for Jesus awakened, I wanted to serve Him, but I didn't know just how. I had to work for a living, but my work seemed to do nothing for the apostolate, and it took me away from prayer, so it was of entirely negative value. Soon I studied for the priesthood and was ordained. Only after many years did the message of the Church and the Gospels really get through to me: that any useful human occupation done in love—whether salaried or not—advances the Kingdom of God. The Gospels—and in fact Jesus Himself—teaches this in telling us beforehand what parameters He will use for judging us when the time comes. He tells us in the twenty-fifth chapter of Matthew that we will be measured by our useful service to others, by whether we provided them with their very material needs out of love. And I find this confirmed throughout the Bible. Ever since understanding this I have felt a responsibility for telling lay people about it, so they can find deeper meaning in their lives and see the unity in them. Then they can work with more generosity and less self-interest.

I have also learned to use the word of God as a healing potion in the ministry of counseling. As I listen to a person's problems, there usually comes to me from Scriptures a passage which provides a specific remedy. I write the passage down and give it like a medical prescription, to be taken until memorized, and then repeated each time the problem arises. These prescriptions have genuine healing powers.

11.

A Lamp to the Pilgrim's Feet

It is impossible to recount here all that Scripture does for the pilgrim's prayer and work and play and personality. Jesus, his commander-in-chief, Himself made Scripture central to His life, and used it to discern what path to take. In the desert He used it as a sword to counter the attacks of Satan. He used it to uncover the false ways hidden in the temptations He had, and so He used it to guide His course of action, His choice of apostolic works and methods. Tempted to proceed by way of spectacles and prodigies He responded: "It is written, *You shall not tempt the Lord your God*" (Matthew 4:7). Jesus used Scriptures to guide others as well, for Old Testament texts lace His teachings.

Jesus both fulfills and makes use of Scripture to explain the Kingdom of God. The sweep of the Kingdom's coming in power is foreshown by Scripture. The seedling of the Kingdom makes its way from time's beginning, and grows to its fullness at the end of time. Its power is irresistible and its victory is assured, not only because of God's infinite power and commitment, but because Jesus has already won the victory over sin, the one obstacle to the Kingdom: "Be of good cheer, I have overcome the world" (John 16:33).

The sole focus of this panorama of salvation history is Jesus. The sole focus of Scripture is Jesus. The Bible begins with words foretelling the Word, then proceeds to present the Word in His flesh, then illumines us with the words of the Word, and finally foretells His word's fulfillment in the return of the Word in His flesh to claim His Kingdom.

He who does not know both the Old Testament and the New

does not know Jesus well, and he who does not know Jesus well has no clear knowledge of His Kingdom or of how to serve it. The Testaments Old and New put Jesus before the pilgrim's eyes and teach him to act like Jesus in every circumstance: "Have this mind among yourselves, which was in Christ Jesus, who, though he was in the form of God . . .emptied himself" (Phil. 2:5, 7).

The first chapter of Mark portrays Jesus as the master sent contemplative. He comes on the public scene and begins by performing a public religious act. He experiences God through it, and experiences His confirmation by God the Father and His guidance by God the Spirit. He sets out and preaches the Kingdom. He gathers followers, preaches and does good works.

In the end, Jesus dies in seeming defeat, yet rises from the dead in total triumph.

It is this Jesus who is the measure and guide of the pilgrim. The Scriptures show forth the body of Jesus in action, and the Father gives to those who heed Him the Spirit of Jesus. Both the body and the Spirit of Jesus are essential norms for the work and the guidance of the pilgrim contemplative. The lamp for his feet is Jesus, the Word of God made flesh, and therefore both the body and Spirit of Jesus.

The Scriptures and the teaching Church not only guide the pilgrim along true ways; they guard him from false ones. They protect him from the unfaith of the times. He is warned away from those falsely liberal Christians who have lost their own way so completely that they doubt even the reality of Jesus' bodily resurrection. He finds Jesus condemning the Sadducees for falling into the same lack of belief in resurrection because of their misuse of Scriptures: "You are wrong, because you know neither the Scriptures nor the power of God" (Matthew 22:29). The pilgrim respects and esteems only those scriptural studies and that scholarship which do not earn the condemnation of the very Scriptures they explain. Some exegetes earn this condemnation by explaining away the right and responsibility which the Scriptures confer on the hierarchy to be the judge of their judgments in accord with Christ's express will to Peter: "I tell you, you are Peter, and on this rock I will build my Church, and . . . whatever you bind on earth shall be bound in heaven" (Matthew 16:18-19).

This charge was the foundation of the Church and even Paul respected it, though he had received the basic gospel message by private revelation (Gal. 1:12ff). He went to meet St. Peter (Gal. 1:18), he preached only what he had received (1 Cor. 15:3) and when other doctrine was disseminated he would not tolerate it:

"Even if we, or an angel from heaven, should preach to you a gospel contrary to that which we preached to you, let him be accursed" (Gal. 1:8). When there was a serious conflict about the true doctrine, he went to Jerusalem to consult the Apostles (Acts 15:1-2), and abided by the common decision of the hierarchy.

The pilgrim abhors the false voices within the Church which pass off Jesus' moral teaching as idealism, and suggest the liceity of premarital and extra-marital sex, homosexual acts, and other sins which the whole sweep of revelation condemns, and which the teaching Church equally condemns. He recognizes in these voices the false teachers against whom Paul cautions: "I appeal to you, brethren, to take note of those who create dissensions and difficulties, in opposition to the doctrine you have been taught" (Rom. 16:17).

He abhors the false doctrinal and moral pluralism, which is in reality syncretism: a jumble of contradictions which is not the work of God's revelation, but a work the devil promotes, as St. Augustine saw: "When the devil saw the human race abandoning the temple of demons and marching happily forward in the name of the freedom-giving mediator, he inspired heretics to oppose Christian teaching under cover of the Christian name as though their presence in the City of God could go unchallenged like the presence, in the city of confusion, of philosophers with wholly different and even contradictory positions" (*City of God* XVIII, 21).

Through his deep faith and knowledge of Scriptures and the Church's teaching, the Spirit gives him a keen sense for distinguishing between those who explain the faith and those who explain it away. He is not looking for wise men who give him ultimate truth on their own authority, but only for wise and learned men who attempt humbly to explain the ultimate truth which God has given His Church. His prolonged contact with the wanderings, reversals, and open contradictions of human wisdom, have exposed its limited value to him. That the record of philosophers is dismal is testified to by St. Augustine, who was one of the greatest of them: "These men in all their laborious investigations, seem to have had one supreme common objective: to understand what manner of living is best suited to laying hold upon happiness. Yet they ended up by disagreeing—disciples with masters, and disciples with fellow disciples. Why, except that they sought the answer to their question merely in human terms, depending solely upon human experience and human reasoning?" (*City of God* XVIII, 41).

Exegetes of Scripture who usurp the hierarchy's right to judge their work are claiming that their human opinion of God's word is more absolute than the word of God they are judging. The truth is that ultimate truth comes only by submission to the Spirit of truth as St. Paul made clear: "For God in his wisdom made it impossible for men to know him by means of their own wisdom" (1 Cor. 1:21 *Good News* version).

The pilgrim is graced with this submission to the spirit, and the Spirit teaches him to read the Scriptures in the Church. And so it is that the Scriptures always remain a lamp to his feet.

SPIRITUAL PROJECT NUMBER FIVE: *Lectio Divina*

"We also thank God constantly for this, that when you received the word of God which you have heard from us, you accepted it, not as the word of men but as what it truly is, the word of God, which is at work in you believers" (1 Thess. 2:13).

Christian tradition teaches us to assimilate the word of God through the senses as well as the spirit, and to train the whole man to live it: the memory to recall it, the mind to conform to it, the motor nerves and sinews to reproduce it, etc. The following spiritual exercises can help to this purpose (they are not meant to be done all at one time).

1. Write out on a scrap of paper the following scriptural revelation and promise of Jesus, and memorize it: "If a man loves me, he will keep my word, and my Father will love him, and we will come to him and make our home with him" (John 14:23). Repeat it frequently through the day for a week. If you can't remember how it goes, draw the scrap of paper from your pocket and refresh yourself, until at length the memory can recall it at will.

2. Repeat John 14:23 and *picture* the Father with you and within you looking at you with fatherly tenderness and devotion. See how He Himself is speaking to you in the following words (and in all biblical words): "He let you hunger and fed you with manna, which you did not know, nor did your fathers know; that he might make you know that man does not live by bread alone, but that man lives by everything that proceeds out of the mouth of the Lord" (Deut. 8:3). Ask the Father to help you taste this food. Chew every single word of this passage, as you chew bread, until you get its spiritual taste.

3. To get the words of God into your body as well as your soul, read Scriptures aloud, pronouncing each word as though you were chewing it. *See* the word on paper. *Feel* the word forming on your lips. *Taste* it in your mouth. *Hear* it in your ear. Concentrate on each

of these sense-experiences of the word individually, and then together. Try to grasp and sense that, soul and body, you are being united to the word of God: "The *mouth* of the just man murmurs wisdom . . ." (Ps. 37:30 JB).

4. Imbue your imagination with the effects of the word of God. Read words of Jesus from the Gospel and try to hear the ringing clarity of His voice as He spoke. Speak the name of *Jesus*, and imagine you can smell it like incense on the air in accord with the words of the Song of Songs: "Your name spoken is a spreading perfume" (1:3 NAB).

5. Say repeatedly the words of Jesus: "I have food to eat of which you do not know. . . . My food is to do the will of him who sent me, and to accomplish his work" (John 4:32-33). Try to *feel your will taking on this same shape and becoming one with His.*

6. Let your body rhythms learn to participate in your *Lectio Divina*: As you breathe out, read a few words of Scripture. Stop and meditate on them while you breathe in. As you breathe out again, read the next few words, etc.

7. As you read the Scripture, try to become *aware* of your own affections rising in response to the word of God. This spontaneous, in-depth response of self to Self, is your deepest word of communion with the Lord. You must learn to wait for it to happen, by walking slowly through the paths of Scripture, and stopping when the beauty of Truth appears, and taking time to chew the nourishment given you.

8. Don't try to *force* flavor out of Scripture any more than you try to *force* flavor out of food. If you chew food and it contains flavor, the flavor will give you pleasure; if it is absent, there is nothing you can do. The Lord is your flavor in Scripture, and you must wait for Him, for He is Lord. He is also Lord-Fashioner of your nature, and you must wait for it to bring forth affections in due season: "Stir not up nor awaken love until it please" (Song of Songs 2:7).

9. Just as the psalmist prayed to God in words that really expressed his moods and feelings of the moment, so should you do when you use Scripture to help you pray. Assess your mood here and now, and try to recall the place in Scripture which best expresses that mood. Turn to it and read it prayerfully. The better you know Scripture, the more helpful this practice will be.

12.

The Apostolate of Truth

God's word has given the pilgrim such a taste of truth and such a hunger for it that he desires to pursue and know truth in all its manifestations, whether in revelation or creation. It is not primarily through imagination or affections that God comes to him now; it is as Truth that God comes into his life, and the Kingdom into being. From now on God will speak less to his senses and more to his mind. But just as his senses had to experience a loss of the pleasures of earth before they could register the pleasures of heaven, his intelligence will have to submit its native light to the higher light of revelation, so that in all things faith may prevail.

This phase of the pilgrim's development makes him a man devoted to truth and the search for truth and the defense of truth. He is hungry for all truth: for revealed truth, and for truth searched out by human ingenuity, whether it be speculative or practical truth. Given the chance, he will search for truth in the past as well as the present, in science as well as the arts, in the East as well as the West —but above all, in the one, true Catholic and apostolic Church. He is no mere gatherer of information; he is a pilgrim of truth. He is penetrating to the truth of things, and this truth is leading him to the Truth beyond things.

At this depth of penetration into the nature of things, it begins to become evident that every legitimate human enterprise is, in the hands of a pilgrim sent to engage in it, capable of advancing the Kingdom of God. It also becomes evident that the teaching profession has special significances for the Kingdom. One pilgrim, who is an ordained priest, addresses this point:

I pursue research in "secular" literature and teach literature and language to college students. Such is my mission. To those who wish to know how a priest can justify such activity, I answer that truth is the essence of revelation and revelation unquestionably linked to redemption. Any advance in any way of knowing, any discovery of anything new, any clarification of perceptions, any development of human faculties gives either facility in comprehending or actual understanding, direct or oblique, of God's word and work. Our problems with revelation are essentially problems of perceptivity. Human perceptivity evolves in each person, but has also evolved over the centuries. It is the function of the Catholic teacher and scholar to hand on and advance the tradition which perpetuates these evolutions. Truth is indivisible. Any understanding is an approach to God. And any contribution to human understanding is participation in God's revealing and thus redemptive work.

The pilgrim is experiencing a fusion of things spiritual and secular, for truth is one, though it comes through many sources. He is experiencing a fusion of personal, spiritual goals and apostolic objectives, because the search for truth and the communication of truth is a primary way to grow personally and at the same time to advance the Kingdom.

He is oppressed by anyone or anything untrue. He gains insight into the psychological destructiveness of untruth. He feels responsibility (and response-ability) for presenting truth, defending it, and arguing for it, even at great cost to himself. This is what Jesus did. The pilgrim with the qualities of affability, patience, and discretion will be blessed now, for he will execute his apostolate of truth without unnecessarily alienating anyone. Most pilgrims will fail by excess in one of two directions: they will be too timid to speak up when they know they should, or they will speak up even when they should not.

The timid will suffer harassment from their own consciences, as they stand by silent and let the day be carried by untruthful or dishonest ways and means. The image and word of Jesus will confront them: "He who is not with me is against me" (Matthew 12:30). It is a bitter potion.

The intemperate will be prey to the abuses which are as common in the war for truth as in every other war: over-fervid attacks, inaccurate striking of wrong targets, defending untenable positions. The result is much suffering and self-recrimination.

The excesses in either direction are difficult to avoid. It is not easy to know when to speak and when to be silent, nor does everyone have the same gift or the same responsibility for speaking up. It is literally true that as regards the question of when to speak and when to be silent, *only God knows*, and that here especially the pilgrim will act rightly only if he is deeply attuned to himself and to the Spirit of God. He must learn to discern between the various impulses that arise in him. Only by long experience and cultivated self-control can he learn to respond spontaneously to the right impulses. One pilgrim reflects on the problem:

> I observed the contrariety between my snap judgments and associated remarks on the one hand, and my deeper convictions on the other. Which is the real 'I'? How can action spring so frequently from the 'non-I'? It is time to excise what is not 'I', and to bring into unity what is. I beg your grace, Lord, to renounce the snap judgments. I resolve to live by my deeper convictions. I will stop being and giving poor example. How can others know me except by my actions?

Scripture takes cognizance of this thorny problem of control of the tongue, and directs us to the answer: "The plans of the mind belong to man, but the answer of the tongue is from the Lord" (Prov. 16:1).

The pilgrim now holds to truth as to his very self, and more, as to the Beloved. The Beloved is the Word, the Logos, the Truth sent by the Father. A trace of Him can be found in any truth whatsoever. To betray truth is to betray Him. To be remiss in the search for truth is to be indifferent to Him.

Truth brings the pilgrim much peace and joy, but also much aridity and suffering. So much truth is abstract, contains so little of the life of the Beloved. So much truth is contested, robbing him of the joy it should bring. He suffers from the crucifixion of truth by the world. He rejoices at his wedding to truth, even though it is also his crucifixion. It is worth everything because one day truth will shed its abstractions like a garment, and he will look on the open face of Truth Incarnate and Truth Divine.

This new growth has deep significance for him as one sent on a Spirit-guided mission by God. He is learning, even in his work in the world, to feed on the word of God, not on his five senses. Never before did he dream how pervasive faith must become. Everything must be judged by faith. Faith is his communications line with the Master whose agent he is. Every directive and order he receives can be heard only in faith. Only by faith can he discern God's work where it goes on in the world. Every value he holds must be held in faith. Every action he performs must be a response to faith. His function is not so much to judge what is good and what is evil as to hear and do the will of God. To judge what is good and what evil is the prerogative of God, who said to the first man: "You may freely eat of every tree of the garden; but of the tree of the knowledge of good and evil you shall not eat" (Gen. 2:16-17). The sent contemplative is called and appointed to listen to God and to act in response. To obey (*obedire*) is to listen acutely (*ob-audire*) and to act responsively. The action God wants can be known only by revelation and/ or inspiration received and understood in his own time and space and circumstances, and his action in response is a work of faith. He can be an effective agent of God only when his contemplative attunement to God and the world proceeds in pure faith. The pilgrim is now an apostle of truth, but he measures all truth by the norms of faith, and he builds up trustworthy norms of faith by having perpetual recourse to God's revelation.

13.

The Pilgrim and Divine Revelation

The pilgrim is quite aware that though he is a friend of Christ, he is also called to serve with Christ. He has been sent to work toward the completion of the mission on which Christ was sent by the Father. All followers of Christ are no doubt called to serve with Christ, but the pilgrim is called to a *contemplative service*. That is, he is given the gift of contemplation, and given it in a unique form as a special mission charism. He is equipped with the grace of a contemplation-of-communication-with-the-Spirit that is ordained to the guidance of his mission in all circumstances. This puts him uniquely at the disposal of the Holy Spirit as one always alert for special assignments given by the Spirit: "I will instruct you and teach you the way you should go" (Ps. 32:8). This charismatic relationship to *mission* gradually leads him to gain insight into God's revelation from his own vocation and vantage point, and with his own special apostolic problems in mind.

A side effect of this orientation is that the sent contemplative is in danger of letting his own special problems cloud his relationship to revelation and the Church, particularly if he neglects prayer, or listens to the wrong voices. He can be irritated by the controls the magisterium of the Church utilizes, and begin to think in the misguided terms of those who set the "Charismatic Church" over against the "Institutional Church," and the "Word of God" against "Tradition," and the "Voice of God" against the "Voice of the Church." He can develop such a compassion for the distress of some certain class of sufferers that he comes to prefer his own militancy in their behalf to the meek doctrine of the Scriptures, or his own more accommodating interpretation of biblical morality to the crucifying interpretation of the Church's magisterium. Even if he does not follow his own misguided counsel to this degree, the pilgrim, embittered by his impotence before the vastness of the troubles of the world, may develop a sense of strain in his relationship to the demands of revelation, or a sense of hostility to the firm teaching of the Church's magisterium. Nor are these necessarily the problems of beginners. They can plague even veterans.

One problem which the maturing pilgrim can hardly escape is the problem that confronts every explorer and every innovator—the problem of traveling beyond the maps, of becoming involved in new situations for which the rules have not yet been invented. The likelihood of this problem arising is great, for his charism of listening-to-execute the Lord's apostolic purposes in every situation puts him *by vocation* on the cutting edge of the Son of God's mission. His charism disposes and trains him for just such situations. He is attuned to the Spirit and response-able to Him. When difficulties and new questions arise, which should he solve for himself, and which should he refer to Ecclesial authority?

Purported developments of doctrine are originating in many quarters, and some of these developments touch directly on his apostolate, for good or ill. How is he to discern true development of doctrine and distinguish it from distortion and corruption of doctrine?

In general, how is he to relate the inner guiding and activating impulse of the Spirit to the outer guiding and controlling word of the magisterium?

With these problems in mind, we need to reflect on the sent contemplative's relationship to revelation. Perhaps guidelines will emerge that will summarize his gradually maturing manner of responding to God revealing.

The pilgrim who has become excessively spirit-minded might here interject a complaint that this effort to formulate the ways of the Spirit is a cryptic effort to eliminate the role of the Spirit. Does not Scriptures say: "They shall all be taught by God?" (John 6:45). Yes, but Scripture also says: "Every one who calls upon the name of the Lord will be saved. But . . . how are they to believe in him of whom they have never heard? And how are they to hear without a preacher? So faith comes from what is heard" (Rom. 10:13-17). And it is in this same vein that Jesus says to the hierarchs He has appointed over His Church: "Go into all the world and preach the gospel to the whole creation. He who believes and is baptized will be saved; but he who does not believe will be condemned" (Mark 16: 15-16).

The two pronged communication of revelation through the preaching of God's word by men and the spiritual infusion of it by God's Spirit is God's own plan. The charismatic and the institutional Church is one and the same Church, just as the incarnate Christ and the Holy Spirit are one and the same God. Scripture itself sets up the two poles of institution and charism, and so the two are in no inevitable conflict. The Scripture confirms the fact that one of the essential ways the Spirit speaks to men is through other men. If we want to hear the Spirit, we must listen to men who claim to speak for Him. There is, then, no conflict between drawing up rules for listening to the Spirit, and listening to Him even when He escapes the constrictions of our rules, for the Spirit is both in such things and beyond them.

The sent contemplative is related to divine Revelation in its fullness, just as every Catholic is; but in accord with his unique apostolic charism, he is particularly attuned to such revelation as it provides the key to the unfolding of Christ's mission *here and now*. Because of this, the pilgrim may, in the beginning, think of himself as an independent apostle. That is, he may not be very sensitive to the fact that he is but one missionary member of a *missionary community*. As times goes by, however, he will gain a vision of the oneness of Christ's mission. There is only one Missioner sent by the Father, and it is Christ-and-His-Body-the-Church. Thus the pilgrim's very mission, rather than setting him apart by himself, knits him more closely to the Church. It was to the Twelve Hierarchs that Jesus officially intrusted His mission after the resurrection: "As the Father has sent me, even so I send you" (John 20:21). The pilgrim's mission can only be a participation in theirs. This relates him not only to the Church in general, but to the bishops of the Church, for they are the formal inheritors of the institutional mission.

This oneness of the Missioner demands norms for the unity of purpose and action among the missionary members of Christ. It is not long before the pilgrim sees the scandal of one Christian working at cross-purposes with another, undoing the other's work, in the name of the same Lord.

There is "one Lord, one faith, one baptism" (Eph. 4:5): there is only one Word-made-flesh. The work of the kingdom is the work of assisting Christ to grow and develop in His members through preaching the word of Christ and responding to His one Holy Spirit, the one Unifier. There can be only one dogma, one doctrine, one holiness, one living faith proffered through lives living it—living the one life of Christ. There must, then, be in the body of Christ some authority for settling the doctrinal conflicts among Christians. Thus the pilgrim's actual experience confirms the need for the authority structure which the Scriptures and Church impose.

One pilgrim, a Catholic priest, saw this insight verified in a non-Catholic Christian friend of his. Eager to help spread the Gospel, the man used to go to a public park and preach Christ. He argued that, just as the founders of our country did not leave the interpretation of the Constitution to each individual, but appointed a Supreme Court, so Jesus who was wiser, did not leave his word to personal interpretation: He appointed St. Peter, the Apostles, and their successors to the job. Strangely, the man did not ask to be received into the Church, nor was he pressed to enter. Only when he was on his death-bed did the priest invite his conversion. He eagerly assented. When the priest asked why he had waited so long he said: *I was not worthy.* He had recognized not only the authority of the Church but its holiness, even though he must have witnessed the unholiness of some of its members.

The source of doctrinal tension in the Church is falsely posed when it is described as the tension between the Church as institutional and the Church as charismatic. To pose the problem in this way is to falsely assume that the members charged with institutional authority do not share in the Spirit or His gifts and charisms. The truth is that the Spirit may speak through every member, but He is in fact promised in a special way to those members who are appointed to certain institutional offices. The real source of doctrinal tension lies in the conflict that can arise between the institutional, charismatic, *social body* of the Church and the charismatic *individuals* in the Church: the *prophets,* true and false.

St. Paul, who was both a charismatic and an authority in the institutional Church, rejected the institutional-charismatic division. He saw that the offices and the charismata are ways of dividing not the *persons* but the *services* in the one body of Christ: "By the grace given to me I bid every one among you not to think of himself more highly than he ought to. . . . Having gifts that differ according to the grace given to us, let us use them: if prophecy, in proportion to our faith; if service, in our serving; he who exhorts, in his exhortation; he who contributes, in liberality; he who gives aid, with zeal; he who does acts of mercy, with cheerfulness" (Rom. 12:3-8). St. Paul laid down regulations for the use of the charism of speaking in tongues, and the teaching Church has through the centuries not hesitated to lay down norms for the use of other charismata, such as the vocation to the religious life. The use of the gifts of the Spirit are not above the authority of the Church hierarchs, for both their authority and the gifts are the work of the same Spirit.

Because the Church is the bride of Christ, and the bride has the same Spirit as Christ the Bridegroom, the pilgrim contemplative must align his Spirit-experiences with the Church's. The universal Church's discernment of the Spirit does not supplant his own, but it *does* guide his own. The more the pilgrim's own life pulses with the life of the true Church, the more readily will he discern the true movements of the Spirit in himself, and distinguish them from all other impulses. This is true simply because the Spirit *is* the Life of the Church.

To be rightly attuned to revelation, then, the pilgrim must be right with *the Church* and *with himself. The Church* means here the deposit of faith, the people who live it, the members who theologize on it, and the members who authoritatively interpret it: the magisterium. The *deposit of faith* is composed of the Scriptures, the tradition, and the people who live it, for they are the *living tradition.* Even this view is constricting, for divine revelation is in the profoundest sense God's *self*-communication. The Church is, therefore, the people of God receiving God through Scripture, tradition, sacrament, worship, and one another, as the Spirit develops the body of Christ in the course of salvation history.

The pilgrim must be right with the Church, for it is the objective source of revelation for him, but he must also be right with himself, for he is the subjective register of that revelation. He discerns the true revelation by means of three kinds of personal experience: by judgments of reason illumined by faith; by being drawn to the truth of revelation through the register of his affections (attraction of the heart); and by noumenal experiences such as private guidance through the inspirations of grace.

Where the teaching and guidance of the Church harmonize with these personal judgments and experiences, all is peace. But at times there will be conflict, not only with the Church, but between his own reason and feelings, or between his faith-judgments and his mystical experiences. It is at such times that the pilgrim must have clearly in mind what he considers the most fundamental sources of the truth of his faith. Is it his own private judgments? Or his religious experiences? His feelings? Or the belief of the whole Church as presented authoritatively by the magisterium?

Let us try to phrase the Catholic answer to these questions. The true Catholic believes the Church to be the one, true Church of Christ. He believes this not simply because the Church makes this claim, but because the Spirit helps him to accept the Church's claim in a peaceful act of faith, as in accord with revelation. Once he accepts the Church as the true teacher of faith, he accepts what it says about revelation and about itself. He then tries to train mind and heart to resonate with the Church according to the obedience of faith. What *does* the Church say about itself? What does it say about the contrary and contradictory teachings on faith and morals heard within the Catholic body today? Ultimately, what does the *magisterium* of the Church say about these things? What norms for discernment does it offer the concerned pilgrim? The sent contemplative must know the answers to these questions to the best of his competence. He must know what the official teaching body of the Church teaches concerning faith and morals; what it says about its teaching authority and responsibility; finally, what it says about its relationship to the theologians. We will treat these matters briefly in the following chapters. Then, hopefully, we will be in a position to distill useful norms to guide the pilgrim in his response to revelation and his search for living union with the Church.

The next three chapters, then, will not even attempt to push forward the limits of the Church's understanding of the role of the Spirit in the offices of the Church; they will simply gather here the magisterium's contemporary teaching on the subject for the reader who wishes to ponder it with the author in preparation for drawing up the *Norms for a Living Union with Revelation* which will follow. It is only in those norms that an original set of contemporary guidelines will be attempted.

With regard to the use of Scripture here and throughout the treatise: in the spirit of what is being attempted in this work, scriptural texts are not adduced as strict proofs, but as God's word relating to the matter under consideration. At times the extended spiritual meaning is all that is intended—surely appropriate in a work addressed to contemplatives who by vocation reach to the essence of God's word, not by ignoring the need for philological and theological exegesis, but by refusing to be trapped into spirit-less literalism. For the believer who reads Scripture in the Spirit, from the perspective of the whole Bible, its traditional three-fold spiritual sense (allegorical, tropological, and anagogical) flows spontaneously out of the literal sense. For the Bible speaks throughout of Christ, of the believer, and of the future life.

14.

The Pilgrim and the Teaching Church

Sent contemplatives are engaged in works too diversified to be catalogued, but their purpose in them all is to herald the Gospel and bring the Kingdom of God—and for this they need the help of the ecclesiastical magisterium. The magisterium is weighted with

Christ's command to spread the Gospel with purity. It guards the Gospel against erroneous interpretations, and it points out the whole range of the Gospel's contemporary relevance to human society. To accomplish these tasks the magisterium must guide the development of doctrine as it relates to ongoing history; it must also guard it against those who would strip it of its message of bodily resurrection and eternal life with God, or reduce it to a mere secular humanism.

The truth the magisterium defends and communicates is God's revelation. Its source is divine, not human, though it reaches us through human agents. "The Church has always regarded, and continues to regard the Scriptures, taken together with sacred Tradition, as the supreme rule of her faith," the magisterium teaches in the *Dogmatic Constitution on Divine Revelation (#21)*.

The magisterium is, therefore, itself only an agent. It can teach as God's word only what it has received, and it has received already the essence of that revelation: "The Roman Pontiff and the bishops, by reason of their office and the seriousness of the matter, apply themselves with zeal to the work of inquiring by every suitable means into this revelation and of giving apt expression to its contents; they do not, however, admit any new public revelation as pertaining to the divine deposit of faith" (*Dogmatic Constitution on the Church* #25).

The Church is, therefore, radically undemocratic because it has a Lord and Master in Jesus Christ. His truth it teaches, and His will it executes. The magisterium rules only in obedience to Him. He, the fullness of revelation, has come, and the magisterium awaits no further revelation; it awaits His return.

The Church, nevertheless, has democratic elements. The Spirit can move any member of the Church to stress a truth, condemn an error, or begin a work, whether or not he holds an office in the Church. Thus, by divine charism an individual can say *yes* or *no* to some ecclesial element even before the magisterium. Though the magisterium has the responsibility of making the final judgment on movements in the Church, it has no monopoly on initiating such movements. The magisterium ought to listen and observe the Church before it teaches the Church. The magisterium itself confirms this when it teaches: "By reason of the knowledge, competence, or pre-eminence which they have, the laity are empowered—indeed obliged—to manifest their opinion on those things which pertain to the good of the Church. If the occasion should arise this should be done through the institutions established by the Church for that purpose" (*Dogmatic Constitution on the Church* #37).

All Catholics moved to speak should be heard, but the magisterium has the responsibility of pronouncing the final judgment. Nor does the teaching of the magisterium lean on the consent of the members, for the magisterium's guidance and authority is not from the members but from God: "Bishops who teach in communion with the Roman Pontiff are to be revered by all as witnesses of divine and Catholic truth; the faithful, for their part, are obliged to submit to their bishops' decision, made in the name of Christ, in matters of faith and morals, and to adhere to it with a ready and respectful allegiance of mind. This loyal submission of the will and intellect must be given, in a special way, to the authentic teaching authority of the Roman Pontiff, even when he does not speak *ex cathedra*, in such wise, indeed, that his supreme teaching authority be acknowledged with respect, and sincere assent be given to decisions made by him, conformably with his manifest mind and intention, which is made known principally either by the character of the documents in question, or by the frequency with which a certain doctrine is proposed, or by the manner in which the doctrine is formulated.

"Although the bishops, taken individually, do not enjoy the privilege of infallibility, they do, however, proclaim infallibly the doctrine of Christ on the following conditions: namely, when, even though dispersed throughout the world but preserving for all that amongst themselves and with Peter's successor the bond of communion, in their authoritative teaching concerning matters of faith and morals, they are in agreement that a particular teaching is to be held definitively and absolutely. This is still more clearly the case when, assembled in an ecumenical council, they are, for the universal Church, teachers of and judges in matters of faith and morals, whose decisions must be adhered to with the loyal and obedient assent of faith.

"This infallibility, however, with which the divine Redeemer wished to endow his Church in defining doctrine pertaining to faith and morals, is co-extensive with the deposit of revelation, which must be religiously guarded and loyally and courageously expounded. The Roman Pontiff, head of the college of bishops, enjoys this infallibility in virtue of his office, when, as supreme pastor and teacher of all the faithful—who confirms his brethren in the faith (cf. Luke 22:32)—he proclaims in an absolute decision a doctrine pertaining to faith or morals. For that reason his definitions are rightly said to be irreformable by their very nature and not by reason of the assent of the Church, in as much as they were made with the assistance of the Holy Spirit promised to him in the person of blessed Peter himself; and as a consequence they are in no way in need of the approval of others, and do not admit of appeal to any other tribunal. For in such a case the Roman Pontiff does not utter a pronouncement as a private person, but rather does he expound and defend the teaching of the Catholic faith as the supreme teacher of the universal Church, in whom the Church's charism of infallibility is present in a singular way" (*Dogmatic Constitution on the Church* #25; cf. Vatican I for the definition of papal infallibility--D 1839f).

This passage represents the magisterium's fundamental self-understanding, and it is therefore the guide of the authentic sent contemplative. The passage was composed during the course of the Second Vatican Council. In 1970, Pope Paul gave an "Apostolic Exhortation to all the Bishops in peace and communion with the Apostolic See, on the Fifth Anniversary of the close of the Second Vatican Council." He reminded the bishops that they must insistently speak out the whole truth in this time when many faithful are troubled about the meaning of some of the most fundamental dogmas such as those concerning Christ and the Trinity, the Real Presence, the ordained priesthood, and Christian morality as in the matter of the indissolubility of marriage. He pointed out that while sociological surveys may be useful, the "Gallup poll" mentality is wrong when applied to religious matters.

The effort to formulate the Gospel in ways which speak to men today was a key aim of the Council, but the Pope warns the bishops that there have arisen "venturesome hypotheses" which are disturbing the faith and ravaging the Christian people. He then exhorts the bishops to carry out their responsibility: "Dearly beloved brothers, let us not be reduced to silence for fear of criticism, which is always possible and may at times be well-founded. However necessary the function of theologians, it is not to the learned that God has confided the duty of authentically interpreting the faith of the Church: that faith is borne by the life of the people whose bishops are responsible for them before God. It is for the bishops to tell the people what God asks them to believe" (*The Teachings of Paul VI: 1970*, U.S.C.C., pp. 465-475).

Here, then, is the teaching Church's authentic presentation of its role. Here, therefore, are the norms which should inform the pilgrim's relationship to the magisterium.

The relation of theologians to the whole Church in general and to the magisterium in particular needs further consideration, for it is one of the most distressing problems for many pilgrims of our day. It will be considered in the next chapter.

15.

The Pilgrim, the Magisterium

and the Theologians

The Church has probably never had a greater need of the work of its theologians and scriptural exegetes than it has today. The great present need of theologians springs from the explosion of knowledge and the cultural developments of our time. Revelation must be plumbed anew, and doctrinal penetration must reach new depths, so that all the erudition of modern times may be enlisted to spread the Gospel in a way which is authentic and yet appeals to the contemporary mind and heart.

And yet great harm is presently being done by some theologians and exegetes. It comes from a radical rejection of tradition, an excessive demythologizing of Scriptures that betrays the word of God, and a rejection of the magisterium and a usurping of its role. Perhaps worst of all has been the failure of theologians to take one another to task for these excesses.

It is necessary here, then, to recall the relation of the theologians, and their diverse interpretations, to the whole Church and to the magisterium, so that the pilgrim contemplative will be judicious in what he accepts from theologians.

The magisterium itself teaches that there is development of doctrine, but it also points out the way it proceeds: "What was handed on by the apostles comprises everything that serves to make the People of God live their lives in holiness and increase their faith. . . . The Tradition that comes from the apostles makes progress in the Church, with the help of the Holy Spirit. There is a growth in insight into the realities and words that are being passed on. This comes about in various ways. It comes through the contemplation and study of believers who ponder these things in their hearts (cf. Luke 2:19, 51). It comes from the intimate sense of spiritual realities which they experience. And it comes from the preaching of those who have received, along with their right of succession in the episcopate, the sure charism of truth" (*Dogmatic Constitution on Divine Revelation* # 8). What appears here is the fact that in the development of doctrine, faith and prayer are more necessary than even study and learning and brilliance. Jesus made this evident when He said: "I thank thee, Father, Lord of heaven and earth, that thou hast hidden these things from the wise and understanding and revealed them to babes" (Luke 10:21). And Paul says: "Has not God made foolish the wisdom of the world? For since, in the wisdom of God, the world did not know God through wisdom, it pleased God through the folly of what we preach to save those who believe" (1 Cor. 1:20).

This point concerning the real source of true theology is so basic and so overlooked it cannot be overstressed. There are two sources of human truth: God and man. Theology is the science of interpreting truth revealed by God. The theologian who does not hold to revelation as to his first principle is as unsound as the scientist who does not hold to the laws of nature as his first principles but instead fabricates laws from his own imaginings. The theologian who is less concerned with revelation than he is with philosophy or sociology has lost his credibility. Contrast his manner of proceeding with the care the magisterium takes in trying to determine the meaning of revelation: "The Roman Pontiffs, according to the exigencies of time and circumstances, sometimes assembling Ecumenical Councils, or asking for the mind of the Church scattered throughout the world, sometimes by particular Synods, sometimes using other helps which Divine Providence supplied, defined as to be held those things which with the help of God they had recognized as conformable with the Sacred Scriptures and Apostolic Traditions. For the Holy Spirit was not promised to the successors of Peter that by his revelation they might make known new doctrine, but that by his assistance they might inviolably keep and faithfully expound the revelation or deposit of faith delivered through the apostles" (Vatican Council I, N-R 385).

In deciding whether to make use of a given theologian's teaching, then, a pilgrim should carefully observe whether his source is the Scriptures and the tradition. Pope Paul VI carefully described the theologians' authentic sources in his "Apostolic Exhortation to All Bishops" earlier referred to. He wrote: "In the recent past it has quite rightly been said: *Theology, being the science of the faith, can only find its norm in the Church, the community of the believers. When theology rejects its postulates and understands its norm in a different way, it loses its basis and its object. The religious freedom affirmed by the Council and which rests upon freedom of conscience is valid for the personal decision in relation to faith, but it has nothing to do with determining the content and scope of divine revelation.* In like manner, the utilization of human scientific knowledge in research in hermeneutics is a way of investigating the revealed data, but these data cannot be reduced to the analyses thus provided, because they transcend them both in origin and content." The theologian or exegete who treats revelation as mere human documents, or who substitutes his own judgments for the Church's traditional doctrinal interpretations, must be rejected. Scripture and tradition must always be used to judge the theologian's judgments.

The final judgment on the theologian's work is neither his nor the pilgrim's but the magisterium's. The magisterium is not necessarily capable of doing the work the theologians do, but it is capable of making the final judgment on the accuracy of their work, for this is the office given it in the Spirit. The relation of the unofficial office of theologians to the official office of the magisterium is traced out by Pope Paul in his "Address to an International Congress on the Theology of Vatican II":

> Both theology and the magisterium seek to further the same purpose: to preserve the sacred deposit of revelation; to look more deeply into it, to explain it, teach it, and defend it. . . . But theology and the magisterium have different duties, and are endowed with different gifts. Sacred theology uses reason enlightened by faith; and it receives no little light from the Divine Paraclete, to which the theologian must pay heed. Its duty is to examine and comprehend the truths of revelation more thoroughly; to bring the fruits of its labor to the attention of the Christian community and, in

particular, to the attention of the magisterium itself, so that the whole Christian people may be enlightened by the doctrine which the ecclesiastical hierarchy hands down; and finally, to lend its efforts to the task of spreading, clarifying, confirming, and defending the truth which the magisterium authoritatively propounds.

The magisterium, on the other hand, has received authority from Jesus Christ, and the gift of the Holy Spirit, through which it teaches the People of God. Its official task is, first and foremost, to bear witness to the teaching received from the Apostles and hand it on, so that it might become the possession of the universal Church and of the whole human family; to maintain this doctrine completely free from errors and distortions; in the light of divine revelation to pass authoritative judgment on new teachings, and on the considerations proposed by theology as solutions to new questions; and finally, to authoritatively propose new and deeper investigations into divine revelation, and new adaptations of this revelation to our times—which it, with the enlightenment of the Holy Spirit, judges to be in full accordance with Christ's teaching.

Thus sacred theology . . . seeks to discover how the Christian community might translate its faith into practice, and it tries to grasp the truths, opinions, questions, and tendencies which the Holy Spirit stirs up in the People of God ("What the Spirit Says to the Churches, Apoc. 2:7") (*The Pope Speaks*, Autumn, 1966, pp. 351-352).

These concise and official statements both show the admirable function of the theologian in the Church and define the limits of his role, and its relationship to the magisterium.

This completes our condensed review of what the magisterium says about itself, its responsibility toward revelation, and its relationship with theologians. Let us now attempt to make a few observations on the consequences of this teaching for the pilgrim contemplative.

The pilgrim knows that he owes his loyalty to Christ and his submission to the authority of Christ. It follows then that he owes his loyalty and submission to those who have inherited the magisterial office appointed by Christ—for they share in Christ's authority and enjoy the guidance of His Spirit in accord with a promise (John 16:5-15). By contrast, a theologian is invested with no authority but his own competence. It is a self-appointed role, and thus the value of a theologian's teaching depends on his knowledge of God's revelation, the subjection of his mind to that revelation in the "obedience of faith," (Rom. 17:26), his use of authentic Catholic theological method in explicating revelation, the native brilliance of his mind, and the degree of graced understanding which the Spirit gratuitously gives him. Since a private theologian has no guarantee of special guidance by the Spirit, his doctrine must be examined for authenticity by those whose authoritative pastoral office assures them the guidance of the Spirit for this very work.

The pilgrim whose spirituality or apostolate requires him to stay abreast of theological developments has a special problem. No one should aspire to such a spirituality or such an apostolate who does not have the competence and the knowledge of the faith to manage the task.

His first task is to know well what the Scriptures and the tradition and the teaching Church say in the matters that concern him. This will enable him to detect readily the more open breaches of faith and theological method. He will easily single out those scriptural exegetes and theologians who count the Scriptures as a privileged record of religious experiences, but not the inerrant word of God. He will be sensitive to the Christian deist whose writings subtly reveal his failure to believe in miracles or in prayer. He will recognize the ethician who parts with him in not holding that the morality of the New Testament is divinely revealed, and in not accepting the terrible warning against sin and the stern command to fidelity which Jesus gives: "If your hand causes you to sin, cut it off; it is better for you to enter life maimed than with two hands to go to hell" (Mark 9:44). He will be alert for the theologian who shows a weakness of faith or character in his penchant for doctrinal selectivity —writing beautifully about matters which appeal to him—such as the humanity of Jesus—and allowing others to sink out of sight—such as the divinity of Jesus and His self-awareness of His divine nature.

He will have no trouble in singling out the theologian who, in his passion for freedom and the cause of pluralistic theology, tends to undermine the role of the magisterium. The clear-minded pilgrim will always remember that the magisterium is not the enemy of freedom but only the guardian of truth, and therefore, of freedom also. For Jesus said: "If you continue in my word . . . the truth will make you free" (John 8:31).

Some unwise pilgrims think they can follow the doctrine of a given theologian until it is condemned as heretical. The truth is that most theologians who teach doctrinal errors and heresies are never condemned, for it is both impossible and unnecessary: impossible because such things occur too frequently; unnecessary because most of them pass in and out of Church history like leaves blowing away in the fall, dying of their own mortality.

The sent contemplative who attempts to forward his mission with anything but the soundest doctrine is at best unwise and at worst one who has gone astray. There is no word so powerful for his work as the Word of God; there is no interpretation of it so effective for his work as that given by the magisterium. (The pilgrim whose mission *is* to assist in the development of doctrine must properly nuance this guideline of course).

It is generally not too difficult to locate the really sound theologians. They manifest their reverence for the Scriptures and for Catholic tradition. They show respect for the magisterium, especially for the Sovereign Pontiff. Their works help to unify Christians by showing the unity of the faith and its harmony with reason. They never foster division in the name of diversity. They teach that pluralism is healthy only when it promotes unity amid and through diversity. They manifest the humility of faith. They are not masters of the truth but its servants. They are servants of the community and the magisterium in their role of explaining Jesus Christ. They are not a counter-magisterium. They recognize full well that they have no authority but their insights into the truths of faith. It is not difficult to locate such theologians, for "you will know them by their fruits" (Matthew 7:16). It is not dangerous to lean on their teaching, for even the mistakes of the humble are not deadly, and can easily be corrected when they come to light, providing that the disciple is himself humble.

One other aspect of the theological enterprise must be considered. The role of some theologians is the role of the pioneer. They put forth new interpretations—they say *yes* or *no* to some movement in the Church—even before the magisterium (as Pope Paul's teaching quoted above clearly indicates). By the nature of things, then, new developments in theology are untested, tentative, and very possibly erroneous. They may be dangerous—and may appear so even when they are not.

This means that an innovative theologian's role carries the labors of a pioneer. Sometimes he is unwittingly a false prophet and his doctrine has to be condemned: "Any one who goes ahead and does not abide in the doctrine of Christ does not have God; he who abides in the doctrine has both the Father and the Son. If any one comes to you and does not bring this doctrine, do not receive him into the house" (2 John 9). Sometimes he only appears to be a false prophet and is persecuted as one even when he is not. This is the burden of the true prophet, that he is often rejected not only by the ungodly, but by those who ought to be hearing the same Spirit as he, but are not hearing. It is a fact in the history of the Church that some of its greatest theologians were for a time treated with suspicion and disciplined by the magisterium.

In order not to add to the inevitable burden of innovative theologians, the pilgrim might well test his conduct against the following norms:

1. Do not condemn a position which the magisterium has not condemned, unless you have the theological competence to do so, or unless you are consciously speaking prophetically in the Spirit to expose a danger to the faithful.

2. Do not *firmly* adopt a novel theological position before the magisterium or the body of the faithful does so. Without private revelation, no man can have the certitude of faith in a matter wherein the whole Church does not have that certitude.

3. If you adopt a novel theological position even for the best of reasons, do it tentatively, and make this evident to others so you do not lead them astray.

4. Do not become exclusively a follower of any one contemporary theologian. Be guided by the advice Pope Paul VI gave to theologians themselves (in the address identified above): "Divine truth is preserved in the whole Christian community by the Holy Spirit. Hence within this community you will find truth more easily, if you cultivate ties of communion with the entire community of the faithful . . . (and) develop more heartfelt communion with the Church's magisterium."

The pilgrim hears many voices within the Church, and he can profit by many of them, but he should attune himself to the authoritative voice of the Church's magisterium, above all to our Holy Father the Bishop of Rome. Revelation itself attests to this, as the documentation of this and preceding chapters makes manifest.

In the next chapter we will consider more interior norms for a union of mind and heart with the whole Church and its faith.

16.

Norms for a Living Union

with Revelation and the Church

Every Christian must cultivate a living union with revelation and the Church, but this objective stands out with special emphasis in the case of the sent contemplative. He has been chosen as a unique agent in disseminating revelation and promoting the growth of the Kingdom-Church. The primary means of his agency is his *incessant contemplative contact* with the living revelation and the Church which communicates it. His living union with revelation and the Church is the source of his own salvation and the means of his apostolate. If his union is perfect enough to form a pattern for others, it may be his most valuable apostolic contribution.

To gather our norms for a living union of the sent contemplative with revelation, let us begin by recalling what revelation is. *Revelation* is God unveiling Himself. *Faith* is man's affirmative response to this divine unveiling. Revelation and faith are, therefore, interpersonal in nature. A man's whole self—mind, affections, experiences —is involved in the response of faith. This recall of the interpersonal nature of revelation and faith makes it evident that authentic norms for a living union with revelation and the Church must include norms for guiding both the mind and the heart, and norms for judging the value of religious experience. If these norms are to do their job, they must instruct us in listening to the Spirit, for it is He who communicates revelation.

Furthermore, since God-made-flesh reveals Himself to and through His people, we respond to Him in the same way: to and with His people. Living union with revelation is therefore ecclesial in nature. It includes union with the Catholic Church. Our norms will be based on this truth.

These norms for union with revelation and the Catholic Church will also serve as guidelines for the discernment of spirits and for all spiritual decision making. For this reason we will have to refer back to this chapter later in our treatise.

In gathering guidelines for this living union, we are not focusing solely on dogmatic or juridical criteria. We are rather putting together practical objective and subjective norms for a vibrant spiritual and apostolic life lived in union with God and His people. The norms we gather will not be the only correct ones, and they may be far from being perfect ones, but they should prove serviceable. To have no norms at all is worst of all.

These norms must contain both objective guidelines and subjective ones. The objective guidelines are necessary because it is part of the revelation through which God instructs and commands us through other men; and so we must have norms covering those whom we ought to hear and believe. The subjective guidelines are necessary because in the end a man must listen to his own heart and obey his own conscience. Our desire and longing is that in actual practice we will find that the objective and subjective norms harmonize and resonate for our peace. To realize this desire we have taken the trouble in the preceding chapters to refresh ourselves on the objective nature of revelation as it comes to us through the Catholic Church; and we now will take the trouble to look carefully at the subjective norms for living union with God and His people. Jesus Himself guarantees the basic possibility of this *harmony* between the truth of objective revelation and our *inner perception of it:* "My teaching is not mine, but his who sent me; if any man's will is to do his will, he shall know whether the teaching is from God or whether I am speaking on my own authority" (John 7:16-17).

The norms we are about to assemble will be chosen on the basis of the following convictions: first, that God *does* illumine our mind in matters of faith so that all true faith-conclusions which a believer draws are instances of grace breaking into consciousness—even though we are usually not aware at the time that it is a work of God, for we are aware only of our own efforts to think; second, that affections stirred by faith are other instances of grace breaking into consciousness, though we may not be aware that it is so except by a reflection such as this, wherein we recall that the Spirit of Love not only thinks through us, but prays and loves through us; third and last, that mystical experiences are another legitimate source of knowledge and "feeling" for the truth, and that mystical experience is a formal experience of grace breaking into consciousness. In making use of these convictions, we are making it self-evident that our hope of a living union with revelation and the Church is a supernatural hope. It is based more on God than on ourselves. We are also making evident the nature of the union we hope for. We hope for union with God and the Church in mind, heart, and religious experiences.

There is another problem which confronts us at the outset of this search for norms of unity. Divine revelation says, "The precepts of the Lord are right, rejoicing the heart; the commandment of the Lord is pure, enlightening the eyes" (Ps. 19:8). If this is so, why are norms for discerning His revelation even necessary? Why is there such disagreement on the content of revelation? God's revelation itself answers these questions. The problem is not with the clarity of the revelation, but with the deviousness of the human heart, which sees only what it wants to see: "The heart is deceitful above all things, and desperately corrupt; who can understand it?" (Jer. 17:9).

Every wrong attachment and hang-up we have clouds our minds and disorders our wills. Before we can think rightly or believe rightly we must be right in ourselves. St. Ignatius Loyola saw this clearly, and provided a help toward the right ordering of the self. He gave us his *Spiritual Exercises,* whose purpose is "guidance in self-mastery and the management of life, and to that end . . . guidance in making the appropriate decisions only in moments of inner personal freedom from those emotions and other biases which militate against authentic Christianity" (#21). From this consideration we can draw up a postulate which antecedes all our other norms for living union with revelation and the Church.

POSTULATE: *A Catholic must make regular use of spiritual exercises to ward off the spiritual blindness and hardness of heart against which revelation constantly warns. Just as a man has to wash his eyeglasses to see clearly, the believer has to wash the mind and heart by prayers and penance and meditation on revelation, if he is see it with clarity.*

We will make our norms more useful if we group them according to our purposes. We need one category of norms for the guidance of the will and affections, another for the guidance of reason, and a third for assessing the authenticity of mystical experiences.

Now that we have organized our categories, we can begin to collect our norms for a living union with revelation and the church. CATEGORY I. *Faith Norms for the Right Use of the Will and the Guidance of the Affections.*

Just as a car cannot propel itself without an engine, man does not move without a motive. None of us will perseveringly seek a living union with revelation in the face of all the obstacles which are bound to arise, unless we put on the mind of Christ. To do the will of God was food and drink to Him. The need for this motivation leads us to formulate our first guideline.

NORM ONE: *Cultivate a growing desire of mind and heart to search out and carry out God's will.*

The revelation concerning God's will makes it evident that He has delegated His authority to legitimate human overseers of both Church and State. Since the rebellion of sin in us biases us against obedience, we will go astray if we do not overcome this bias by conscious effort. This leads us to our second norm.

NORM TWO: *Cultivate obedience to ecclesiastical authority in matters of faith and morals, and to other authorities in their proper spheres.*

To use our will and affections rightly, we must have a *right heart.* The heart cannot be wholly right if the mind is wrong, for mind and heart work closely together—so closely in fact that the Scriptures use the heart as a symbol of both mind and affectivity. The heart can readily go astray without the head—so readily that western man has become so distrustful of his affections that good men sometimes ignore them in making their decisions. Their excessive distrust is warranted only when the heart has not been purified by long obedience to God's law, or by many years of a life of true love. A purified heart can often excel the formal act of reason in discerning the right way. The reason for this is that the pure heart is full of love, and love is the best judge of the way of love. This is simply the *principle of connaturality* at work. Blessed Peter Faber reports that St. Ignatius, that gifted discerner of spirits, said: *Unctio doceat te de omnibus, Let your devotion guide you* (let us remember that *devotion* is an affectionate readiness to do *what God wants*). Revelation confirms this belief that a good heart is the best discerner of spirits—provided its reliance is on God, not itself: "Establish the counsel of your own heart, for no one is more faithful to you than it is. For a man's soul sometimes keeps him better informed than seven watchmen sitting high on a watchtower. And besides all this pray to the Most High that he may direct your way in truth" (Sir. 37:13-15). This reflection on the heart helps us to formulate our next norm.

NORM THREE: *A pilgrim must pay attention to his own heart, and favor those ways of living which bring him stable peace and joy.*

There is only one case in which it is easy to do what we ought with our will and feelings, and that is when we love what is commanded. Since God's revelation commands us to belong to the Church, this command will sour us if we do not cultivate an attitude of affection toward the Church. Yet many members of the Church cultivate those who never cease attacking the Church. Their spirit toward the Church is not right. What lover ever listened readily to one who even verbally abused his beloved? Since love is the building force of human hearts and a spontaneous discerner of the right relationship to the one loved, we will not have a healthy relationship to the Church without affection for it. This truth leads to the next guideline.

NORM FOUR: *Love the Church loyally. Put up with her failings generously. Correct disorders in the Church with the gentleness of love. Yet boldly denounce outright evils (cf. Matthew 21:12f; 23:1f).*

The will and affections are the central actors in our relationship with God and the Church. Faith without love is dead. Since *personal religious experience* is what most readily awakens our love and most spontaneously attracts and forms the heart's relationship to God and the Church, the value of personal religious experience should not be underestimated. Personal religious experience is the *subjective* foundation of a pilgrim's faith. It is also a major source of his own religious identity and personality. If this is so, a pilgrim ought never to forget his own religious experiences.

The pilgrim who loses contact with his own past religious experiences has lost his subjective religious identity, just as a Catholic who drifts out of the Church has lost his objective religious identity. The ex-Catholic is bereft of objective norms of faith and morals; the forgetter of his own religious experiences is bereft of a sense of personal relationship with God and the sense of direction which that personal relationship would give his life.

It is imperative, therefore, that a pilgrim never cease contemplating those personal religious experiences which have affected the direction of his whole life. Once a personal religious experience gives him *the feel* of some truth of faith (the joy of loving God, the holiness of chastity; the sense of an apostolic call, etc.), he is in possession of the best norm for subjective judgment of anything related to that truth. Does this new proposal, this new direction, which is supposedly an authentic development of what he has experienced before, resonate with or grate against the feel he has for it? Let it be judged accordingly, providing the judgment does not conflict with the objective norms of revelation. This gives us our next norm.

NORM FIVE: *Keep in contact with the springs of your first graces, because they provide living measuring rods for later religious experiences.*

In the first five norms we have affirmed the guidance-value of the heart even though we know that the history of religion tells of many deluded pilgrims driven to heresy and madness by their enthusiasms. We affirm the high place of the heart because it would be unchristian and inhuman to do otherwise. We affirm it with confidence because, taught by revelation and by experience, we do not let the heart stand alone. The affections are most dangerous when the mind is empty. How can the heart resonate with truth if both mind and heart have fed on errors and do not know the truth? So we turn now from guidelines for the heart to guidelines for the mind.

CATEGORY II. *Faith Norms for the Guidance of the Mind.*

Faith comes by hearing, and so the first way we enter into living union with revelation is with the mind. To grow in this union and to safeguard ourselves from error, we need to ponder the content of our faith, day and night, as the Scriptures exhort us. We ought also to keep up with the Church's understanding of the practical meaning of revelation for our day. This imperative suggests our first guideline for the mind.

NORM ONE: *Know the deposit of faith and its exposition in Scripture, tradition, the teaching of the magisterium, and the lives of the people of God, especially the Saints. Meditate these sources perpetually, trusting in the Spirit to give understanding.*

When the truth is known, the whole mind and heart can learn to resonate with it wherever it appears, and to detect, often readily, the false note of religious untruth.

The pondering of revelation is a sacred use of the light of the mind. While this sanctifies the mind, it does not make it inerrant, or remove freedom of judgment. The proof of this is that some heretics have been brilliant, and knowledgeable in faith and theology.

In our meditation, therefore, we ought to remember that while nothing can be judged without the intellect, not everything can be judged by the human intellect alone. Therefore, while authority may be the weakest argument in matters of human knowledge, it is the strongest argument in divine knowledge. We believe revelation *on the authority of God revealing,* and we interpret it according to the authoritative teaching of those in the Church to whom Christ has in a special way extended His teaching authority and the guidance of the Spirit. Further, the history of the magisterium, as well as the word of God, indicate that Church authority has the right and responsibility of setting the pace for the development of doctrine according to the wise pedagogy of the Spirit: "And I tell you, you are Peter, and on this rock I will build my Church . . . Whatever you bind on earth shall be bound in heaven" (Matthew 16:18-19). This brings us to our next norm for a living union of the mind with revelation and the Church.

NORM TWO: *Know the authority of the ecclesiastical magisterium and abide by it with devotion, without grudging, to the extent a good conscience permits it, in accord with the teaching of Scripture: "Obey your leaders and submit to them; for they are keeping watch over your souls, as men who will have to give account. Let them do this joyfully, and not sadly, for that would be of no advantage to you" (Hebr. 13:17).*

Thus reasons's pride will be subdued, and the sweetness and peace of the believing heart will be cultivated. Our attitude should be: to always believe what the whole Church believes; to believe what the magisterium teaches as far as an informed conscience permits; never to disbelieve what the magisterium teaches by dogmatic definition.

Though the magisterium guides us in matters of objective faith and morals, it does not relieve us of a multitude of personal decisions in other matters, large and small. How is a pilgrim to know whether to marry, or to apply to a religious community, or to live the single life in the world? What career should he pursue, what apostolate should he serve in? What spiritual books should he read?

An event from the life of St. Ignatius helps provide an answer. Because a book by Erasmus was repeatedly recommended to him, he began reading it. He noticed it was disturbing his burning love of God and devotion to His will. He threw the book away. The discernment of the spirits which moved him had given him what he needed to know to make the right decision: Anything decreasing peace and joy in God and causing unrest and sadness is wrong for me (unless I am sad at having to make a sacrifice for God). This brings us to our next intellectual norm.

NORM THREE: *Know which problems you have to solve for yourself, and how to go about it through appropriate gathering of the facts, and through reflection, and discernment of spirits.* (This norm and this whole chapter make it evident that not only every sent contemplative but every human being has the responsibility of learning *how* to distinguish between good and bad impulses; and above all he must learn *how* to discern and do the will of God).

There are many matters in which one should supplement his own judgment by heeding the axiom: *No man is a good judge in his own case.* This axiom is especially pertinent in religious matters, for serious wrong judgments can be very destructive. It is accordingly the practice of serious Catholics to find a knowledgeable spiritual guide. He can listen to a pilgrim's experiences, take an objective view of them, examine them in the light of revelation and of broad personal religious experience, and then either confirm or question the pilgrim's own decisions regarding them. Through this interchange the pilgrim learns how to gain a more objective view of his own experiences, and how to be more aware of the impulses that move him, and subject them to discernment. If he has any doctrinal problems the knowledge of a learned director will often make them evaporate. Our next norm, then:

NORM FOUR: *Consult a wise spiritual director, regularly if possible, but at least at times of major decisions, and in times of crisis.*

We all have to make judgments about such things as to whom we should go for spiritual direction, what spiritual writers and theological writers we should read, what movements to join, etc. What criterion should we use to make these judgments besides that of religious doctrine, which is not always adequate? One of the best of all criteria for assessing the activities and teachings of a fellow Catholic whose doctrine at least appears sound is *his effect upon the community.* Does he operate in an orderly way in the community? Does he unite the community, or splinter it? Is he a peacemaker or does he fire up unnecessary controversy? Does he have the primary effect of enlightening and inspiring or of negating and protesting? Here again Jesus is exemplar. Though He engaged in controversy when attacked, His doctrine is a web of truth and inspiration, not of fulmination and condemnation. To arguers and murmurers Jesus once said: "Do not murmur among yourselves. No one can come to me unless the Father who sent me draws him" (John 6:43-44). Since it is union in love, peace, and joy which are signs of the Kingdom, we should be wary of revolutionaries and dissidents and their tactics. Our next guideline then:

NORM FIVE: *Discern the spirit of persons and movements by their effects, especially their effect on the community. "You will know them by their fruits" (Matthew 7:16).*

We ought not only avoid aligning with doctrinal revolutionaries and dissidents in the Church, but also to shun their tactics. One of their most imflammatory tactics is to exaggerate and exacerbate differences by couching them in falsely irreconcilable polarities like "Scripture or tradition," "conscience or magisterium," "rigid moralism or situation ethics," "dead doctrine or process theology," etc. Faith problems rightly put never present such irrational choices. The spirit of the man who poses them is not right.

Erasmus once said: "There is no reason to believe black is white, even if the Pope were to state this in a proclamation. And I know he will never do this." Contrast the spirit Erasmus manifested in this statement with that of St. Ignatius, who wrote: "If we wish to proceed securely in all things, we must hold fast to the following principle: What seems to me white, I will believe black if the hierarchial Church so defines. For I must be convinced that in Christ our Lord, the bridegroom, and in His spouse the Church, only one Spirit holds sway, which governs and rules for the salvation of souls" (*Spiritual Exercises*, Puhl transl., #365). Our next guideline adopts this spirit:

NORM SIX: *Avoid setting up problems according to irreconcilable polarities, and have faith that all seeming irreconcilables will yield in time to the wisdom of the Church.*

The most fundamental intellectual guideline for our doctrinal position ought to be our faith, which is our acceptance of what God has revealed. Divisions in the Church often have their source in members who adhere to some doctrinal position *for reasons other than faith.* Some *firmly* accept a *questionable* doctrine on the authority of their favorite theologian. This is *bad faith.* The only adequate motive of faith is God and His authoritative representatives. When a pilgrim's own faith-knowledge is not adequate to deal with an issue, he should not take a firm stand on it until the magisterium makes its authoritative judgment (cf. Gal. 1:6-9; 1 Cor. 1:10-13).

It is wrong to join a doctrinal party in the Church, wrong to become polarized as a liberal or conservative because faith demands we listen for truth in every quarter, and incessantly think and meditate and pray and purify our faith-understanding. We ought to imitate the theologian who said: "I am in the extreme middle!" Our next guideline:

NORM SEVEN: *Take a doctrinal stand on no criterion of judgment except revelation itself, and the faith response due to it by a Catholic.*

As members of the faith community, we should feel the responsibility of subjecting our use of our theological innovative powers to the good of the community. With regard to the use of words, even secular communities keep rather careful watch on neologisms, for their uncontrolled proliferation would cause a breakdown of communication. The history of heresy in the Church cautions us against theological neologisms. So our next guideline:

NORM EIGHT: *Be wary of new theological terms for traditional doctrines. We should not hasten to use or accept them because in the past they have often cloaked fuzzy thinking or wrong and heretical doctrine.*

Christian as it is to esteem human emotions and affections, and right as it is to give them an honored place in our religious life, we have to reject the anti-rational conduct of those who measure the value of religious practices almost solely according to the emotional response they evoke. This is no more sound than measuring the value of food solely by the pleasure it gives, and the value of medicine by its taste. This emotional approach to religion is sensate, and more a religion of the body than of the whole person. It is contrary to revelation, the Church, and common sense. It is nevertheless a common fault. Our next guideline then:

NORM NINE: *Do not evaluate a religious practice solely or even primarily according to the degree it stirs the affections, or the amount of satisfaction it provides.*

Reason illumined by faith can easily know the truth in some matters of faith and morals, but there are many gray areas in which it can go either way in its judgment. In such cases reason is assisted more by the *life* than by the *doctrine* of Christ. He lived in such holiness that He was far removed from sin, and so could say: "Which of you convicts me of sin?" (John 8:46). Accordingly:

NORM TEN: *Avoid not only outright doctrinal errors and moral evils, but every position and every action which compromise clear and unambiguous adherence to Christ and the Church. "Abstain from every form of evil" (2 Thess. 5:22).*

History shows that even brilliant and holy members of the Church have at times been divided within themselves, their subjective experience drawing them in one direction, and the objective body of revelation and/or the magisterium drawing them in the other. In such circumstances, the Catholic Saints have embraced the mystery of the Cross and the crucifixion of their own impulses in favor of union with the whole Church:

NORM ELEVEN: *When rended by a clash of objective and subjective norms for union with revelation and the Church, be patient in the mystery of the Church. Pray and reflect, seek wise coun-*

sel, and await the resolution God will provide. Living union with revelation is more His work than ours: "The Lord is God, and he has given us light" (Ps. 118:27).

CATEGORY III: *Faith Norms for Assessing Mystical Experience.*

We affirmed (under category one) the central place of personal religious experience in every pilgrim's religious life. We are presently considering a privileged form of personal religious experience called *mystical.*

A mystical experience is one which cannot be produced voluntarily, even for an instant, by the human will or by any human means. It is the work of God. While this description tells us in a general way *what* a mystical experience is, it does not tell us in a concrete instance if an experience is genuinely mystical. That is one reason we need further norms.

Mystical experiences are divided into various types such as visions, locutions, profound experiences of God, illuminations, sudden surges of faith, hope, or love of God not explainable except as grace, inspiration to adopt some course of action, prophetic knowledge of the future, etc.

Mystical experience has its own unique importance for the sent contemplative. Mysticism is implicated in the fact that, having been assimilated to Christ, the *Servant of Yahweh* (Is. 42:1, 5), the pilgrim now depends on the perpetual guidance and inspiration of the Holy Spirit for on-going knowledge of his mission and of the manner in which he is to carry it out. This divine guidance need never take place *dramatically*, but it takes place constantly in the apostle who faithfully discerns the spirits that move him. After all, the foundation of Christian discernment of spirits is the conviction that God moves minds and hearts by grace, and that at times this impulse from Him is distinctly felt and can be clearly distinguished from all others, as when some feel so definitely called to religious life, to the priesthood, or to some other commitment and service. Such distinctly conscious experiences of grace are mystical experiences. (Note how they fulfill the definition of mystical experience given above).

Every Catholic ought, then, to accept and not reject the possibility of mystical experience. To reject it out of false humility or fear is to corrupt one's faith in a way which can render him wholly insensitive to the origin and meaning of any mystical impulses which may stir in him.

NORM ONE: *Cultivate an attitude of faith-acceptance of mystical events, whether as regards yourself or others, particularly those others for whom you may act as a spiritual guide.*

A mystical experience is a gift from God. It has its effect instantaneously *if it is genuinely from Him.* If it is not, it will have no such effect. In either case it is wasteful to spend time and energy trying to discern whether or not it was really a mystical experience. (Overconcern with mysticism can also lead to pride, delusions, and an empty set of religious values.) There are two general exceptions to this rule of not giving time and attention to a mystical experience: if recall brings a spontaneous increase of love of God; or if the experience calls us to carry out some action. In the latter case we *have* to discern the source, lest in carrying out the action we waste our energy on some burden not from God, and perhaps even contrary to His will for us.

NORM TWO: *Unless it is necessary or certainly profitable, neither spend time recalling a putative mystical experience nor spend time and energy assessing whether or not it was mystical.*

We accept mystical experiences because they are vouched for by revelation, and they consist to some degree in private revelation, that is, in God revealing something of Himself *to me subjectively.* Genuine mystical experience is valuable but not as valuable or as necessary for salvation as baptism or the Eucharist (John 3:4; 6:53). Its major value lies in the increase of love and union with God that it produces, and the service of God and man that it engenders. Without love it is nothing (1 Cor. 12—13), and divorced from humility it is a menace. Therefore:

NORM THREE: *Do not exaggerate the worth of mystical experience.*

Mystical experiences and revelations that purport to be genuine are by that fact subject to the objective norms of revelation and the teaching Church. Therefore:

NORM FOUR: *If mystical experience runs contrary to faith or morals, reject it outright as from a source other than God, or contaminated by an influence other than God.*

It can happen that someone is so taken by what he thinks is a mystical experience that he will feel obliged to adhere to it even if it sets him in opposition to revelation or the teaching Church. He should be exhorted to study revelation and pray over it and the example of the Saints, and speak openly with a wise counselor.

NORM FIVE: *Every person must follow his own conscience, but when there are objective signs questioning its soundness, he ought to take every step he can to test himself so that he does not allow a false conscience to make him stand against God and the Church.*

The Christian religion draws a man to union with God in total love, and union with man in the likeness of Christ's union. Every genuine religious experience contributes to this purpose. Hence:

NORM SIX: *A mystical experience which does not increase the theological virtues of faith, hope, and love is not from God and not genuine.*

God sometimes invites to something or commands something through the medium of a mystical experience. If personal conviction tested by consultation is that the invitation was from God, it must not be refused lightly; if the command is certainly from God, the mystic's responsibility is evident:

NORM SEVEN: *A pilgrim is bound in conscience to carry out a command which stands as certainly given him by God (cf. Acts of the Apostles 4:19, and passim; St. Joan of Arc, etc.).*

NORM EIGHT: *For more refined and subtle norms a pilgrim should study the works of the recognized Saints and teachers of mysticism: St. Teresa of Avila, St. John of the Cross, and, as regards the discernment of spirits, the writings of St. Ignatius of Loyola, especially his "Rules for the Discernment of Spirits," in* THE SPIRITUAL EXERCISES OF ST. IGNATIUS.

17.

Trials of Growth

The pilgrim's progress has led him into a strange world which is the contrary of the one he had hoped to enter. He had sought a world in which God and man were completely reconciled, a world in which he could find the Divine everywhere, a world where God's Kingdom was established. Instead, he finds that the world says little about God now, and even in his own person there is a vast region in which God does not appear, and a deeply interior region, hardly accessible to himself, into which God has withdrawn. He knows of the presence of God and His Kingdom there only by a deep, living faith, and an enduring peace unaltered by the storms in his other regions and in the world around him. Speaking in a general way, God is experienced as neither absent nor present, but, as it were, dormant.

The pilgrim is exhausted from years of intense work and prayer. He is feeling the strain of relationships with many around him. He is worn down by the struggle to do God's will without rigidity and without laxity. His mind, so long attuned to God, is now relatively free of wayward phantasms and daydreams. His five senses lie supine, having given up hope of attaining their fill of natural pleasures. He no longer experiences the former unruly impulses to pursue bodily comforts and pleasures to excess. The world of sense desires has lost its hold on him. He knows too well that it has no power to fulfill its wild promises, and even its wildest promises do not speak to his own true desires. He has chosen austerity because it leads him to his true desires, however slowly. His true desire is simply told in prayer: "A day in thy courts is better than a thousand elsewhere. I would rather be a doorkeeper in the house of my God than dwell in the tents of wickedness" (Ps. 84:10-11).

The distress which the senses endure during this period is extreme. A dream which one pilgrim recounts will illustrate this:

> In my dream I felt pain, and I looked over my body to discover the cause. With horror I saw that millions of layers of rock shale were imbedded deep in my flesh like razor blades. I pulled out one piece and felt exquisite relief. But when I looked at the uncounted shards remaining, I gave up in despair.

This dream expresses figuratively the many sufferings which the pilgrim finds inescapable so long as he remains true to his calling.

There is distress of both body and soul from the strain his way of life puts on human relationships. The pilgrim has continued to pursue the Father's Truth in earnest. It is a mysterious Truth, but this he knows, that it is Christ, and this he experiences, that whoever pursues this Truth is persecuted with Christ, even by many who claim to be pursuing Christ themselves.

To know Jesus is to know the Truth that is the Father Himself: "He who has seen me has seen the Father" (John 14:9). Yet how hard to really know Jesus! Many saw Him and did not know Him. Many heard Him and did not believe Him. Yet the pilgrim trusts the Father. The Father will not conceal from him the Truth that is Jesus. Was not the Father compelled by His friendship with Abraham to confide in him, according to the Father's own words: "Shall I hide from Abraham what I am about to do . . . ?" (Gen. 18:17). Surely the Father will share with him the mystery of Jesus.

It is, in fact, what the Father has already shared with the pilgrim that gets the pilgrim in trouble. To have conviction about the Father's Truth revealed to him through constant pondering of Scripture and Church teaching has become second nature to him. He speaks about the truths of revelation with conviction and lives them with commitment, and this brings him into conflict with the many who hold that truth is hardly attainable. They are annoyed, inconvenienced, even scandalized by his certitude.

Yet he can make no apology, for his certitude is not a product of neat reason but of faith. He is willing to be corrected, but not intimidated. He is insistent in speech because he cares less for what people think about him than for what they think about the word of God. He has received the Lord's truths in trust, and he is responsible for sharing them with the Lord's other disciples. He is not asking them to believe because he speaks, but to believe what he speaks because if they are God's own offspring they must recognize that what he speaks is from God. This is what Jesus teaches: "My teaching is not mine, but his who sent me; if any man's will is to do his will, he shall know whether the teaching is from God or whether I am speaking on my own authority" (John 7:16-17). In accord with these words, the pilgrim is asking others not so much to believe his word, as to listen to it, and to believe what the Spirit says about it in their own hearts.

The pilgrim is only too aware that the way he speaks or lives the Truth is itself inadequate, and this awareness is itself suffering. His efforts to understand and incarnate the revelation have brought him into sharp encounter with one after another of his own limitations. The only adequate way to speak the Word of the Father is the way the Father speaks it—with unspeakable love. But until the pilgrim can speak the Word adequately, he must speak it as best he can.

The pilgrim also continues to experience the hostility incurred by anyone who does not hide his bold aspirations to Christliness. He observes that the faults of one who confesses no such aspirations are often treated indulgently, even approvingly, while the least fault of the Christ-committed person provokes attacks on him ranging from mockery to condemnation as a hypocrite. What he is only trying in hope to become he is condemned for not being now.

There are certain pilgrims excepted from this hostile treatment. They are the men and women who are endowed with such natural gifts of intelligence and personal charm that their fellows indulgently grant them leave to add sanctity to all the rest. But let the person whom the world considers a "no account" aspire greatheartedly to the grace of God and he will be abused for his presumption. The world does not understand that such a one is neither presumptive nor proud, for it does not understand a hope that is placed in God alone.

A pilgrim does not need the world's permission to aspire to such holiness and the bold pilgrim does not ask it. If the world's permission were awaited, how few would respond to Christ! The pilgrim who boldly aspires to Christliness forges ahead, though he may be assailed like the blind man in the Gospels who persisted in clamoring to Jesus for help.

The timid or unsure pilgrim is upset by those social pressures which "put him in his place," and wonders if he *is* foolish and presumptuous. The efforts to repress him and the umbrage which even his friends sometimes take undermine both his self-esteem and his conviction that his aspirations are from God.

What is to be done in such distress? It helps to make a distinction between the *call* to Christliness and the presumption that one has achieved Christliness. A pilgrim need have no fear of not being called to perfection, for *all* are called. But a pilgrim may well fear he is "putting on airs" about a perfection he has no wise reached. One pilgrim writes:

> When I hear talks on prayer, I wish that more stress could be put on the importance of living a genuine Christian life first of all. I have come across so many who make formal prayer every day but they have never really learned the A B C's of Christian living. They do not associate their prayer life with genuine Christian living and this has led them into great delusions about themselves. It is true that we are all weak and we all fail now and then. But when it is habitual and these failures do not lessen gradually, one is led to wonder if their prayer life is authentic. There are people who have delusions of sanctity, and one should examine himself in the matter.

My own experience as a spiritual director, however, gives me reason to believe that often these people know their imperfection, and their airs are simply defenses against those who would write them off as "no accounts."

The well-balanced pilgrim does not feel persecuted in a personal way by these harassments any more than does a soldier on a battlefield. He realizes that whoever forges ahead in the likeness of Christ will have to bear the brunt of the counterattacks of a sinful world. Even his *own* sinfulness within him rebels against him. The world's hostility is predictable and inevitable. All men make their demands on one another, but the pilgrim demands an end to sin, and society finds this the most outrageous demand of all.

The pilgrim who does not allow himself to be suppressed or soured by hostility will in the end gain great advantage from it. The world's contempt purges any residual inflated self-esteem, and teaches the pilgrim that pride and holiness are an absurb contradiction which none can tolerate. The world's contempt schools him in the necessity of being God's agent in a spirit of heart-felt lowliness without which he is useless. It frees him from excess dependence on the approval of men; it teaches him he cannot please two masters, and so frees him to please God alone. It fortifies him with St. Paul's attitude toward illegitimate human judgments: "With me it is a very small thing that I should be judged by you or by any human court. I do not even judge myself. I am not aware of anything against myself, but I am not thereby acquitted. It is the Lord who judges me. Therefore do not pronounce judgment before the time, before the Lord comes" (1 Cor. 4:3-5).

These experiences are hard on human relationships, which are already strained by the pilgrim's condition. He is exhausted by the demands of this life of total faith. He finds it difficult to patiently endure—and at times he denounces—the gossip and shallow, vain and cutting witticisms in which groups often find recreation; and yet, because of his own exhausted condition, he himself has little to contribute in place of these things. He sympathizes with the need for recreation, and sometimes feels he has so little to give that he is reluctant to inflict his company on anyone. Still, he feels resentful and angry if people deliberately avoid him. Pride is hardly his problem; self-esteem slips dangerously low in the seas of his own consciousness, "Lord, save me!" (Matthew 14:30).

One pilgrim in these straits described the help he found through prayer:

> I was depressed by my limited success and my failures despite my best efforts. I was saddened by my lack of status and by animosities which I felt I could not shake off and be faithful to grace. I thought of Jesus rejected by Judas and run out on by His friends. I prayed, and realized how completely I was in God's hands, and I came up with three practices to sustain me in these trials. The first was to repeat over and over in faith: "What is better for me than your will, O Lord?" The second was to make a petition: "If I am really as poor as I feel, then You make me rich, O Lord!" The third practice came out of my admiration for King David. When his own son made war on him and he had to flee, an enemy followed him hurling curses and denunciations. Instead of killing or punishing the man, David said: "If he is cursing because the Lord has said to him, 'Curse David,' who then shall say, 'Why have you done so?' Let him alone and let him curse . . . it may be that the Lord will look upon my affliction, and that the Lord will repay me with good" (2 Sam. 16:10-12). My third practice was to say: 'Lord if I deserve this unjust treatment for my sins, I accept it; if I do not, I gladly endure it with Jesus.' These practices supported me in all I had to endure.

The pilgrim who can accept all from God as David did is secure. Yet some pilgrims are so hard-pressed they feel threatened by an emotional or mental breakdown. In such cases, counsel ought to be sought, but not even counsel should persuade a pilgrim to turn back when he knows God is calling him on.

18.

Difficulties in the Apostolate

The difficulties in the pilgrim's personal and social relationships were considered in the last chapter as they affect his own well-being; now we must look at their effect upon his role as God's agent in the world.

Judged in a human way, the man of God who is unpopular is at best only marginally successful. The man of God who is rejected is a failure. This manner of assessment is not without merit *in some cases.* The emissary of God who *through his own fault* incurs the hostility of the ones to whom he has been sent is himself impeding the spread of the Gospel.

We must, however, be ready to judge God's rejected emissaries in another way—the way we look at Christ, Son and Servant of the Father. Though sent by the Father, and though He gave no cause in Himself, He was despised and rejected by men because they wanted not His Gospel. Son though He was, He became the Suffering Servant foretold by Isaias (42:1ff). His own generation deemed Him a pitiable and miserable failure. Tested by the customary norms of *acceptibility* and *accomplishment of tangible goals*, Jesus *was* a failure. Tested by the true purpose of His mission from the Father, He was more than a success. He won the salvation of the world.

Jesus is the pioneer and archetype upon whom other sent contemplatives pattern their lives and their judgments on their success and failure. Like Jesus, they desire to be well received by men; they desire to accomplish all the objectives of service at which they aim. Yet, in a terrible passion of identification with the Lord of the Cross, they hunger and thirst to be rejected, spat upon, made fools of, condemned and destroyed, their mission frustrated as far as human eye can judge.

Caught in the grip of these two contrary drives—to succeed completely and to fail miserably—how are they to conduct themselves? The answer is embodied in Jesus. He did nothing to fail, and He failed to do nothing that would bring success. His one norm was that all He did be done in fidelity to His mission.

The pilgrim should nurture his desire to be crucified with Christ, but he must cultivate every help to the success of his mission that is compatible with his identity as another Christ. He must balance the cultivation of humility with the quest for effectiveness; the desire to be scorned with the need to be accepted; the desire to suffer with the imperative of pouring all his energies into service; the readiness to be despised with the responsibility to maintain his own psychic health. He must be quite ready to be turned down and cast out, but he must also cultivate all the human qualities that will make him acceptable to men in his own right, so that he can gain a hearing for the Gospel in its own right. This is only to do what Jesus did: "He has done all things well!" (Mark 7:37). Only after the pilgrim has given every cause to be accepted by men has he earned the right to find the joy in rejection which Jesus counseled: "Blessed are you when men revile you and persecute you . . . rejoice and be glad, for your reward is great in heaven, for so men persecuted the prophets who were before you" (Matthew 5:11-12).

This dialectic between natural values and supernatural ones is productive of the mature pilgrim contemplative. He is forged in the fusion and interplay of nature and grace at work in him. Only then is he in a position to be acceptable to God and acceptable to man. Only when he has determined that the hungry will be fed, the shelterless sheltered, the unjust social structures dismantled, the Good News preached by word and deed, all to the best of his ability—only then has he absorbed the Scriptural principle for embracing the contrary experiences of life in such a way that instead of destroying him they will make him flourish and develop to maturity.

The reflection we have just made sheds light on many problem areas of a life given to both prayer and service. This light can help us pinpoint problems and set priorities where values clash.

With regard to personal and social relationships, the pilgrim must take every reasonable means to solve problems and enhance his personableness. Some pilgrims have a neurotic tendency to tune in on every hurt inflicted on them, and prematurely draw consolation out of being afflicted for Christ. A more healthy procedure would be to examine oneself critically and constructively. Is the basis of the problem some personality defect which can be corrected, or which at any rate should be endured without a martyr complex? Is the affliction the result of psychic hypersensitivity that needs to be overcome? Is it the result of a nursing of grievances that should be quickly forgiven and forgotten? Is it the result of unreal expectations of gratitude? Problems in these areas may have little to do with the Gospel directly, but indirectly they interfere with the pilgrim's functioning as the ambassador of the Gospel.

Sent contemplatives express and communicate the Gospel through every legitimate human enterprise and service. Each one should cultivate the talents and skills that enhance his expertise, and the qualities that make him appealing and acceptable. Each one ought to pursue whatever learning he needs to make him more acceptable to his peers. He will be more successful if he develops the diction to express both himself and God's revelation in a manner that is both authentic and appealing. He will enhance his acceptability by cultivating the civility that gives grace to his firmness and boldness. The humble and holy pilgrim is undoubtedly joined to God; the suave and competent pilgrim is undoubtedly acceptable to men. The humble and holy, suave and competent pilgrim is pleasing to both God and man. He is the ideal sent contemplative.

Another area of the spiritual life which the pilgrim must adopt and personalize to suit his vocation is asceticism. Asceticism is the practice of self-denial, under the impulse of grace, to atone for sin, to renounce it, and to turn in freedom to embrace God in love. Anyone who has seriously given himself to the demands of contemplation in action knows that the primary asceticism of this form of life is the asceticism of service. This is in accord with the prophetic message: "Is such the fast that I chose, a day for a man to humble himself: Is it to bow down his head like a rush, and to spread sackcloth and ashes under him? Will you call this a fast, and a day acceptable to the Lord? Is this not the fast that I choose: to loose the bonds of wickedness, to undo the thongs of the yoke . . . is it not to share your bread with the hungry, and bring the homeless poor into your house; when you see the naked, to cover him, and not to hide yourself from your own flesh?" (Is. 58:5-7). The apostolate of service carried on in a spirit of constant attunement to God is in itself a crucifying spiritual and ascetical exercise. It fulfills both the duties of one's state of life and many of the demands of asceticism.

There is also the *asceticism of dialogue*, the asceticism involved in the effort to understand others and patiently explain oneself to them. It is an asceticism of community, a work of peace.

In our day of environmental pollution, and of incipient shortages of many natural resources, we could also advocate an asceticism of conservation. As a man in the world, the contemplative in action should set a pattern for the brotherly use of our finite resources.

In the end, however, all these forms of asceticism are not in themselves enough. They involve the restraint of right usage and right action, but asceticism puts a further constraint even upon right usage. It is a doing with less than one's due, and for short periods, even with less than one's need, to train for a higher goal and fill a higher need. Just as the athlete may enter into many contests but in addition must have his training periods, and the pianist gives many recitals but never omits his hours of practice, the spiritual athlete too must adhere to his formal spiritual exercises.

Proof of this abounds in the Scriptures and in the life of the Lord and the Saints. Jesus fasted for forty days. Paul chastised himself. St. Catherine of Siena, taken to a spa to find health, was found by her mother scalding herself in one of the baths, to do penance. St. Ignatius went to his native place to recover his health. He was observed to be wearing a chain for penance when he was sick in bed. St. Francis Xavier hobbled across the snows of Japan on bare and bleeding feet singing for joy and carrying the Gospel in his heart. All of these people were sent contemplatives.

It becomes evident, then, that in ascetical matters, humanistic norms will not adequately guide a pilgrim. We owe God a reasonable service, a worship "worthy of thinking beings" (Rom. 12:1 JB), but we are dealing with reason impassioned by love and made divine by grace. We can be guided somewhat by norms such as we have discussed here, but finally each individual must weigh his own situation and respond to his own graces. Since many settle too readily for too little penance, experimentation to learn by experience what is appropriate can be helpful. We can experiment, and discern from the results (joy in the Lord, and equal or improved ability for our work) what practices of asceticism to adopt. A missionary Sister in India describes this procedure:

> I am personally feeling a little overwhelmed with the whole world hunger problem and the question of the basic inequalities in the economic systems which, for now, allows part of the world to be overfed while other parts starve. I'm thinking of skipping the evening meal for a while, and offer the time usually spent, in

prayer for a world which will look a little more at the other "guy's" problem through the same other "guy's" stomach. Not sure yet whether it is an inspiration of the Lord or just one of my own crazy ideas to satisfy my guilt complex for past sins, but it is coming to me in prayer and I'll take it seriously, hoping to discern and praying for the courage to accept the challenge either way.

If the dialectic between asceticism and efficiency is a thorny problem, it is only one of many in the life of a zealous pilgrim contemplative. Another is the balance between work and play. Play includes recreation, rest, and leisure. Play is a humanizing activity. It enriches the personality, wards off dullness and heaviness, enhances creativity, promotes good spirits, and leads to a more appealing way of doing things. Many pilgrims encroach on their time of play for the sake of their work. It is right to do this when necessary, but it is not necessarily more virtuous (or even as virtuous) to do it when unnecessary. It harms both the person and his effectiveness. Is the good it produces worth what it costs? This is the question that must be asked. Perhaps the answer of the Lord will be: "Come away by yourselves to a lonely place, and rest a while" (Mark 6:31).

We would never come to an end if we considered all the pairs of values in tension within the life of a zealous pilgrim. He must take reasonable means to preserve his health, yet be ready to embrace sickness. He desires to be in disrepute with Christ, yet he acts to promote his reputation so that he may have opportunity to serve, and to spread the Gospel. He works to succeed and prays that the Father will give his works a higher efficacy than success—the efficacy of being a fool with Christ, which will make him "more than conquerors" (cf. Rom. 8:37).

Through and in these adjustments, the pilgrim is growing ever more aware of mankind's insatiable needs. He suffers from the widening chasm between the projects he would like to undertake and what he can undertake. There is too much to do, and he is ineffective in even the little he sets out to do. He persists in aspiring to do great things for the Kingdom, but he aspires in pure faith now, for experience has disabused his hopes in his own powers. Abram the wandering Aramean is his model. Having not even a country of his own, he believed he would become father of many nations.

Experience and observation have convinced the pilgrim of the futility of human works done independently of the divine plan. Such works do nothing to bring the Kingdom, and may in fact hinder it, just as uncoordinated works in any enterprise lead nowhere.

The pilgrim jettisons any remaining hope in man's autonomous plans and purposes: "Our Father . . . Thy will be done."

Now that he has less difficulty in executing God's will, he is learning how difficult it is to *know* God's will. How hard for the finite to open to the Infinite! Again, it is one thing for the pilgrim to learn God's will concerning his own spiritual affairs, and another to be guided by God's will along all the paths he must travel as His agent in a very complex world.

He is discovering more and more for himself the importance of a daily examination of conscience. In that spiritual exercise he no longer concerns himself solely with sin, but with all the aspects of his life of service, and with the adjustments of personality and life style which he must make to grow into a mature servant of the Lord.

Difficulties and troubles in the spiritual order, when they are properly diagnosed, tell us not only where we must direct our energies to avoid disaster, but where we can direct them to achieve new growth. It is in accord with this principle that the daily examen helps the pilgrim to continue his advance along the path of the sent contemplative.

19.

Prayer in Process

The events within the pilgrim's interior life remain shadowy and elusive. Apostolic fatigue coupled with the intangibility of his imageless and wordless prayer make him susceptible to distractions in the course of prayer, and also to falling asleep. His present austere prayer teaches him no longer to doubt that the rich insights and affections he formerly enjoyed in prayer were God's gift and not his own accomplishment. Despite the austerity of his present prayer, he is convinced it pleases the Lord: "Ice and cold, bless the Lord" (Dan. 3:49). Many pilgrims spend an hour a day in this uncharted and featureless prayer.

Although this stage of interior prayer is marked by few events, God does pay distinct and consoling visits to some, though not necessarily during the actual time of prayer. One pilgrim paid a visit to the Blessed Sacrament one night. When he returned to his room, he felt it filled with the presence of God:

> I saw no visions, I just felt God's presence touching me. A stillness and a silence fell upon me so deep that Quiet became a new experience. This Quiet was Presence. It was God. The Presence continued until I fell asleep. It recurred at times for about a year.

For the most part, the pilgrim's prayer continues to be austere. Its results have to be gauged by faith and by the quality of his life, and it is thus that a capable spiritual director will assess it.

It is at Mass that the pilgrim most finds God. He listens to the priest's words, *This is my body*, and he believes and knows with all certainty that the risen Lord is once again present. Other religious experiences wax and wane, and their substance is open to varied

184

and uncertain interpretations; but the Eucharist remains always the same, a meeting with the Lord God that is complete and certain, independent of the presence or absence of felt experience, because it is guaranteed by His own word. The pilgrim goes to the Eucharist sometimes joyous and sometimes with painful longing. It invariably comforts him even when he is aware of feeling no comfort.

At Mass the Lord's presence and power and love outweigh all divisions and join him to all present and to all men. He repeatedly experiences it to be the Sacrament of Community, the Mystery of Christ's total Body, the center of His growing Kingdom. One pilgrim, a young Sister, was able to trace out the communitarian and apostolic influence of this sacrament upon her growth:

> Not too long ago, a priest friend of mine said, "What has the Lord been doing in your life?" I thought to myself, "Wow! I really don't know." I knew that I had changed, that I was growing in the Lord but I never really asked myself specifically in what way. I knew that Jesus was speaking to me through the Eucharist, melting me, molding me and fashioning me in His way, but nobody ever asked me to verbalize to them how Jesus works in me. So I took time to sit down and reflect.
>
> When I was in the ninth or tenth grade, I started to go to daily Communion. Sometimes I wouldn't make it for the whole Mass but I always managed to receive the Eucharist. Then there would be times when the priest would give me part of his Host, and I always thought that this was the Lord's way of saying "Everything's all right!" It doesn't happen often and it's such a joyful surprise when it does—a beautiful gift.
>
> When I made my Initial Commitment in Religious life . . . part of my ceremony for Initial Commitment was part of a tape I listened to as a novice:
>
> "Vocation: Jesus takes bread (selects and chooses it). He blesses it and makes it holy (makes it more than what it is). He breaks the bread and gives it to the Apostles.
>
> "We are called to be somebody. We are blessed with the whole life of Christ—to be broken and to be given for others.
>
> "We become the living Eucharist. Vocation is living out the Eucharist—the heart of Christ's life. Continuous Call! Continuous Creation! Continuous Amen!"
>
> Again, I didn't realize in its living out what I was saying. The cover of my ceremony book had on it the words "Through Him, with Him, in Him, July 19, 1971," with a design composed of a cross, the Good Shepherd staff, a little branch of wheat, a chalice and a broken Host. Since then, Jesus the Master Teacher, has been instructing me in the meaning of this theme. The Lord is using this

simple devotion to the Eucharist to show me how to be Eucharist. And this is where the action in my life takes place.

I have found that in the Lord's School, as in any other, there must be testing, something that allows me to know whether or not I am really willing to "be broken" and given to others as Jesus' Body. In all my tests, Jesus has always let me know that He is here with me. My willingness to make a permanent commitment in a human community is really the degree of my faith in Jesus' unfailing fidelity to me.

My renewal of promises last summer was a faith renewal. I really wasn't sure of myself. I had a rather difficult year in the apostolate and I wasn't too sure of myself in community. When it came time to renew my promises I was kind of blah—the spirit was willing but the flesh wasn't too sure. So it was a faith commitment—saying yes to all that was and would be (even though I wasn't too happy about the whole thing). At Communion, the celebrant gave me half of his Host: He said as he was ready to consume the Host, something inside told him to give half to me. So again, Jesus said, "Everything's all right, N.; I am with you."

And because of that faith commitment, the Lord has reinforced His call and is drawing me deeper and deeper into Eucharist. At a recent lecture, a priest said that for the fullness of Eucharist, the people present offer themselves totally at the offertory and the Father accepts and blesses the gift. When the bread and wine are consecrated and made the Body and Blood of Christ—we are also changed and become Eucharist. When we receive the Body and Blood of Jesus, we are also receiving the community. What an impact this has made! To the degree that I offer myself, I am made Eucharist, I am Jesus for others. And each member of my community is Jesus for me. I receive each one at the Eucharist.

In reflecting, there is a pattern. The Lord has accepted a child's love for the Eucharist and is bringing it to maturity. Now at Mass when the priest says "This is my body to be given up for you" there is a new dimension. Jesus needs my body to be given for others. This is where I am in the apostolate and in community. I see a different picture—one that has its center in Jesus—and that makes all the difference in the world. The human problems are still there, and always will be, but the grace I receive from Eucharist enables me to see with different eyes. I am more willing to give, to be available, to be of service.

During this period of interior and Eucharistic growth, certain pilgrims undergo the following unusual experience. If they visit the Blessed Sacrament during a time when they are enjoying the felt presence of God referred to above, they experience a confusing two-fold Presence, one of the omni-present Divinity, and the other of the bodily Presence of the Lord in the tabernacle. This experience seems to illustrate concretely the Lord's two-fold manner of joining us to Him: through His all-present Divinity, and through His risen Body, whose presence is assured us only in connection with the consecrated Host.

One of the deepest joys and strongest supports a pilgrim can have at this time is the companionship of a few friends in a like state with himself. It matters not whether their companionship be shared in worship, on a walk, or in a game. Conversation can range over any subject, though frequently it turns to the Lord. It is one of the deepest happinesses of life. Out of it comes nourishment for love, and a desire for the Lord that still further deepens devotion to prayer and the Eucharist. When such companions walk through the countryside, where God still sometimes hovers, the experience is all the richer. Pilgrims called to the religious life generally have by far the greatest opportunities for this blessed companionship.

Pleasantly enough, some of the old ways of finding God cyclically recur, making the pilgrim suspect that the capacity for them is still there, coursing below the surface. He wonders whether they went underground to prepare for new growth, or because search for novelty made him turn his back on them. The truth is that visitations from God, which are thrilling at their onset, after a while seem so commonplace that one tires of the effort to be faithful to them, unaware of what a terrible tragedy this is. At any rate, the pilgrim is learning to be flexible and even inventive in the way he brings everything into his prayer and his prayer into his whole world. Thus he is becoming a sent contemplative.

During this hard period the pilgrim is winning many marvelous freedoms: freedom from enslavement to the senses; freedom from the tyranny of a wayward imagination; freedom from worldly plans; freedom from inordinate fear of suffering; freedom from human respect; freedom to tread his own unique path, in awareness that not even the Saints' examples can show him his way in all its particulars; freedom from the illusion that God's truth or His will is easily learned, or readily grasped without error; freedom from any sense of personal persecution; freedom from the illusion that spiritual consolations are of his own making or subject to his power; freedom from an inflated self-image; freedom from the delusion that he has it within his own power to accomplish great things; freedom from the fear of aspiring to great things, if God should draw him. With these freedoms he is free to be an ambassador sent by God, an agent who can reasonably well hear His instructions and execute them.

The years pass, and even in trials he calls himself blessed: "The Lord is my chosen portion and my cup; thou holdest my lot. The lines have fallen for me in pleasant places; yea, I have a goodly heritage" (Ps. 16:5-6).

End of BOOK ONE